REGNUM STUDIES IN MISSION

Christianity and Cultures

Shaping Christian Thinking in Context

REGNUM STUDIES IN MISSION

Series Preface

Regnum Studies in Mission are born from the lived experience of Christians and Christian communities in mission, especially but not solely in the fast growing churches among the poor of the world. These churches have more to tell than stories of growth. They are making significant impacts on their cultures in the cause of Christ. They are producing 'cultural products' which express the reality of Christian faith, hope and love in their societies.

Regnum Studies in Mission are the fruit often of rigorous research to the highest international standards and always of authentic Christian engagement in the transformation of people and societies. And these are for the world. The formation of Christian theology, missiology and practice in the twenty-first century will depend to a great extent on the active participation of growing churches contributing biblical and culturally appropriate expressions of Christian practice to inform World Christianity.

Series Editors

A full listing of titles in this series
appears at the end of this book

REGNUM STUDIES IN MISSION

Christianity and Cultures

Shaping Christian Thinking in Context

Edited by
David Emmanuel Singh
Bernard C. Farr

First published 2008 by Regnum Books International

Regnum is an imprint of The Oxford Centre for Mission Studies
and Paternoster Press
P.O. Box 300, Carlisle, Cumbria, CA3 0QS, UK
and
P.O. Box 1047, Waynesboro, GA 30830–2047, USA

09 08 07 06 05 04 03 8 7 6 5 4 3 2 1

British Library Cataloguing in Publication Data
A catalogue record for this book is available from the British Library

ISBN: 978-1-506475-22-6

Typeset by BB Ltd

The publication of this celebration title for the silver jubilee anniversary of OCMS is made possible through the generous financial assistance of The Commission on Theological Education of Evangelisches Missionswerk in Deutschland (EMW, Dr. Verena Grüter), Hamburg, Germany.

Distributed by 1517 Media in the US and Canada

Contents

PREFACE

David Emmanuel Singh and Bernard C. Farr

Dr. David Emmanuel Singh is Research Tutor and Dr. Bernard C. Farr is Academic Dean of the Oxford Centre for Mission Studies, U.K.

Twenty-five years' existence of the Oxford Centre for Mission Studies (OCMS) may seem minor in relation to the history of Oxford and its university but for those who have been part of this recent past these have been eventful and significant years of advancing holistic mission through scholarly engagement. This volume on Christianity and Cultures: Shaping Christian Thinking in Context is a way of marking this important milestone in the relatively short story of OCMS.

The papers contained in this volume have been exclusively sourced from Transformation: an International Journal of Holistic Mission Studies (formerly, An International Dialogue on Mission and Ethics) which is known to its subscribers and partners simply as Transformation. These papers date from the very foundation of the journal, roughly coinciding with the origins of the Centre in 1983/4, to the issues appearing in 2007. Transformation is owned wholly by OCMS but published and distributed by Paternoster Periodicals.

The impetus for the publication of this volume came last year as the management team at OCMS was brainstorming possible ways to celebrate OCMS' 25th anniversary in 2008. It was originally decided to focus on papers on the theme of 'the Bible and Culture', which in itself was a worthy theme to highlight, in an effort to show the variety of contributions on the relationship between the Bible and its reception in different cultures and the equally diverse body of contributors ranging from practitioners to scholars. This theme was broadened in two ways: first, to include aspects other than the sacred Christian text by replacing 'the Bible' with 'Christianity' used in a generic sense in recognition of the plurality of cultural contexts where Christianity expresses itself and takes shape; second, by changing the word 'culture' to 'cultures' in recognition of the many cultures which Transformation represents.

This volume provides a tripartite view of Christianity's engagement with cultures by focusing on the question: how is Christian thinking forming or reforming through its interaction with the varied contexts it encounters? As Christianity has taken and still takes shape in multiple contexts, it naturally results in a variety of expressions and emphases. One can gain an appreciation of these by studying different strands of theological-missiological thinking, socio-political engagements and forms of family relationships in interaction with the host cultures.

The three parts of this volume contain altogether nineteen papers. These papers represent different geographical regions including North America, Europe, Africa, South East Asia, South Asia and Latin America and both male and female contributors. The papers by Thomas and Hoole are being republished posthumously.

In the first part, the papers are concerned with the theme of Christian thought in the context of cultures. Carver argues that culture is a gift of God to humanity expressing a sense of the sacred and a communion with others. However, cultures are liable to imperfections and distortions which can be addressed by the reconciling work of Christ. Accordingly, Asian theologians ask difficult questions about the nature of the Christian faith and its place in Asian cultures. For example, Hwa Yung writes about the revival of Asian cultures and the positive role Christians can play if they embrace their host cultures and engage them in dialogue instead of rejecting them without serious engagement. Ranger demonstrates how the Christian use of idioms from the African culture enables African men and women to respond to Christianity more naturally. These uses of local idioms have had a tremendous influence on African churches, even though some churches went to extremes with the idea of embracing the host culture and despite the mechanisms that control these excesses internally without discouraging experimention with new ideas of inculturation. The process of the inculturation of Christianity into any culture can be both creative and syncretistic. Where local cultures are shaped by deeply rooted traditional religions, it becomes a more difficult issue. Change does not need to involve the rejection of the culture but rather its re-orientation to Jesus Christ. Inculturation should define, therefore, the nature and shape of this re-orientation.

This volume also provides examples from different regions. Schmidt speaks of Afro-Caribbean religions as instances of the coming together of different religious traditions and the emergence of synthetic religious forms. In the Catholic tradition, for example, the presence of the practice of devotion to saints may indicate that these forms are uniquely Afro-Caribbean and, thus, do not simply constitute a Catholic cult. Many of these traditions incorporate elements from West Africa, Europe and Native America. Devasahayam reflects on the Indian context and suggests that underlying all Indian culture is the caste system. There are two significant theological responses to this system, both of which have historical roots. Whereas one accepts the caste system as part of Indian culture, the other rejects it from the Dalit or untouchable standpoint. Devasahayam believes the latter to be more holistic in its approach. Kirsteen Kim looks at the rediscovery of pneumatology and the contribution Indian theology makes to this discussion from a 'Spirit-Christology' rather than a 'Logos-Christology' perspective. Various terms, such as *atman*, *antaryamin*, and *shakti* have been used by Indian theologians, which suggest the contribution Indian pneumatology can make to international discussions on Christianity and cultures.

Several articles focus on Christian political thinking in different contexts. Thomas, who served as a governor of Nagaland, reviews the ideological crisis amongst the Indian middle class as manifested in the recent political success of fundamental Hindu nationalism. As an Indian Christian from the southern state of Kerala, he draws our attention to three Christian anthropological insights: the spiritual transcendence of selfhood, moral realism, and the interaction of individuals in society regarding the Indian crisis of secular democracy and global economics. In his view, as religious freedom safeguards other freedoms faiths must reach an understanding on divisive issues. Christians should not oppose the profit motive in modem market economics, but demand social development initiatives from the state which acts as the organ of the whole community. Thomas emphasizes two alternatives of Christian witness in politics: either a critical mainstream participation or a withdrawal to create ideal alternatives. His call is for Christians to choose the former model as he sees Christ at work there.

There exists a deeper relationship between rights, democracy and liberal economic principles than is often acknowledged. O'Donovan believes this to be important especially at a time when many Christians are beginning to entertain serious doubts about how global market forces affect the majority in the world. She finds that looking back in history is helpful and concludes that seen from this perspective the secular liberal-democratic rights culture is beginning to collapse. Furthermore, Gitari who is deeply involved in Kenyan politics as a powerful moral force, from a theological base reminds us that God creates and sustains His creation. God commands us to be participants in divine creativity in the totality of human life and history through the incarnation of the gospel.

There is a need for a wider debate, as Freston proposes, incorporating the two major continents which constitute the new heartland of Protestant political militancy. According to Freston, evangelicalism is overwhelmingly a Third World phenomenon. The examination of the historical and social background of Protestants in politics in Latin American countries, particularly Brazil, Guatemala and Peru, reveals not only parallels, but also significant differences. This also appears to be true in Africa although African countries have a more acute economic crisis, more non-evangelical Protestants and less experience of multi-party democracy. However, there is a correspondence between some African and Latin American cases which could illuminate the future.

Evangelicals today appear to have an increasing political influence in America but, as Sider believes, they lack a clear political philosophy. Inconsistency and confusion prevail and there is a need for a serious study of society, political philosophy, specific issues, and, most importantly, the Bible. For Sider, Jesus Christ is at the centre of Christian politics formed by certain Biblical paradigms, such as the sanctity of every human being, justice, a concern for the poor, laws promoting community and family values, the need to work and the right to life. Petersen focuses particularly on Pentecostals who have historically rejected political involvement (mainly because they have suffered under political repression) as the way to challenge social injustice. Their programmes have brought personal regeneration to the most disadvantaged sectors of society which may have far-reaching implications for both social transformation and, in our modern world, for politics. Petersen suggests that direct political action should begin initially with local structures, and involvement in national politics should occur only to bring change for the powerless through an integral ministry as exemplified by Christ.

A reference was made above to the need for laws to promote family values. The section on the family includes contributions from Wright, a British Biblical scholar who sets the family within a Biblical moral framework by asking the question: is the family a good thing or not? He reviews what the Bible says about the family and concludes that it was created for good, but can often be distorted for evil. Glaser focuses on the positive role of the family in an individual's spiritual life, but acknowledges that the link between family and faith differs from culture to culture. Writing from a Nigerian context, Kwashi agrees with Glaser in supposing that the 'family is the most important factor in moulding a human being' and, likewise, acknowledges that the very meaning of the family is variable. Such variability is not necessarily religion specific i.e. a Christian state does not necessarily guarantee an ideal family, as Chang-Him shows in the Seychelles where a good proportion of children are born out of wedlock. In many households, the father does not play a significant role in the family and leaves it to the mother to carry the full responsibility of bringing up the children alone. The father sees nothing wrong in relationships with other partners and with more children. Chang-Him believes that not only culture may have something to do with this state of affairs but also the experience of slavery in the nineteenth century. As Hoole suggests in writing from South Asia, the traditional notions of interdependence and stability in the traditional South Asian family life are breaking down. If the old kinship structure is to be redeemed, the gospel must be allowed to impact on the extended family so that the individual is able to participate in the new humanity of Christ. There is a need for re-socialization of people from broken families as individuals adopted by God and received into a new family of Christian brothers and sisters. This requires challenging the power of some institutions such as the caste system and the joint family. There may be a new opportunity for building a new family that will transcend the restrictions of the caste system.

This volume is evidence, therefore, of the extent and depth of the struggle of committed Christians from across the world to relate Christianity to their specific cultures. This is an unending story of the search for relevant and meaningful beliefs and practices. It is also a testimony to the adaptability of the gospel and its power to become variously incarnated. OCMS, through its journal Transformation, has been privileged for over 25 years to bring these struggles for intelligent and embedded faith to wider communities of interest and offers this volume both as a thanksgiving and as a celebration.

PART ONE

CHRISTIAN THINKING IN CONTEXT

Culture from an Evangelical Perspective

Carver T. Yu

Dr. Carver T. Yu is President and Professor at the China Graduate School of Theology, Hong Kong

Culture as a Gift for Fulfilment

Barth gives us perhaps the most succinct definition of 'culture': 'Culture means humanity'.[1] In other words, humanity does not live *in* culture, but its very being is actualized and concretized as culture. In so far as humanity is a gift from God, culture is also a gift from God. At the same time, 'seen from the point of view of creation, the kingdom of nature (*regnum naturae*), culture is the promise originally given to man he is to become'.[2] With that promise intrinsic to its being, humanity cannot stop striving to draw out and complete what nature holds for it. Even as sinners, as those who alienate themselves from self, they nevertheless strive for wholeness as if answering the call to a certain destiny. The French definition of 'civilization' as 'the sum of the *aims* proceeding from human activity…' and the German definition of *kultur* as 'the idea of the final *goal* and the totality of norms by which human activity should be guided' point to the directedness intrinsic to culture. All culture, no matter how inadequate, aims to achieve a certain degree of wholeness for human existence. The wholeness of humanity, however, can only be found in the fulfilment of human beings as the image of God. 'The image is not in man; it is man'.[3]

Humanity Shares God's Sanctity

As the image of God, humanity shares the sanctity that belongs to God, a sanctity, which confronts even God's absolute freedom and power as its boundary, in so far as God has chosen to use his freedom to affirm it and not violate it. We can even say that humanity shares the kind of absoluteness that belongs to God. In this sense, it is quite understandable that early church fathers

---

[1] Barth, 1962:338
[2] Barth, 1962:341
[3] Heschel, 1972:152

like Athanasius as well as Basil the Great, and subsequently the Eastern Orthodox tradition, have put so much emphasis on the idea of the 'deification of man'. Athanasius if referring to the logic of Christ's incarnation would say, 'He was made man that we might be made god'. Basil would also put it thus: 'man is nothing less than a creature that has received the order to become god'.[4] Referring to the biblical tradition, Heschel points out:

> It is an important fact, however, that in contrast with Babylonia and particularly Egypt, where the preoccupation with death was the central issue of religious thinking, the Bible hardly deals with death as a problem. Its central concern is not, as in the Gilgamesh Epic, how to escape death, but rather how to sanctify life. And the divine image and likeness does not serve man to attain immortality but to attain sanctity.[5]

Ensuring the sanctity of the human person as that which is holy to God is the most fundamental directive of culture as the manifestation of humanity. A culture, if it is to fulfil its task for the actualization of humanity, cultivates a sense of sacredness for his neighbour. 'Thou shall love thy neighbour as thyself' (Leviticus 19:18) is an inevitable implication drawn from the fact that behind and above each human person, there is the absolute God. At the same time, humanity hears the call from God, 'you shall be holy for I, the Lord, your God, am holy' (Leviticus 19:2). Culture should also give expression to the sense of the sacred (or holy) intrinsic to humanity. A culture which cultivates commitment to the unconditional is being true to its task. In so far as God's freedom expresses his absoluteness, humanity has a kind of freedom reflecting God's freedom of self-determination, self-initiation and self-limitation. As God created Adam, a distinct individual, and not created a mass of humanity as the bearer of His image, the individual with a distinctive identity (with a specific name) and freedom is of supreme significance in the Christian definition of humanity. Yet the individual does not exist in abstraction from the ground of his being, nor from his intrinsic relation with other men. He has his identity only in the very act of communion with God as well as with others. 'God created man in his image. Male and female he created them.' The moment Adam knows his individuality, he knows it as something that bears within it the presence of others. Thus humanity's being is in relation. Sociality and solidarity is basic to his humanity. God's presence is intrinsic to humanity. Covenantal commitment and individual distinctiveness are inseparable correlates. Freedom is also exercised within this being in relation. There is no genuine individuality and freedom without commitment, and there is no true covenantal commitment without real individuality. Culture in its authentic manifestation of humanity brings freedom and commitment together as two inseparable mutual

---

[4] Mantzaridis, 1984:7

[5] Heschel, 1972:152

determinants. An authentic culture cultivates freedom as freedom-for. It cultivates a freedom that enables the self to transcend itself. The magnitude of self-transcendence is another measure of the authenticity of culture.

Individuals in Community

On the basis of humanity thus constituted, each person receives two mandates from God as part of the fulfilment, to administer the created order (Genesis 1:26–27) and to give names to the living creatures. Humanity is to till and guard what has been entrusted to him, so that the land prospers. Ensuring prosperity and enjoying abundance from it as the sign of God's goodness is also a significant mandate of culture. To till and to keep, humanity is to bring out the values intrinsic to nature, to articulate nature in such a way that it gives glory to God and abundance to human beings. Material abundance is also a sign of authentic culture. At the same time, Adam is to give names to the living creatures. To give a name is to define and thus give meaning and allocate values. Meaning-and-value creation is another task of culture. This gives space for human creativity and imagination. God's world can be explored and related to in many possible ways. In tilling and keeping, in naming and defining, humanity draws the land, the living beings and all into a unified structure of meaningfulness with God as the ground. Each person builds his/her world of meaning and values based on reality. This is the realm of knowledge, and wisdom mediates his relation with the created order. An authentic culture cultivates openness to the life-world in which each human being is being actively engaged by God's created order. He does not stand outside the created order as subject over against objects, subjecting the world into a world-picture (world-view) of his sheer imagination. Rather he sees his reality as part and parcel of a totality.

Sin and God's Promise

The reality of sin puts authentic culture on the defensive. What has been a promise now hangs over humanity as a judgment of their unfaithfulness. In so far as the freedom of humanity is a real gift from God, then their will to distort the promise of God is allowed with its full effect, even if it is contained in God's providence. Thereafter the distortion of humanity sets in and permeates every aspect of culture. The land still prospers, but prosperity can become destructive. There will be thorns and thistles, which will block and disrupt man's attempt for order and abundance. What should have been positive directives for fulfilment can now become vortices drawing every being into stifling cul-de-sacs.

Culture thus contains implications of the curse from God as well as the working of humanity's sinful design. In the face of the reality of sin, all cultures, including those deeply touched by the Christian gospel and even those which claim to be Christian cultures, are mixtures of what is reminiscent of God's promise, God's preserving grace and human distortion. All encounter God's judgment and God's affirming grace so that when Christians are confronted with cultures other than their own, they ought to be humble, knowing that no culture, including the culture in which Christianity prospers, can claim to be true to God's promise. Even Christians cannot but live in cultures which are still under the judgment but also the preserving and redeeming grace of God. All cultures are to be judged by the Word of God and are to be affirmed by the Word of God as God's gift, even in their corrupted form. The distortions and frustrations of God's promise work themselves out in a variety of cultural forms.

Culture thus becomes the arena where humanity acts out his disobedience and rejection of God. In various degrees, institutions in culture may violate the integrity of humanity's being human. There may be cultural forms which blatantly deny the sanctity of each person, treating them as an object or commodity, or as means to certain ends. There may be cultures where human freedom is structurally stifled, and their individuality is dissolved. There may be cultural forms in which alienation is the condition of existence, where humanity's communal and communicative character is seriously hampered. There may be cultures in which human solidarity with nature is damaged, and desacralization of nature is a fact of life. There may also be cultures which polarize humanity's spiritual and physical dimensions. Humanity is either reduced to the physical or his spiritual quest for liberation from the world displaces all concerns for the well-being of worldly life.

God's Judgment and Grace

Where do we begin to identify these distortions? As each person is bestowed with the gift and the mandate to create meaning and values on the basis of reality, it is the structure of meaning and values that provides the magnetic centre and directive for all cultural syntheses. It is in these structures of meaning – their inner contradictions, the discrepancies between the ideal and the real – that we sense the deviations from the promise of God. To put it in another way, when the creative structure of meaning and value is turned into ideology, we see clues to the problem. It is the ideology of each and every culture that has to be identified, to show the inner contradiction and discrepancies, to see how God's promise, his preserving grace has been distorted in the light of the *crisis* of God's Word. Despite humanity's wilful distortion, God's grace continues, his promise still stands. Here we share Barth's conviction when he says, 'This gift, his humanity, is not blotted out through the fall, nor is its goodness diminished'.[6]

---

[6] Barth, 1972:53

This conviction is based on the humanity of God revealed in Jesus Christ, that 'in his sovereign decision, God is human. His free affirmation of man, his free substitution for him – this is God's humanity.' 'From the point of view of reconciliation, the kingdom of grace, culture is the law in reference to which the sinner, sanctified by God has to practice his faith and obedience.'[7] Culture seen from this perspective has now become God's instrument as a preservation order preventing humanity from falling into total chaos. From then on, culture is a mixture: it contains God's original promise and human rebellion as well as God's providential reference for preservation. The church fathers see laws and government (even the persecuting Roman government) as necessary evils under the providence of God to prevent men from consuming each other.

In this sense, culture has to be affirmed. As an instrument for preservation, culture contains a curse, which is also a blessing in disguise. Humanity is subjected to toils and labour, to the adversity of the created order, which questions his dominion, to disciplines of life which call his freedom into question. Even in this way, culture reflects the preserving and redeeming grace of God. As Augustine puts it in his *City of God*:

> There is a common use among both kinds of men and households of things necessary to this mortal life…For the earthly city, which does not live by faith, seeks an earthly peace; and interests itself in the harmony of rule and obedience among its citizens to the end that there may be a certain agreement of men's wills regarding the things that pertain to this life. But the heavenly city, or rather that part of it which only makes pilgrimage in mortality and lives by faith, is likewise obliged to make use of this peace…Hence while it continues to live in the earthly city as a captive in its pilgrimage … it does not hesitate to conform to the laws of the earthly city whereby are administered the things suited to the maintenance of mortal life; and since this mortality is common to all, a harmony is preserved between the two cities in respect of things which pertain to it.[8]

As preservation order, culture has in many ways become reactive attempts to sustain rather than to create. At the same time, the distortions and aberrations of what originally belong to God's promise work their way into all aspects of man's life, even affecting what had been intended as part of the preservation order. Culture has now become at once both a pointer to the fulfilment of God's promise, a preservation order, and a stifling structure of man's sinfulness.

Critique of Culture

The contingent 'absoluteness' of humanity bestowed by God to ensure his sanctity has in one way or another been distorted in cultural forms as human self-absolutization. The deification of humanity as a possibility in Christ is

---

[7] Barth, 1962:344

[8] Augustine, 1984:xix.17; cited from Baillie, 1945:9

taken over by the human spirit. 'Man becomes god to himself.' Such self-absolutization of humanity comes to its height in the form of the structure of meaning in which the transcendent is radically denied. In such cultures, the *saeculum,* the present or the facticity of human existence is taken as the totality of meaning. Anthropocentrism prevails, and 'the whole creation has been groaning', 'for the creation was subjected to frustration, not by its own choice, but by the will of the one who subjected it' (Romans 8:18–23). Such deification has appeared in history time and again. However, radically secularized modern culture coming out from the 'Christian' west and the postmodern narcissistic culture as an outcome of the radicalization of the Romantic reaction against the Enlightenment is a form of self-absolutization that is most damaging to humanity and to nature. Within such a culture, humanity gets shut off from the sense of transcendent mystery and the sense of the sacredness of being. This ultimately undermines man himself as the foundation of meaning. Reason and freedom thus conceived, the two pillars of the cultural project of the Enlightenment, finally become highly problematic and threaten to break down completely under the full impact of skepticism and subjectivism.

Human Persons and Divinity

Freedom bestowed by God can also be misconstrued in a totally individualistic way. Freedom is taken as freedom without commitment. The social evils coming out from the market economy reveal the true nature of such freedom. Here again, functional rationality has undermined the personal realm of being so much that the values vital to the development of capitalism are withering. In the social dimension, social fragmentation has become so severe that modern society is in danger of the total collapse of the public realm. The integratedness of humanity as a unity of diverse dimensions is also violated. Under the pressure of positivistic reductionism, humanity is reduced to their physical realm of being. Humanity thus becomes one-dimensional. The spiritual dimension is disregarded. What is supposed to be a creative construction of meaning and values based on reality becomes an ideology – ideology as false consciousness. Again, this creates a pervasive sense of spiritual predicament in modern culture. The validity of science itself is in question as scientific truth itself can be reduced to an epi-phenomenon of biochemical reactions. Scientistic reductionism in the final analysis negates itself. We can see from the above analysis that within a culture that absolutizes itself, or violates the integrity of humanity, an inner dialectics of self-negation always sets in, until finally it collapses under its own weight.

We can see that outcome as a principle designed by divine providence, to reveal to humanity their inauthentic existence. However, even in such a situation, culture as a gift from God and as the preservation order provided by God to sustain sinful beings so as to keep them open for redemption is set to work. The deep yearning expressed in various spiritual forms point them to their spiritual predicaments, and thus to the unfulfilled promise of what he should be. The rule of law, the various advances for the enrichment of humanity, the various movements in response to personal and social fragmentation, the prophetic calls for justice and liberation, stand as signs of God's affirmation of culture as the fulfilment of his promise for humanity. Indeed, before we look at Asian cultures, it is the West, developing out of its abandonment of the Christian tradition, placing human rationality and freedom at the centre of the universe that ought to be radically criticized. If we fail to criticize western culture, we have discredited ourselves for the prophetic claim of the gospel. While we encounter human beings in the West as secular anthropocentric individuals, we encounter them in Asian traditions more as *homo-religiosus*. The sense of the sacred and the sense of sanctity of life are relatively stronger. Society is structured more as a communion than as an association. Covenantal commitment takes precedent over individuality. The awareness of cosmic solidarity stands out rather clearly.

The drawback of Asian tradition when placed alongside the technological power of the West seems to be the inner inertia hindering scientific development. Also, from the missionary-evangelistic perspective, their religions confront the gospel as closed systems. In Asian cultural traditions, we see the promise as well as the judgment of God. In so far as the sanctity of humanity is affirmed without losing sight of his dependence on the transcendent, Asian humanistic insights to this effect have to be taken as a sign of God's original gift. At the same time, insights about the contingency of human existence can also be taken as a sign of gift from God. In Hinduism, Buddhism and Taoism, the nothingness of human existence is stressed. This understanding of the nature of human existence in itself agrees in a profound way with the Christian belief in *creatio ex nihilo*. It depicts the condition of man in alienation from God. Humanity is keenly aware of the fact that existence grounded on their self is nothingness so that attachment to the self is a delusion leading only to suffering.

Humanity and Jesus Christ

From the evangelical perspective, however, the nothingness of the differentiated human person does not have the final word. In Jesus Christ, humanity is created to be real. The sanctity and integrity of the human person has, of course, its ground in divine reality, but divine reality does not absorb the human person, thus rendering it an insignificant epiphenomenon of the unfolding divine drama. No, God takes human existence so seriously that he became a human being, so that humanity may become as holy as God, i.e., as that which is 'separated', but 'separated for' divine-human communion. In the Christian tradition, genuine communion goes hand in hand with the act of covenanting. The very act of covenanting ensures the integrity of both parties.

The Hindu tradition as a life-system in many ways reflects the promise for authentic humanity. The utter devotion to the Absolute, the calm self-surrender, the non-attachment to the fruit of one's self-sacrifice, and the single-minded discipline for the quest of deliverance, reveal a deep awareness of humanity as they are and what they should be. It would seem rather arrogant for Christians to brush it aside as valueless paganism. With such deep spirituality, however, one is puzzled as to why Hindu culture is riddled with extreme poverty, with a vast gap between the rich and the poor, and with a caste system which has for centuries been so inhuman and yet well justified by the same spiritual tradition which calls for our deepest admiration. Where has been the prophetic judgment of social injustice and inhumanity? Why is there no inner dynamic for social change? What is the intrinsic problem to the historical and social process? The problem of Hinduism, however, lies not in what appears to be polytheism, for in fact it may be regarded as intensely monotheistic:

> To admit the various descriptions of God is not to lapse into polytheism. When Yajnavalkya was called upon to state the number of gods, he started with the popular number of 3,306, and ended by reducing them all to one Brahman. "This indestructible enduring reality is to be looked upon as one only." These different representations do not tell us about what God is in himself but what he is to us. The anthropomorphic conceptions of the divine is relative to our needs.[9]

The problem lies in the fact that it is a system of self-absolutization in another direction. It stresses the identity between God and humanity so much that on the one hand the world and the self is so relativized that it may even be interpreted as *maya*, as the great *samkara* would express it, or as moments in the life process of Brahman, as Radhakrishnan would express it. On the other hand, this amounts to the affirmation that whatever is, is Real and Divine. Let us quote from the Upanishad:

> There is nothing that is not Spirit. The personal Self is the impersonal Spirit. It has four conditions. First comes the material condition – common to all – perception turned outward…This is known as the waking condition. The second is the mental condition, perception turned inward … wherein the Self enjoys subtle matter. This is known as the dreaming condition. In the deep sleep man feels no desire, creates no dream. The undreaming sleep is the third condition, the intellectual condition. Because of his union with the Self and his unbroken knowledge of it, he is filled with joy; his mind is illuminated…He is neither that which is known nor that which is unknown…The only proof of His existence is union with Him. The world disappears in Him ….[10]

---

[9] Radhakrishnan, 1960:22–23

[10] Monk *et al.*, 1987:151

If the phenomenal world, the world process, and the self are moments in the drama of divine unfolding, then each moment is absolute and necessary. All events in the historical process, or all structures in the social process, may then be justified as part and parcel of the Absolute. It is the drama of the poor to remain poor, as the lot is fallen to them in a designated scene of the drama. The oppressive caste system would appear totally justified. It is not the individual person who is absolutized, but the historico-social process. With this absolutization, the society closes in on itself. Transcendent critique proves unnecessary and impossible. In contrast, a society touched by the gospel would acknowledge distance between God and humanity, the historical and social processes around man are not completely determined by the divine but to a large extent reflect humanity's own making. As soon as humnaity also acknowledges their sin, there is openness for a transcendent critique of society.

The Poor among Us

While acknowledging the spiritual depth of Hinduism, we must point out the fact that the promise of God for the distinct characteristic of being human, and freedom bestowed on humanity to find and create meaning and value on the basis of God's creation, does not mean that humanity has to be absorbed into the divine and lose himself in order to find fulfilment. The individuality and freedom of humanity has its own right, protected by God and accompanied by God. Prophetic justice has to be proclaimed as a demand from God as his gift in ensuring the sanctity of each and every created being; it is also his mandate for humanity to bear covenantal responsibility. Christ is the fulfilment of the promise that all are one in him. It is also a gift of God that humanity is an integrated being, who receives both physical and spiritual blessings from God. Hinduism seems to have placed relatively less attention on physical reality while putting great emphasis on spiritual quest. Poverty can be a result of the neglect or even tacit negation of the physical world. The material world is real and it is a gift from God for the fulfilment of mutual engagement and involvement between God, humanity and cosmos. If we are to meet Hindu culture with the Word of God, it would not be to condemn but to affirm, to affirm the gift of God already manifested, and to affirm what fulfilment there could be in the promise of God for all cultures.

Christ and Fulfilment

The promise of what humanity can become has already been given. It is up to man to bring the promise to fulfilment in working out his structure of meaning and values. Christ as the mediator of creation and redemption has, in his concrete incarnation, revealed the fulfilment of what man can become. The reality of human wholeness and the fullest disclosure of divine-human love are unfolded in him. Not only unfolded in him but made available through him.

Through his sacrifice the estrangement from God is overcome. God is infinitely close to man in Jesus Christ. Humanity is once again confronted with the free grace of God and his promise for humanity. The fulfilment of the promise becomes genuinely possible. Christ then may be regarded as the crown of what every culture is striving for and yet frustrated by its inner contradiction.[11] A culture confronted by Christ does not need to be a clean empty page rid completely of its intellectual, moral, aesthetic or religious *a priori*, so long as all these *a priori* become open to self criticism as to whether they have been the source of inner contradictions and stumbling blocks for the fulfilment of God's promise.

[11] See Farquhar, 1971:85

TOWARDS AN EVANGELICAL APPROACH TO RELIGIONS AND CULTURES[1]

Hwa Yung

Rt. Rev. Dr. Hwa Yung is a bishop in the Methodist Church at Petaling Jaya, Malaysia

Resurgence of Asian Religions and Cultures

Perhaps one of the most discussed papers in international academic and political circles in the last few years is Samuel Huntington's 'The Clash of Civilizations?'[2] Huntington argues that in the evolution of conflicts in the modern world, clashes first occurred between kings and princes, then between nation states, and finally between ideologies as in the Cold War period. But we have now arrived at the stage of world history when increasingly the clashes will be between civilizations. Huntington writes: "It is my hypothesis that the fundamental source of conflict in this new world will not be primarily ideological or primarily economic. The great divisions among humankind and the dominating source of conflict will be cultural. Nation states will remain the most powerful actors in world affairs, but the principal conflicts of global politics will occur between nations and groups of different civilizations. The clash of civilizations will dominate global politics. The fault lines between civilizations will be the battle lines of the future."[3] Civilizations are shaped by history, language, culture, tradition and, especially, religions. With the end of the Cold War, ideological differences will increasingly be overcome by cultural and religious commonalities. The net result is that civilization conflicts will be inevitable and the most important players in these clashes will be the Confucian, Islamic and western civilizations. Huntington's thesis is built partly on the fact that all over the world there has been a resurgence of traditional cultures and religions. This is especially so amongst the educated elites of non-western societies. Indeed there has been a sharp reversal of trends. In the past, elites of non-western societies tended to gravitate towards western cultures and values, while the common people remained dominated by indigenous cultures.

---

1 Hwa Yung, 2000:86–91. See another version Hwa Yung, 1997:61–80

2 Huntington, 1993:22–49. See its expanded version in Huntington, 1996

3 Huntington, 1993:22

But today, 'a de-westernization and indigenization of elites is occurring in many non-western countries at the same time that western, usually American, cultures, styles and habits become more popular among the mass of the people'.[4]

Whether Huntington's central thesis is correct or not only time will tell. But one of the key presuppositions of his thesis, that there is a resurgence of traditional cultures and religions in non-western societies, especially amongst the elites, finds confirmation everywhere in Asian societies today. To begin with, through West, Central, South and South-East Asia, Islam's resurgence is common knowledge. The case of Iran is already well-known. The news on Afghanistan is that the Taliban, led by people who until few years ago were nothing more than a group of Islamic theological students in Pakistan, is likely to rule the whole country soon. In Malaysia, one of the key issues facing Christians is how do we cope with Islam's resurgence and its consequences for non-Muslims? In neighbouring Indonesia, the present President, B.J. Habibie, is also the leader of ICMI, the Muslim Intellectuals Association of Indonesia. Here Islamic resurgence is increasingly perceived as threatening the character of the country, even though the Pancasilla supposedly ensures that all recognized religions will have an equal place in Indonesian society. This resurgence is not confined to Islam only. The dominance of the Hindu fundamentalist Bharatiya Janata Party in India's politics today is the result of a protracted effort over many years to bring together all segments and layers of Hindu society into a united political and social front. The same resurgence is seen in societies traditionally defined by Confucianism. Lee Kuan Yew, the former Prime Minister of Singapore, in the mid–1980s called for a return to moral values with a Confucian base in order to protect Singapore from degenerating into 'a nation of thieves and robbers'.[5] Similarly, Tu Wei-Ming has drawn attention to the revival of Confucianism elsewhere in East Asia.[6] Finally, writing on the most economically and industrially advanced country in Asia, H. Byron Earhart argues that it is a misconception to think that modernization and westernization have loosened the grip of traditional beliefs on Japan. Rather, it appears that the distinctiveness of Japanese religion will persist in the future. 'Kami, Buddhas, ancestors, and holy persons will probably remain at the core of Japanese religion and continue to form a distinctive pattern or sacred way that has always been characteristic of the Japanese religious heritage'.[7] Given the above evidence, we are, therefore, forced to the conclusion that the resurgence of traditional cultures and religions in Asia is here to stay and that if the Asian church is going to take mission seriously in the twenty-first century, this will be one reality that it cannot afford to ignore.

---

4 Huntington, 1993:27

5 Compare Lu, 1992 with Wei-Ming, 1984

6 Wei-Ming, 1991:740–781

7 Earhart, 1984:133

But before we look at how then we should respond to it, we will take a quick glance at what attitudes the church has taken towards indigenous cultures and religions in the modern era.

Christian Responses to Non-Christian Cultures and Religions

Christian responses to non-Christian cultures and religions in the past five hundred years can probably be summed up, with some over-simplification, as accommodation, rejection, capitulation, and confrontation. We will look briefly at each in turn.

Accommodation: The sixteenth to seventeenth century Jesuit experiment

The work of Matteo Ricci (1552–1610) in China and Roberto Nobili (1577–1656) in India is well documented.[8] For our purposes, we will focus only on the work of Ricci in China. Through sheer determination, Ricci entered China in 1583, and finally reached Beijing in 1600. In order to gain maximum acceptability for the gospel, he mastered the Chinese language and the classics, dressed as a Chinese scholar, and in every way possible tried to accommodate the gospel to the culture and religious practices of the Chinese. For example, he was not afraid to use terms like *Shangdi* (Sovereign on High) and *Tian* (Heaven) from the Confucian classics for God. In modern missiological terms, these represented real efforts in indigenization or contextualization. But did the Jesuits go too far in their experiment? This appears to have been the case as seen in the historic Rites Controversy in Roman Catholic mission history. Ricci, in the face of all the evidence, argued that the Chinese ancestral rites had no more than civil significance. Commenting on the whole controversy, Kenneth Scott Latourette notes that, 'Whatever may be true of a few of the educated, for the great masses the prohibited rites had in them much of animism'.[9] Latourette is almost certainly right in suggesting that, had it not been for the papal decision to prohibit participation in ancestral rites, the church would have eventually lost its distinctiveness through too much compromise.[10] Thus the evidence indicates that Ricci and his co-workers appeared to have been too accommodating in their 'accommodation' approach.

Rejection: The nineteenth century view

It is probably correct to say that the predominant nineteenth century view of non-Christian religions and non-western cultures amongst western Christians is one of rejection. David Bosch has argued that one of the results of the Enlightenment paradigm on mission thinking was that the belief in the

---

[8] See Neill, 1986:138–141 & 156–165

[9] Latourette, 1929:154

[10] Latourette, 1929:152–155

superiority of the Christian faith led also to beliefs of cultural superiority.[11] Theologically, this translates into the later position, perhaps best identified with Karl Barth, that Christianity is totally discontinuous with non-Christian religions. Nothing good can be learnt from them. Culturally, it simply meant that non-western cultures were generally denigrated. As J. Pobee observed, up to his time, 'all the historical churches by and large implemented the doctrine of *tabula rasa*, i.e. the missionary doctrine that there is nothing in the non-Christian culture on which the missionary can build and, therefore, every aspect of the traditional non-Christian culture had to be destroyed before Christianity can be built up'.[12] Indeed, Bosch further points out that, 'until fairly recently virtually all westerners (and in many cases, non-westerners) took it for granted that the reshaping of the entire world in the image of the West was a foregone conclusion'.[13]

Yet this view has come to be recognized as being far from adequate. It is theologically inadequate because it ignores the whole dimension of what is usually called general revelation in Protestant theology. It is culturally inadequate in view of the evident decline and increasing lack of appeal of western culture today on the one hand, and the resurgence of non-western cultures on the other.

Capitulation: Twentieth century religious pluralism

In recent years, from out of liberal Christian circles has emerged a strident religious pluralism which affirms not only universal salvation for all, but also the equality of all religions.[14] Arguments for this come from various directions. Some suggest that the claim of Christian uniqueness is an extension of western imperialism into the religious realm. Others argue that all claims to religious truths are merely human perceptions of the divine, and are therefore relative at best. Still others argue that the 'cosmic Christ' or 'spirit' is at work in all cultures and religions, and, therefore, any claims to uniqueness is arrogant to say the least. Increasingly it is now recognized that the real impetus behind religious pluralism today comes from the western world struggling with the problems of modernity. This is perhaps most frankly stated by Tom Driver, a pluralist himself:

> It will be better part of wisdom to acknowledge, even to stress, that the whole discussion about 'religious pluralism' ... belongs to western liberal religious thought at the present time ... The agenda...is certainly western...couched in

---

[11] Bosch, 1991:291–298

[12] Pobee, 1982:168–172, quoted in Hiebert, 1994:76

[13] Bosch, 1991:292

[14] See e.g., Knitter, 1985 and Hick and Knitter (eds.) 1987. This can also be seen in the writings of Asian theologians like S. J. Samartha and C.S. Song.

western terms, addressed to western audiences, and aimed at the western conscience.[15]

Similarly, Lesslie Newbigin has argued that Enlightenment thought has created a 'plausibility structure' which relativizes all truth claims and which exalts doubt over faith.[16] That this cannot be an acceptable Christian position has been clearly demonstrated by evangelical and other scholars.[17] It can only be sustained by ignoring clear affirmations of the uniqueness of Christ and his atoning work in Scripture, and the impact of sin and the demonic in humanity's religious quest. In effect, this is nothing short of capitulation to the Enlightenment relativization of all religious and moral truth claims. It may well turn out to be nothing more than the swan song of western liberal Christianity!

Confrontation: Pentecostal-charismatic-spiritual warfare

The fourth view is one that is found in many Pentecostal and charismatic circles today. This view really builds on the second, but takes it further by linking much or all of non-Christian religions (and, by association, cultures) with the demonic. Hence they are not only to be rejected, but also to be actively confronted through spiritual warfare. This is not something that is explicitly stated often – it would appear too crude. But it is a popular view held in large sections of Pentecostal-charismatic circles.[18] The strength of this position is that it takes the demonic dimension seriously, something which evangelical theology in general has paid only lip service to at best, and which liberalism has usually ignored. Consequently it has opened new avenues through prayer for greater effectiveness in pastoral and healing ministries. However, its weaknesses must not be overlooked. Like the second position, it has little or no place for God's general revelation to humanity. Further, in rejecting non-Christian religions as wholly demonic, it often rejects much of non-Christian cultures on the same grounds by association. For example, in the Chinese Christian world, Christians are often told that acupuncture and the martial arts must be rejected because of their pagan demonic associations, without analysing as to which aspects of such practices are good and redeemable, and which are demonic and ought to be rejected. These examples can be multiplied. The net result is that often only what comes out of the West will pass the test of having no pagan or demonic associations. With such a theology, the cultural

---

15 Driver, 1987:206

16 Newbigin, 1989:1–65

17 As well as Newbigin, 1989, see especially Netland, 1991 and Ramachandra, 1996. Religious pluralism is not unambiguously native to Asian thought. Both in China and India, the categories of orthodoxy and heterodoxy are clearly found in Confucianism and Hinduism respectively. See Hwa Yung, 1997:115–118.

18 What is pleaded for here is to have a more careful analysis and greater discernment on such issues.

deformation of Asian Christianity is now complete! But that cannot be the way forward for Asian Christianity if we are not to lose our own cultural identities. If the four responses above are deemed inadequate, what then would be considered to be a proper Christian response? It is to this that we will now turn.

Rooted Theology of Religions and Cultures

Evangelical theology has rightly rejected any relativization of Christian truth claims which have been classically understood to be taught by Scripture and the ecumencial creeds of the early church. It has rightly rejected universalism and pluralism, drawn attention to the sinful and demonic in non-Christian religions and cultures, and emphasized the need to call men and women to repentance and faith in Christ in order to escape from the wrath and judgment of God against sin. Yet, while having rightly stood firmly on these truths, evangelical theology has sometimes been less than biblical in its total understanding of how we should perceive non-Christian religions and cultures. Consider the following examples.

a. Are all without Christ eternally condemned? In seeking to avoid the danger of universalism and compromising the uniqueness of Christ's atonement on the cross and the centrality of evangelism, evangelical theology often feels compelled to insist that all without explicit knowledge of Christ's salvation stand eternally condemned. This means all who have never heard of Christ and his offer of salvation are without any hope whatsoever. But this rigid position appears to be less than biblical. For example, Paul's view is somewhat different. In speaking about the atonement, he speaks of God demonstrating his justice in having 'left the sins committed beforehand unpunished' (Rom. 3:25). Here he refers to the Old Testament saints who have been saved, even though they do not have explicit knowledge of Christ. Some will say that this is an exceptional case since they already know the God of the Old Testament. This would not apply to others outside the stream of Old Testament revelation. But this position cannot be defended in light of Paul's preaching in Athens, where he explicitly states: 'In the past God overlooked such ignorance' (Acts 17:30). This clearly refers to Gentiles who have never heard of the gospel. Of course, he does not say that they will all be saved; but neither does he say that they are all eternally condemned. But to say that 'God overlooked such ignorance' to Gentiles who have never heard of the gospel implies that hope exists for some at least. This does not mean that their salvation comes through good works or non-Christian religions. Rather, if they are saved, it is still because of what Christ has done for them on the cross![19]

b. Light from general revelation: Evangelicals probably all agree that there is a general revelation given to all humanity, apart from the special revelation through the Judeo-Christian tradition. But is there not a tendency for us to

[19] Among evangelicals to articulate a similar position are Anderson, 1984:137–175, Green, 1990:70–81 and Crokett and Sigountos (eds.) 1991:257–264.

think, like Karl Barth, that much or all general revelation is pretty useless, especially in regards to our salvation? Of course, this is again out of the fear of compromising the uniqueness of our salvation in Christ!

And yet here again, is there a possibility that our theology is less than biblical? For example, Melchizedek (Gen. 14:17–20) is never described in Scripture as having received the same revelatory tradition as has been given to Israel in the Old Testament. Yet Christ is described as 'a priest forever in the order of Melchizedek' (Ps. 110:4; Heb. 5–7). Again, the Magi (Mat. 2:2–12) were almost certainly astrologers from the 'East' (Persia? India?). Yet, each Christmas we are reminded that, in their search for the truth, from out of their pagan religious backgrounds, the Magi came from afar to worship the king. In spite of these and other scriptural sources, evangelical theology has, as a whole, systematically taken an entirely negative view of non-Christian religions (and often cultures as well).[20]

c. Understanding non-Christian religions: If we look at the numerous Ph.D.s by Asian evangelical scholars in the field of theological studies, we find hardly more than handful are in the field of religions. Most prefer the more 'Christian' fields of theology, biblical studies, church history, missiology, and the like. Our aversion, and possibly fear, of the study of other religions certainly has crippled our witness to those of other faiths, especially when probably more than 90% of Asia's population adhere to one non-Christian religion or another.

It is instructive to compare our present attitudes with that of Daniel and his three friends in Babylonian captivity. Their 'university' training involves studying 'the language and literature of the Babylonians' (Dan. 1:4). Any commentary will tell us that these include not only the ancient languages, mathematics and astronomy, but also Babylonian myths and legends, magic, astrology, divination through dreams, and the like. Daniel and his friends excelled in their studies and did far better than their companions (1:18–20). The important point to note is that they were not afraid to master a hostile worldview, even though in their lives and witness they were constantly dependent on God. Is it any wonder that God could use them so powerfully in an environment which was so hostile to their faith? Surely we need to ask what lesson this may have for us?

d. Relationship with non-Christians: As evangelicals have tended to view other religions negatively, we have also often ended up viewing non-Christians negatively – mainly or merely as objects of our efforts at evangelism. Many of us do not have many real friends amongst those who are not Christians. Yet again, how strangely this differs from Paul. Paul spent just over two years in Ephesus and there was a riot in the city, largely because of the problems caused to the pagan temple business because of his missionary work (Acts 19). When he wanted to go and try to pacify the rioters, one important group of people

[20] See Pinnock, 1992. One does not have to agree with all of Pinnock's conclusions to note the validity of much of the scriptural materials that he draws our attention to.

who stopped him were the asiarchon, who are described as 'friends of Paul'. But who were these asiarchon? They were the provincial officials of wealth and influence, and who were also leaders of the temples in the area.[21] In other words, Paul has good friends among the non-Christian religious leaders of his time! Does this not also in part explain the effectiveness of his missionary work?

e. The good in non-Christian cultures: All cultures are usually a complex mixture of both the good and the bad, the divine and the demonic. There are, therefore, those things that are good and divine even in non-Christian cultures. To write off everything in pagan cultures that appears to have some association with pagan religions is to adopt an over-simplistic view of reality. It represents not only a failure to take general revelation seriously, but also it fails to take the goodness of God's original creation seriously. We need to be reminded of that final vision at the end of the Bible when 'the kings of the earth' will bring 'the glory and honour of the nations' into the Holy City (vv. 24 & 26; cf. Isa. 60). Whatever else this may mean, surely that which is good and pure in every culture will find a place in the eternal city! I have attempted to show, using the five examples above, that evangelicals often have a less than biblical understanding of religions and cultures. This has resulted in part from the tendency in evangelical circles to emphasize the doctrine of redemption at the expense of the doctrine of creation. A further and related problem is that evangelicals do not have a very strong grasp of the doctrine of general revelation which deals with God's work outside the church. We need to work towards a more biblical and robust theology of religions and cultures, especially within the Asian context. This requires of us a mastery of Asian cultures and religions which is not often found within evangelical circles at present. Only then will we be able to deal effectively with the issues of apologetics, dialogue and inculturation. This leads us to the next point.

Renewed Emphasis on Apologetics

One of the ways used by the early church for evangelism among the Gentiles was the development of an effective apologetics.[22] Most of the books we have on apologetics in Asia are of western origin or address the questions from a western perspective. We have very little good apologetics written on Asian religions and cultures. One exception is N. Goreh's *A Rational Refutation of the Hindu Philosophical Systems,*[23] although written almost 150 years ago. He employs the *reductio ad absurdum* approach to show the inner contradiction and incoherence of the various Hindu philosophical systems. It is a pity that his book appears to have become forgotten when so much of the West has been turning to Hindu spirituality for answers in recent years. In this connection we

---

[21] Bruce, 1954:400

[22] See e.g. Green, 1970:127-143

[23] See Paradkar, 1969 and Boyd, 1975:40–57

need to look also at L. de Silva's *The Problem of Self in Buddhism and Christianity*.[24] It should be noted that de Silva's work is not meant as an apologetic towards Buddhists. His concern is for a dialogue with Buddhism in the sense that both religions can help illumine each other. This is not the place to give an extended treatment of his argument. We will go straight to the climax of his thesis instead.

In his concern for dialogue, de Silva shows by careful arguments that if the Buddhist doctrine of *anatta* (no-self) is real, God must be necessary. Otherwise there is no escape from nihilism. 'Because man is *anatta*, God is indispensable; because man is absolutely *anatta* God is absolutely necessary.'[25] There is no doubt about the basic correctness of de Silva's thesis. But the main problem is not with the cogency of his argument, but rather his apparent inability to see where it ultimately leads. His proposal of *anatta-pneuma* (a mutual reshaping of each other's meaning by bringing together the Buddhist concept of no-self and the Christian understanding of the human as spiritual) is obviously highly original and creative for the purpose of bridging key anthropological concepts from two different religious traditions. But it can only be sustained by filling the Buddhist *anatta* with Christian meaning. Despite his dialogic concern, there is no real corresponding need to fill *pneuma* (spirit in the Christian sense) with Buddhist meaning.

It is doubtful that a Theravada Buddhist will be at all happy with such a dialogic exercise. But de Silva's argument goes beyond even this. What he has done is to demonstrate with relentless logic that the only way to prevent the Theravada Buddhist view of the person from sliding back into either nihilism or eternalism (the human having an eternal soul), is to attribute to *anatta* the quality of *pneuma*. But this can only be done if we affirm the existence of a personal God. 'If God is not, then *anatta* necessarily implies final extinction.'[26] This is one conclusion that Theravada Buddhism cannot accept without surrendering its identity. What de Silva has accomplished is not so much an able exercise in dialogue – although it is that also – but, rather, a brilliant Christian apologetic addressed to Theravada Buddhists. Evangelicals will not agree with some of de Silva's dialogic presuppositions. But we can learn from him the lesson that a careful and sympathetic understanding of another religious tradition can open up new doors for the communication of the gospel through a cogent Christian apologetic. This is the sort of work we need to engage in much more. Unless we begin to address this much more seriously, the work of evangelization in Asia will again be crippled.

---

[24] De Silva, 1979
[25] De Silva, 1979:138
[26] De Silva, 1979:145

Dialogue with other Faiths

Evangelicals have been very hesitant to engage in dialogue with non-Christians because of the fear of syncretism, of being misunderstood, and of the tendency in some circles to use it as a substitute for evangelism. But it is now increasingly recognized that genuine dialogue is not an optional exercise. As S.P. Athyal puts it,

> In communities where people of different religions live together as neighbours, it is inevitable that they will be conscious of their interdependence and seek to promote peace and mutual understanding. It is also necessary for us to be well aware of the beliefs and convictions that shape people if we wish to communicate the gospel effectively to them. These are the considerations that lead to interreligious dialogue.[27]

In other words, for the sake of inter-religious harmony, mutual understanding and effective witness for Christ, we need to be engaged in genuine dialogue. In a similar way, Vinay Samuel has argued that both for the sake of social transformation, which in a religiously plural context cannot occur 'without a religious reality that promotes that change', and for the effectiveness of our evangelistic approaches, serious dialogue is inescapable.[28] Careful reflection will show that these points are unavoidable.

Of course we will need to approach dialogue with wisdom and caution. This is especially so in the present context where many liberal scholars, including many within Asia, are pushing stridently for a pluralistic theology of religions. For example, C.S. Song, throughout much of his writings, has argued that Christians forget that theological truth is found everywhere. Consequently, for him, 'Life without Immanuel is an illusion ... But life is God-is-with-us ... That is why in Asia we have Gautama Buddha, Mo Ti, Shinran, Gandhi.'[29] What Song is trying to emphasize is that we can sometimes (or, often) find that God has worked through non-Christian religious experiences. This, as we have argued earlier, is something that we cannot totally deny. But at the same time, he is obviously overstating his case because of his pluralist presuppositions. In the same passage, Song insists that Gandhi is 'a sign of God for us Christians also'.[30]

We need, however, to ask Song whether Gandhi is 'a sign of God for us' even in his rejection of Christ's unique divinity and atonement for sinful humanity, or only in his acceptance of Christ's 'Sermon on the Mount'? Nowhere in his writing does Song makes this clear. The ambiguity of his position is clear. It is against such a background that Vinay Samuel helpfully

---

27 Athyal, 1993:63

28 Samuel, and Sugden, 1984:274 and 286

29 Song, 1986:26

30 Song, 1986:25

lays down some of the parameters of an evangelical approach to dialogue. These include a clear affirmation of the uniqueness of Christ in Christian revelation, the need to distinguish between Christ's own exclusive claims from those made by the institutional church, the willingness to discern the presence of God in others' religious experiences, the recognition of the sinful and demonic in religions, and to work wherever possible for the redemption of all creation.[31] This approach clearly avoids two opposite dangers which an evangelical theology of dialogue must guard against: that of the extreme conservatives on the one hand who see nothing good and redeemable in non-Christian religions (and sometimes, cultures as well), and that of the present-day pluralists who recognize no essential differences between the Christian and non-Christian faiths.

Inculturation: Incarnating the gospel in Asian cultures

A few years ago while on sabbatical I met a Japanese Christian girl, a Tokyo University graduate, in the US. One day, rather excitedly she said to me, 'You know for the first time in my life, I could relate Christianity to my own culture!' I asked her why? She then explained that she was attending an Old Testament class and looking at the last chapter of Job. After telling Job's three friends that he was angry with them for saying false things of him, the Lord told them to go and ask Job to pray for them. And the Lord goes on to say, 'I will accept his prayer and not deal with you according to your folly' (42:8b). Then to her pleasant surprise, the American professor said next, 'We Americans don't understand this, but you Japanese people do.' The point was that prayer was rooted in our *relationship* with God, and that people whose cultures prized relationships above individualism can understand Job 42:8b much more easily! This incident, however, has raised a real question in my mind. Why is it that it took so long in this Japanese sister's pilgrimage for her to be able to relate her faith in Christ to her culture? Is it because, as one Asian writer puts it, much of Asian Christianity is 'culturally deformed'? My own observations indicate that that is unfortunately the case.

The African missiologist, L. Sanneh, reminds us in his seminal work, *Translating the Message – The Missionary Impact on Culture*,[32] that the gospel is eminently translatable into other cultures. But this is something that much of Christianity in the nineteenth and twentieth century has forgotten for various reasons. The present emphasis on indigenization or contextualization is certainly a step in the right direction. After all this is what the incarnation is all about – the Word took on flesh in a specific culture and historical context. Unfortunately, in certain circles, contextualization has come to refer mainly to relating the gospel to the socio-political issues of the day in liberation theology terms. However, indigenization or contextualization should mean not only how

---

[31] Samuel, 1991:162ff

[32] Sanneh, 1989

the unchanging gospel of Christ relates to the socio-political context, but also how it relates to the culture of the people to whom we bring the gospel, and to the way we carry out our work of evangelization and pastoral ministry among these people. Increasingly, the term 'inculturation' is being used within missiological circles for the efforts made to relate the gospel to culture. Perhaps the best definition of this term is 'the intimate transformation of authentic cultural values through their integration in Christianity and the insertion of Christianity in the various human cultures'.[33] It involves, in the words of David Bosch, 'a *double movement*: there is at once inculturation of Christianity and Christianization of culture.'[34] If the gospel is truly going to take root in Asian soil, if it is going to make the advance into Asia that we believe that God desires of his church in the next century, we will need to make much more serious efforts in this direction.

What are some specific areas where the gospel must be more related to Asian cultures? I will give two examples. The first concerns our evangelistic methods and pastoral practices. For example, individualistic approaches in evangelism must be replaced in many places by more community and family based ones. Again, evangelistic and pastoral practices developed out of the secularized West, where the spiritual dimension (involving spirits, magic and charms, astrology, etc.) is often ignored, must give way to more Bible-based practices which takes the deliverance and healing ministries seriously.[35] Yet again, Christian functional substitutes must be sought and pioneered for traditional non-Christian practices of ancestral veneration, funeral practices, cultural festivals, etc. if the Asian church is not going to be seen as being against Asian cultures *per se*.[36]

Second, much of the way we think about Christian ethics has been shaped largely by modern western Christian thinking on the subject. Christian moral thinking formulated in the West invariably prioritizes principles over relationships. But how do Christian ethics operate in a culture where the order is often reversed? For example, family ties are so close in many Asian societies that nepotism invariably results. Yet, if a Christian fails to 'take care' of family members, he or she is also damned in the eyes of his or her culture. Or again, where is the dividing line to be drawn between a bribe and a gift given in appreciation and to cement a relationship? There is obviously a need for the development of a more culturally sensitive ethics.[37]

---

33 Pope John Paul II 1990:89. See also Kraft, 1979, Stott and Coote (eds.) 1980) and Hiebert, 1987:104–111.

34 Bosch, 1991:454

35 See the analysis by Hiebert, 1994:189–201. It is in part due to western Christianity's failure to address this issue. See also Kraft, 1989:37ff.

36 See, e.g. Ro (ed.) 1985 and Sng and Pang (eds.) 1991.

37 See for a significant effort in developing a culturally sensitive ethics, Adeney, 1995 and Hwa Yung, 1998:153–180.

Conclusion

We have looked at the resurgence of Asian religions and cultures today and some of the challenges this poses to the church. We have noted that existing responses within the church to the challenge of non-Christian religions and cultures have been far from adequate. We have suggested some directions which the evangelical church must take if we are to develop an adequate theology towards non-Christian religions and cultures. And unless we do so, our concern for the evangelization of Asia and for the gospel to make a serious impact upon Asian cultures and value-systems will probably not go very far. Let me, therefore, close by giving one specific example. In China in the 1920s, during the May 4th Movement, Christianity was severely attacked and strongly rejected by the intelligentsia because it did not seem to have any adequate answers to China's concern for modernization and cultural rejuvenation. The church simply lacked an effective apologetic to commend the gospel to the nation as a whole.[38]

Thus at a time when China, for the first time in her long history, opened herself to and welcomed all sorts of foreign influence – intellectual and educational, scientific and technological – in her search for national salvation, *she rejected the gospel of Christ*. But the greater tragedy is that, in spite of the lesson of the 1920s, up until today, more than seventy years down the road, the Chinese church has yet to develop an adequate Christian response to Chinese thought in general, and to the Confucian tradition in particular. Do we wait for the May 4th Movement to repeat itself in the twenty-first century before we set about the task of developing an adequate Christian apologetic? And without such an apologetic, can we ever hope to have an adequately contextual theology for the church to effectively penetrate Chinese soil and go very far in evangelizing the world's largest mission field in the coming generation?

[38] The story is told in full in Wing-Hung, 1983:91.

AFRICAN INITIATED CHURCHES[1]

Terence Ranger

Dr. Terence Ranger is former Rhodes Professor of Race Relations, University of Oxford, Emeritus Fellow of St. Antony's College and Honorary Fellow of the Oxford Centre for Mission Studies, U.K.

Introduction

I have argued before that various idioms of African religion enabled African men and women to respond to Christianity and to place their hopes in it. These idioms were the experience of prophecy, the desire for spiritual healing, the desire to eradicate witchcraft, the experience of spirit possession, and the passion for creating holy places. All of these had interacted with mission Christianity but in the end the mission churches were uncomfortable with all of them, leaving unsatisfied spiritual needs to be met by later African-initiated churches.

I may, therefore, be expected to write about African churches with prophetic leaders, specialising in spiritual healing, focussing on the healing of the witch, using the Holy Spirit to subdue all other spirits, and taking possession of the mountain tops. In the later sections of this paper, these expectations will certainly be realised and I shall make a reference to churches of precisely this type.

Firstly, I have to make two further arguments. One is to take up the point about the African desire for enabling education and the missionary failure to provide it. This led to African churches of a very different kind. Secondly, I have to amplify the comment I made previously on the influence of Pentecostal missions from outside Africa. The idioms and ideas of such missions had a tremendous influence on the prophetic, spiritual African churches, helping to ensure that they would emerge as Christian churches rather than as re-statements of African religion .

---

[1] Ranger, 2007:66-72

Education and Ethiopianism

The late great Bengt Sundkler whose *Bantu Prophets* (London, Lutterworth, 1948) was the first academic analysis of African-initiated churches, divided them into two types, the 'Zionist' and the 'Ethiopian'. Sundkler was writing about South Africa churches and derived these names from the language of the churches themselves, so many of which called themselves churches 'in Zion', while others appealed to the idea of topia, Ethopia.[2]

These names are famously misleading. The word Zionist is usually employed to refer to the advocates of a Jewish homeland – but African 'Zionist' churches are not at all concerned with this idea, nor do they have connections with Israel. If we talk about Ethiopian Christianity we normally mean the ancient Coptic Orthodox Church, but South African 'Ethiopian' churches have no connections with Orthodoxy.

The two names embody quite different ideas from these normal meanings – and from each other. The 'Zionist' churches focus on the holiest of all holy places, Zion City. These are the churches of prophecy, healing, and the Holy Spirit. The 'Ethiopian' churches focus on the idea of Ethopia as an independent African state, resisting Italian invasions, and on the biblical references to Ethiopia, stretching out its hands to God. These churches are about African independence from missionary control and about the superior biblical legitimacy of African Christianity. Many of them were stimulated by black American breakaway churches, particularly the African Methodist Episcopal Church which sent Negro missionaries to South Africa and the Rhodesias. The power of the Ethiopian image was invoked by the AMEC Bishop Turner when he came from the United States to South Africa to commission African evangelists in 1898: 'The time has now come to replace [European missionaries] Arise Africa, for Ethiopia is holding out her hands, not as suppliant, as the white men call her, but to incite us to ... conquer the first place among our people'.[3]

These were the churches which focussed on education for modernity and which tried to set up their own schools and colleges. Forty years ago, two of my own early articles were about Ethiopanism and education.[4]

It amuses me to begin with my (almost) earliest published writing on African religious history, 'The "Ethiopian' Episode in Barotseland, 1900-1905'. The article began with a summary which still remains true:

> It has become something of a historical commonplace that one of the most important vehicles for the growing opposition to white domination in Southern Africa in the period between 1890 and 1914 was the independent church movement which contemporaries entitled 'Ethiopian'. Drawing heavily upon the

---

[2] See Sundkler, 1976

[3] A wonderful study of the AMEC is by Campbell, 1995.

[4] Ranger, 1965a and 1965b. Also relevant is Ranger, 1969.

> experience of American Negro separatism and asserting a claim to independence and mastery in a sphere which was seen as central rather than peripheral to the new world created by colonialism, the 'Ethiopian' challenge was taken seriously by both European Mission societies and Governments. It was experienced first in South Africa, where Africans had been much longer exposed to the pressures of colonization and the teachings of European mission and then spread into British Central Africa where it played an equally important role in the growth of African opposition.[5]

For Central Africa, and Malawi in particular, I cited the classic study of John Chilembwe by George Shepperson and Tom Price, which is still very worth reading and which was republished in Malawi last year.[6] Shepperson had drawn attention to the so-called Ethiopian episode in Barotseland, which took place between 1900 and 1905, wondering how 'it could have developed at all' at such an early stage of Lozi contact with mission and empire.[7] When I explored it, I found that the story was very different from the way in which it had previously been described. It was not as the Paris Evangelical Missionaries described it, a movement back to polygamy and sexual licence. It was not, as J.V.Taylor and Dorothea Lehmann described it,[8] a mass adoption of 'the exotic and confused gospels of prophet movements and Ethiopian sects'. Indeed it was no a popular movement at all and had nothing to do with prophetism. As I wrote:

> 'Ethiopian' activities were concerned primarily with the Lozi aristocracy and not with the people at large andthe 'Ethiopians' were welcomed by that aristocracy not because they offered an indigenous form of Christianity but because they promised to provide a relevant education and to assist in the 'modernization' of Lozi society.[9]

King Lewanika and his Indunas had many ambitious projects for economic development in Barotseland. They wanted their young men to learn English and technical skills. (They also maintained Lozi royal religion). They received no help from the British South Africa Company which was nominally responsible. The Protestant missionaries would only help in the job of education 'on their own terms': 'The Mission regarded education as primarily a preparation for the Christian life; Lewanika and his indunas regarded it as a means of providing the Lozi state with qualified clerks, interpreters, artisans and so on.'[10]

This missionaries closed the 'English school' in 1906 because 'the boys did not attend the Prayer Meetings regularly'. The mission schools were criticised

---

5 Ranger, 1964:26

6 Shepperson and Price, 1958

7 Shepperson, 1963

8 Taylor and Lehmann 1961

9 Ranger, 1964:27

10 Ranger, 1964:30

for concentrating on 'the Bible, singing and a smattering of imperfect English'. Whereas the missionaries wanted a network of Lower Primary schools, open 'to young chiefs and serfs alike', the King wanted the sons of the aristocracy to be trained in elite schools.

In 1900, one of the PEM's Sotho evangelists, Willie Mokalapa, broke with the mission. In the 1980s, Mokalapa advised Lewanika not to trust the political advice of the missionaries. 'Do no listen to these whites', he wrote to Lewanika. 'They do not love you. It is only we who love you'. He was sacked by the mission. However, in 1903 Lewanika sent him down to South Africa to invite the African Methodist Episcopal Church to come to Barotseland and open an advanced school. In South Africa Mokalapa was ordained the 'Presiding Elder' of the AMEC in Barotseland. Mokalapa promised Lewanika that soon 'the Barotse would be able to learn to read, write and speak English in two or three months'. He also promised technical education. Lewanika paid the travelling expenses of the AMEC teachers and their salaries when they arrived. He gave them 'an excellent Mission site and placed unlimited slave labour at their disposal.' The AMEC schools were at first very popular with the young elite. 'The natives deserted the Mission churches and joined the Ethiopians.' The AMEC emissaries acted as secretaries to the King and helped with his plans to open up a wagon road for the marketing of Lozi produce. Mokalapa was sent back to South Africa to buy through the AMEC wagons, boats, carriages and a scotch cart.

The story ends in disaster. The money taken to South Africa was lost in the bankruptcy of the firm recommended by the AMEC; no boats or wagons ever arrived; nor did money to support the teachers. By 1905, the AMEC school had closed down and the teachers had left. In order to prevent the Ethiopians from returning, the BSAC allowed Lewanika to set up the elite Barotse National School paid for out of the national revenues and independent of the missionaries.

The themes which emerge from this sad story bring out some of the essential characteristics of Ethiopian churches everywhere, though there were few African kings able to offer patronage. Three themes dominate – the frustration of African evangelists and teachers at being held back in the mission church; African suspicion of colonial motives; and the desire for advanced education. The period at which these frustrations emerged varied widely.

One moment which stimulated the emergence of Ethiopian churches in eastern Africa was the First World War. The fighting and epidemics of disease undercut white claims to represent civilisation and progress. In many places first British and then German missionaries were interned and African Christians ran the churches until white control was re-established after the war. A student at Makerere, T.H.I. Guga, collected oral testimony from African Lutherans in the Usambara mountains in north-east Tanzania. The German Lutherans were interned but:

> The word of God was further spread when the Church was being run by natives. There was no opposition. Those who accepted Christianity were helped by the Holy Spirit and had a burning zeal without being forced by any circumstances. It was never because of poverty that they accepted Christianity. During that time there was a free manifestation of love. At festivals many came from afar and sang hymns and played trumpets. [But] when the missionaries came back there were signs that the Holy Spirit had left for the desire to co-operate to work for the Lord was no more seen. Trouble started when they started grading workers. Hatred started.[11]

Another place where German missionaries were interned was in south-western Tanzania among the Nyakyusa. Here African Moravians clashed with the Scottish Presbyterians who had come to run the stations. Nyakyusa Christians were deeply committed – they took names like 'The Word has taken hold of me', 'He has roused me', 'He has died for me'. Like the Lutherans of Usambara they felt they could run the church. So they were responsive when Ethiopian church leaders came into the district from Nyasaland.

There were two main Ethiopian churches in Rungwe, the African National Church and the Last Church of God and His Christ. In the ANC there was an additional element. Its leaders were all well-educated men – printers, clerks, storekeepers, teachers – who had been suspended from the Livingstonia Mission in Nyasaland for polygamy. One of them was Levi Mumba, a leading figure in the Malawi Native Association; another was Robert Sambo, founder of the Industrial and Commercial Workers Union in Southern Rhodesia. They drew up an elaborate constitution: 'We believe in the fatherhood of God and the brotherhood of man regardless of colour and creed and that the African religion with its traditions, laws and customs was instituted by Him so that the Africans may realise him by their own observance.'[12]

In May 1967, one of my University of Dar-es-Salaam students, Mwambuluktu, interviewed members of the Ethiopian church in Rungwe. One of the members of the ANC told him:

> Africa was given to the Africans and Europe to the Europeans. God helped us to get rid of the Europeans so that we could be left free to manage our affairs in our own ways. But our Government is using what the British left to run our country, that is things like laws and administrative machinery. The only difference here in the ANC is that those techniques of administration are interpreted according to our traditions. In the same way when we break from European churches we don't make a new Bible, we use the same but make our own interpretation of it, according to our own traditions and values.[13]

---

[11] Guga, 1965
[12] Wilson, 1959
[13] This quotation is from Ranger, 1969

A final example of the importance of the desire for higher education combined with the frustration of African evangelists and clergy within the mission churches comes from Southern Rhodesia in the 1930s. The first generation of Anglican and Methodist missionaries promised 'equal rights to all civilised men' and promised to 'civilise' Africans by educating them. The more radical missionaries trained up an African clergy, expecting them to take over the churches and to play a prophetic role. However, with the onset of the Great Depression the mission churches withdrew. Many schools were closed down. A new generation of missionaries kept the African clergy firmly in their place as subordinates.[14]

There was great African resentment about this betrayal. Summers' *Colonial Lessons* has chapters headed 'African School Activism, 1920-1934', 'Demanding Schools', 'Struggles and Stalemates'. I have myself written the biography of an African Methodist minister, Douglas Thompson Samkange, who responded bitterly to his repression by the new generation of missionaries and their refusal to support his efforts to provide higher education in the Reserves.[15] Samkange and his friend Reverend Esau Nemapare tried every way they could to set up African agencies. They planned a Methodist African Society which would run its own schools. In the end Nemapare broke away altogether and founded his 'Ethiopian' African Methodist Church. He wrote to Samkange about their joint struggle with the missionaries: 'You must know and know at once that as far as I am concerned the defensive phase is ended and that from now on a new phase is set for life and death: the offensive phase'.[16]

As he set up his own church and schools, Nemapare was pompously rebuked by the missionary Howarth – 'Esau, you have been a child of light' he wrote in June 1947, 'and now you are living in darkness': he replied that 'as an African I must teach the bully to be a gentleman'.

In the 1950s, Nemapare set up a Synod which brought together a number of independent African churches, each indicating in its name the missionary tradition it had broken away from – African Presbyterian, African Lutheran, African Methodist, and so on.

Pentecostal Mission

At a conference in Uppsala in 1987 I argued that:

> Independent churches have been seen as drawing upon African religious traditions in a uniquely direct way and I think this is misleading. Churches which emphasise ecstatic possession by the spirit, which foster prophecy and spiritual healing and exorcism have been seen as continuations of African beliefs and practice. Yet

---

[14] See Summers, 1994 and Summers, 2002

[15] Ranger, 1995

[16] Ranger, 1995:83

> these very features, which are taken as being most African, are in reality the most Christian aspect of such churches. They spring directly from increasingly strong tendencies in world Christianity in the late nineteenth and twentieth centuries. They spring in fact either from anti-establishment Christian Pentecostalism, as it developed in Europe and North America, or from revivalist tendencies within the major mission churches themselves.[17]

In the latest issue of *Transformation*, Allan Anderson writes on 'The Origins of Pentecostalism and its Global Spread in the Early Twentieth Century'. Anderson writes that, 'Canadian evangelist and former elder in Dowie's Zion City, J.G. Lake, travelled to South Africa in 1908 and established the Apostolic Faith Mission, now the largest Pentecostal denomination in that country. Others left for British East Africa in 1911.'[18] Anderson emphasises that white Pentecostal missionaries were as paternalist and racist as any others. However, the ideas of Zion City and of Pentecost rapidly escaped their control. Anderson and Hollenweger describe how the Apostolic and Zionist movements became Africanised in South Africa.[19] Comaroff, in her extraordinary book about Tswana Zionism, describes 'The Cultural Logic of the American Zion' before she comes onto the African version.[20] She finds an extraordinary resonance between the experience of the impoverished white urban groups in America's Mid-West, who flocked to Zion City outside Chicago, and the proletarianised and marginal Tswana.[21] Maxwell's *Gifts of the Spirit* shows in astonishing detail the emergence of prophetic movements in Rhodesia out of a sea of wandering Apostolic Faith evangelists.[22]

However, indigenisation of the Pentecost and the ideal of Zion did not mean a conscious return to African religion. What it meant was that African Christians, through the power of the Holy Spirit, could at last absorb the modes of African religion into Christianity. All over the world, as Anderson shows, people were experiencing Pentecost, speaking in tongues, healing, prophesying, gathering in holy cities. These had been the major idioms of African religion. They were now global. Some scholars have argued that this was no accident. As Anderson writes of the famous Azusa Street revival in Los Angeles, its black American leader, Seymour, 'was deeply affected by an African spirituality, a holistic spirituality that made the Pentecostal and Charismatic message so suitable to cultures all over the world, where experience of divine intervention was more important than creeds, controversies and doctrinal arguments'.[23]

---

[17] Ranger, 1987
[18] Anderson, 2005
[19] Anderson, 2000 and Hollenweger, 1997
[20] Comaroff, 1985
[21] Comaroff, 1985:177, 179, 181-182
[22] Maxwell, 2006
[23] Hollenweger, 1999:183

African Zionist and Pentecostal Churches

So at long last we come to the sort of African initiated churches which took advantage of the failure of mainline mission Christianity to adapt to prophecy, spiritual healing, spirit possession, the idea of the holy mountain, and the preoccupation with witchcraft. But in fact 'took advantage of' is the wrong expression, smacking too much of missionary resentment at the success of these 'enthusiastic' movements. It would be better to say that the prophetic founders of these churches responded to these unfulfilled needs, striving to make African Christianity deeper and more effective.

There have been many sociological and political analyses of these movements which have often been seen as disguised anti-colonialism or as an expression of the resentment of the underclass. I explored such interpretations in my long review essay, 'Religious Movements and Politics in Sub-Saharan Africa', African Studies Review, 29, 2, June 1986. But I also quoted there Archbishop N.H. Ngada's repudiation of such analyses on behalf of the South African prophetic churches:

> There is one enormous omission throughout the whole history that has been written by outsiders. The work of the Holy Spirit throughout our history has simply been left out. The events of our history have been recorded as if everything could be accounted for simply by sociology and anthropology. We would like to write our own history from the point of view of the Holy Spirit ... Everything comes from the spirit of God. Our prophets are called by the Spirit and they dream dreams and see visions.[24]

In my own most recently published chapter on African prophets, I have taken something of this perspective.[25] My chapter is situated in the 1930s, that time of economic depression and of retreat by the mission churches. In the first section of this lecture, I discussed the Ethiopian response to this crisis. In my recent chapter, I discuss the prophetic response.

The prophet on whom I focus is Shoniwa Masedza Tandi Moyo, later and well known as Johana Masowe, John of the Wilderness, founder of a church which today numbers millions. Johana had a complex denominational background – a Methodist uncle, an Anglican father, a series of encounters with the Apostolic Faith Mission, an admiration for the Roman Catholic Church.[26] This had left him with a profound sense of mission Christianity's inability to confront the real needs of Africa.

As I wrote in 2002, 'his main objective was the divine transformation of the African people':

---

24 Ngada, 1986:20-21

25 Ranger, 2002

26 For the first study of Johana Masowe, see Dillon-Malone, 1978); for Johana's interaction with the AFM, see Maxwell, 1999

> Masowe's founding vision [in 1932] was of his death; his journey to heaven; his witness of dead African twins. 'suffocated by their ancestors', and other children killed by witches; the clamour of these slain innocents that 'the world would come to an end so that they could bring their case against their fathers'; and Christ instead commissioning him to return and purge the African people of witchcraft and evil spirits in preparation for the Second Coming. This was an African prophet sent to the African people ... Masowe's work, seen in this light, was not so much a continuation of the missionary's work, the taking up of the task in which the missionaries were faltering. It was rather that the missionaries had been incapable of redeeming the African people. Only an African prophet could so that and thus achieve what the missions had proclaimed but could not do.[27]

The early days of Masowe's movement saw 'great gatherings at which the Holy Spirit descended and Africans flocked to surrender their witchcraft charms and to see them consumed by holy fire. So far from returning to traditional religion, many Africans were giving it up for the first time. As his following grew, Masowe 'began to praise the white mission churches for preparing those who were to become his followers [familiarising them] with his Word before he had come in person to lead them'.[28]

The Masowe Apostles have become the most studied prophetic church in Africa. Books about them are in press by Bella Mukonyora, who concentrates particularly on their gender relations, and by Matthew Engelke, who focusses on the *we chisanu* faction of the church which contrasts the 'dead' Bible to the live Holy Spirit. The Apostles conform almost perfectly to my model – they rely on prophetic leadership (and Engelke) is able to trace the whole sequence of *we chisanu* prophets; they offer spiritual healing; their mission is to exorcise witches and evil spirits; Johana's mountain top burial shrine has become the focus of annual pilgrimages for hundreds of thousands of people. Yet they are totally opposed to African religion. They drive out ancestor spirits as well as demons; they seize mountain tops from spirit mediums and holy pools from the priests of the High God, Mwali. The Zimbabwean Zionist churches enter into direct conflict with the Mwali priests for the control of sacred sites.[29] They undermine African religion by meeting the needs it fills.

Conclusion

I end this paper with a series of paradoxes. The great idioms of African religion in the long nineteenth century, which still find expression in African religion itself, have found their most spectacular adaptation in Apostolic and Zionist churches which seek to destroy traditionalism. Meanwhile the Ethiopian churches, which arose out of a desire for education and a resentment of

---

[27] Ranger, 2002:118
[28] Ranger, 2002:119
[29] See Daneel, 1971

missionary betrayal of the civilising promise, have come to value aspects of 'tradition'. I am currently writing on the social history of the Bulawayo townships, for example. African cultural nationalists there in the 1950s supported the African Methodist Episcopal Church or one of the churches in Nemapare's cluster. They advocated the performance of ancestral rituals for the burial and bringing back of the spirits of the dead. However, at the same time they stressed dignity, sobriety, preaching, the Bible. They strongly disapproved of the noisy ill-disciplined enthusiasm of the Apostles. Meanwhile the historic mission churches, faced with this double challenge, were experimenting with new ideas of inculturation.

INCULTURATION: HISTORICAL BACKGROUND, THEOLOGICAL FOUNDATIONS AND CONTEMPORARY QUESTIONS[1]

Brian Stanley

Dr. Brian Stanley is Director of the Henry Martyn Centre in Cambridge, U.K.

Historical background

Writing of Europe in the early modern period, Professor Andrew Walls has said this: 'Events so welded Christianity and the West together, and the domestication of Christianity in the West was so complete, the process of acculturation there so successful, that the faith seemed inseparable from the categories of European life and thought.'[2]

What to the *insider* can look like remarkably creative and successful inculturation, to the *outsider* can look like domestication of the faith or syncretism. By the late medieval period Christianity had become so deeply ingrained within European culture and social institutions that Christian profession and identity bestowed through baptism became virtually automatic for all who were born within the boundaries of European Christendom, with the notable exception of the Jews. But this apparent triumph of Christian inculturation in what had once been barbarian and pagan territory became a distinct liability once European Christendom went into expansionist mode and attempted to export the faith in its Western form (first Catholic, then Protestant) to parts of Africa, India, China and Japan. The Christian message was generally presented as an integral part of a package of European 'civilisation' to such an extent that Christianity appeared to be an essentially Western product. This was despite the fact that Christianity had preceded the political expansion of Europe to Africa south of the Sahara and to Asia by many centuries: the faith was in Ethiopia from AD 340, South India from 350 at the latest, China from 635. But these ancient roots of Christianity in Africa and Asia were largely forgotten or ignored by the new forces of European missionary expansion. As a result, a false equation between Christian and western identity was propagated to Asia and Africa, with consequences that

---

[1] Stanley, 2007:21-27

[2] Walls, 2002:49

have been and continue to be immensely harmful to the Christian cause, especially in Asia. In some Indian languages today, the word for 'Portuguese' is also the word for 'Christian': for most Indians, formal Christian profession is fundamentally incompatible with Indian, 'Hindu' identity. In a similar way for the majority of Chinese from the eighteenth century onwards, and even to an extent today, Christian identity has appeared to be intrinsically incompatible with what it means to be Chinese.

It is not surprising, therefore, that inculturation has become one of the most prominent themes of the Asian, African, Pacific and Latin American theologies that are now so much a feature of world Christianity. The quest for inculturation is a quest for a secure and integrated identity, motivated by a concern to find ways of being *both* authentically Christian and authentically Chinese, Indian, African, or whatever. It is all about finding a way of being comfortable with the hyphen which for all of us links our particular social and cultural being as Chinese, Nigerian, Indian, or whatever we may be, with our common being in Christ, so that when we call ourselves 'Chinese Christian', 'Nigerian Christian' or 'Indian Christian' we do not feel torn apart by two mutually contradictory allegiances.

'Inculturation' is a fairly recent term in missiology, widespread only from the late 1970s, though cultural anthropologists had employed the concept of *enculturation* (or '*acculturation*', as in the quotation from Andrew Walls). In the earlier part of the twentieth century, Protestant missions had tended to use the term 'indigenisation' to describe their aim of establishing churches which should be authentically indigenous in governance, financial viability, and ownership of their own mission, in other words the famous 'three-selves' of nineteenth-century mission theory that were subsequently appropriated by the official Chinese Protestant church after 1949. Protestants, however, had generally been reluctant to allow insights from indigenous non-Christian cultures to shape theology itself, for Reformed theology has had a sharp awareness of the potential of all human culture to gravitate to a default position marked by human sinfulness.

Indigenisation, therefore, was more about ecclesiological form than theological substance. However, from the early 1970s, Asian, Latin American and African theologies began to emerge both in Catholic and in Protestant circles which insisted that it was not simply inevitable but also legitimate that theological formation itself should be shaped profoundly by the social, political, economic and religious context in which theology was done. Protestant mission theory began in 1972 to employ the concept of 'contextualization'. That term of Protestant origin was itself gradually (but never totally) supplanted from the late 1970s by a different term of Catholic origin. In 1962 the French writer J. Masson used the phrase 'Catholicisme inculturé'. Following extensive discussion of the concept at the 32nd General Assembly of the Jesuit order in 1974, the Superior-General of the Jesuit order, P. Arrupe, introduced the term 'inculturation' to the Synod of Bishops in 1977.

It was taken up in the Apostolic Exhortation issued as a result of the Synod, *Catechesi Tradentae*, and from this point on entered wide currency first in Catholic and then in Protestant circles.[3] Inculturation is arguably the most far-reaching of the three concepts, for it implies that the whole body of the Christian message, not just its external wrapping, needs to take flesh, become incarnate, in the patterns of thought, language, and symbols of a particular culture.

The idea of inculturation is, of course, much older than the term. It is no accident that it was the Jesuits who first introduced the term to modern theological discourse, for it was the Jesuits who were the most distinguished and controversial proponents in mission history of an inculturated approach to evangelization. They did so without the benefit of a developed systematic concept of plural cultures of the kind that we have come to accept as normative. It is only since the late nineteenth century that the idea has become generally accepted that each society has its own culture, functioning as an integrated system of assumptions, practices, and symbols. We should also note that the Jesuit enthusiasm for inculturation was not in fact a universal principle to be applied to all systems of belief. Matteo Ricci, for example, was much keener on expressing Christian faith within the categories of Confucian humanism, which bore some similarities with Italian Catholic humanism, than with Chinese Buddhism, which he believed to be idolatrous and fundamentally at variance with a biblical understanding of reality.[4] Nevertheless, Ricci in China, Alessandro Valignano in Japan, and Robert de Nobili in India, pursued missionary strategies which were ultimately judged in the eyes of their opponents and of the Vatican to be so radical as to place the integrity of the faith in peril. The opposition of the Propaganda de Fide to such rites as ancestor veneration in Confucian societies was not motivated by blind adherence to European ways or total inability to distinguish between matters of faith and matters of national custom. Propaganda in 1659 had indeed issued an instruction to the new Vicars Apostolic to be appointed to Indo-China and China, saying:

> What could be more absurd, indeed, than to transport France, Spain, Italy or some other European country into China? Do not bring them our countries but the faith, which does not reject or harm the customs and habits of any people, so long as they are not perverse; but, on the contrary wishes to see them preserved in their entirety.[5]

Rightly or wrongly, Propaganda felt that the heart of Christian Catholicity was at stake.

---

[3] Bosch, 1991:447

[4] Ross, 1994:150

[5] Cited in Ross, 1994:185

Theological Foundations

Heated debates over the boundaries between authentic and inauthentic inculturation are thus nothing new. As we are all aware, we find them in the New Testament. The first cultural frontier which Christianity crossed in its missionary expansion was that between Jew and Gentile: Acts 15 records the debate at the Council of Jerusalem between the pioneers of the Gentile mission and the defenders of Judaic orthodoxy. It was a debate about how to fix the boundaries of legitimate inculturation of an originally Jewish message in a Gentile environment.

The passion with which opposing views have been expressed in debates over inculturation reminds us that inculturation is not just about external matters such as ecclesiastical dress, church music, or church architecture. If it were, it would be relatively simple (though perhaps deeply depressing, for it is strangely these external facets of church life that often strike Europeans as being *least* inculturated when they visit churches in Africa or Asia). But inculturation has to do more fundamentally with the way in which the faith is received, understood, and expressed in corporate worship and personal devotion, and then lived out in codes of Christian ethics, which may be understood theologically as the worship of consecrated Christian living. Inculturation may be a profound reality at this level, even if the external forms of inculturation in dress, music, and architecture are not present. Conversely, though this may be less likely, it is quite conceivable for a church to indigenise such areas as its clerical dress, musical style and architecture, but to leave the deeper levels of integrated theological and ethical reflection unaffected.

The process of inculturation therefore impinges on the heart of Christian doctrine, for worship is the shaper of orthodoxy, determining the terms in which we give glory to the triune God: as the classic liturgical Latin tag puts it: 'Lex orandi: lex credendi': the law of prayer determines the law of belief. The way in which we worship shapes what we actually believe (as well as vice-versa). Inculturation, therefore, must have implications even for Christology, which more than anything else makes it a highly sensitive and controversial area for Christians. John Mbiti, one of the great pioneers of African theology, has said that 'Christian Theology ought properly to be Christology, for Theology falls or stands on how it understands, translates, and interprets Jesus Christ, at a given Time, Place, and human situation.'[6]

From the beginning, Christians have understood Jesus in terms of the linguistic and cultural categories available to them from the world in which they lived. The term *kyrios*, for example, had a rather different resonance for the Greek-speaking Gentile Christians of Rome or Corinth than it did for the Greek-speaking Jewish Christians in Palestine. For the former, the creedal claim that 'Jesus is Lord' meant that ultimate authority belonged to Jesus, and

[6] Mbiti, 1971:190

not to any of the numerous cult divinities of the Graeco-Roman world, nor to the Roman emperor, with his claim of quasi-divine status. For the latter, to say that 'Jesus was Lord' was to apply to Jesus the same term that Hellenistic Jews had increasingly applied to Yahweh himself, as a substitute for the divine name, which first-century Jews were increasingly reluctant to use. The same term carried different connotations within different sections of the early church, though these differences were variations of nuance rather than mutual incompatibilities.

What is interesting is the evidence from the New Testament that there were linguistic cross-overs between the worlds of Jewish and Gentile Christianity. For example, in I Cor. 16:22: Paul uses the Aramaic *Marana tha* in a letter addressed to a Greek-speaking Gentile congregation in Corinth, and he does not have to translate or explain the phrase. Larry Hurtado comments 'The likely reason is that he himself had introduced the expression to the Corinthians earlier as a verbal link to the devotional practices of their Aramaic-speaking, Jewish Christian co-religionists.'[7] In other words, Paul probably taught the Corinthian Christians 'This is how your brothers and sisters in Jerusalem and Antioch express their faith in the fact that Christ is one day coming again: it's a great catch-phrase: let's use it here as well'. The early church did not regard the cultural frontier between Jewish and Gentile as a closed one: it had all sorts of crossing-points and border traffic was encouraged. That is a vital point as we consider how to affirm both the catholicity and the manifold incultured-ness of world Christianity today.

Contemporary Questions

In the remainder of this paper I should like to suggest five crucial issues that need to be addressed as Christians grapple with the challenge of inculturation:

How much does inculturated language matter?

I have suggested that vernacularization of the faith necessarily means that we are committed to inculturation, even if there is plenty of room for argument over which are the most appropriate terms to use. Linguistic choices in theology do carry major long-term consequences. The centuries-long 'Term Question' in which Catholics eventually opted for *Tianzhu* (sometimes rendered as 'Lord of heaven'), as the term for the Christian God, while Protestants preferred either *Shangdi* (Lord on high') or *Shen* ('Spirit') is a good example. The fact that Catholics and Protestants in China continue to use different terms to address God has undoubtedly contributed to the impression that Catholicism and Protestantism represent quite different religions, an impression that may lie behind the entirely distinct structures created by the post-1949 government to supervise Protestant and Catholic church life.

---

[7] Hurtado, 2003:110

However, it is debatable whether culturally alien or archaic theological language is *always* a liability for the church. As Europe became Christianized during the period that also saw the development of a feudal system of society, Europeans were taught to venerate Jesus using language drawn from feudal relations. Europeans still call Jesus 'Lord', using a term that originally denoted the lord of the manor, the master who did not merely own our land but even our own selves, as we were his serfs or vassals. A person wishing to place himself/herself in feudal service to a new lord would place his hands together between the outstretched hands of the lord as a symbol of submission, dedication to service, and acceptance of the lord's protection. That is why European Christians have been taught to pray with hands clasped together, rather than arms outstretched, as in Judaism.[8] We have retained the feudal language and even the symbolic gesture long after the context which gave rise to them has ceased to apply.

Does that mean the language and the symbols need up-dating? Much modern inculturation theory would suggest that it does, but I am not so sure. In an age when most Western people are profoundly cynical about and suspicious towards those who currently exercise supreme political power, Christology has more to lose than to gain by associating Christ with the Presidents or Prime Ministers whom we know rather than the lords or kings whom we no longer know much about! Nevertheless, language that has *no* cultural resonance within a particular context cannot perform any useful work in bearing theological meaning. It does help to know what a lord was, and what feudal homage involved, if we are to confess Jesus as Lord.

What are the criteria for authentic inculturation?

The perennial issue throughout Christian history has been how to distinguish good inculturation from bad, or – what are the boundaries which separate legitimate inculturation from syncretism? The question is often posed in the form: 'Is there an irreducible core of Christian truth that should be universal in its application to all contexts and cultures, and if so, what is it?' 'What is the essential "DNA" of Christian identity?' The problem about posing the question in this way is that Christians from varying cultural backgrounds will differ on where to draw the boundary between what is kernel and what is husk. For some North American conservative evangelicals, for example, a strict doctrine of verbal inerrancy is 'kernel': unless you subscribe to it, you are not an orthodox Christian. Other Christians, however, would wish to say that the doctrine of verbal inerrancy was a product of a particular Christian culture at a certain period – it is 'husk'. But this is not to deny that there is a kernel: it is simply to say that the cultural conditioning that all Christians share, simply because we are human, means that the ideal of an eternal universal supra-cultural 'gold standard' of what the kernel is will never be attained. Even when

[8] Bloch, 1965:I.145-6, 233

we attempt to verbalize what the kernel is, we cannot avoid the influence of our culture on the language which we employ. Even the Roman Catholic Church, which professes to define such a theological gold-standard through the *magisterium* of the papacy, proves this point by its own history: post-Vatican II Catholicism defines the kernel of orthodoxy rather differently from Tridentine Catholicism.

But does this mean that all boundaries fall, and that all formulations of Christian orthodoxy are pointless? If we were to accept such a tenet, then it would become impossible to maintain any meaningful idea of the catholicity of the church. It would be impossible, for example, to rule out of court as illegitimate such bastard nationalistic 'inculturations' of Christianity as were developed by those who called themselves German Christians during the Nazi period or by Afrikaaner nationalists during the apartheid era in South Africa. It is significant that one of the few contexts in which ecumenical theology since the 1960s has felt compelled to employ the medieval vocabulary of 'heresy' was in response to the theological legitimation of apartheid by the Dutch Reformed Church. The question 'What is the DNA of the Gospel?' has in fact to be continually posed and provisionally answered by Christians of every age and every culture. The answers have to be framed in and through inter-cultural Christian conversation on the basis of seeking faithfully to interpret the scriptural witness. No one portion or indeed generation of the world Church is able to answer that question in isolation from the others. Hence the current argument within the Anglican communion over whether or not the endorsement of physical relationships between Christian homosexuals can be viewed as a legitimate inculturation of the gospel in modern northern-hemisphere society cannot be decided by northern-hemisphere Anglicans alone, nor can it be decided without reference to the judgment of Christians from those other cultural epochs that are now history. As Robert Schreiter insists, one of the essential criteria for authentic Christian identity must be catholicity: 'Is a local church willing to stand under the judgment of other churches in the matter of its Christian performance or does it close itself off, assured of its own truth?'[9] The church which is so convinced that it stands alone in proud possession of the truth is in fact the church which stands in greatest peril of heresy.

Inculturation from outside or from inside?

A third issue relates to the choice between inculturation 'from outside' and inculturation 'from inside'. Inculturation from outside has been the approach of many Western missions from Matteo Ricci onwards. It is about the missionary outsider deciding how the message that they bring can best be packaged in order to promote maximal reception of the message by the host culture. Although to an extent appropriate and necessary, the danger of this approach in a context in which European cultures were taken as the default

[9] Schreiter, 1985:119-20

setting is that it could carry the false implication that the Christian gospel itself was naturally foreign or alien to Asian or African cultures in a way that it was not to European cultures, and that therefore some kind of re-engineering had to take place to remove the inherent problem of foreignness. As a 'religion', in the institutional form that it was carried to Asia and Africa, Christianity undoubtedly needed and doubtless still needs such re-fashioning, but we get into theological difficulties if we say that the gospel itself is more indigenous to some portions of humanity than it is to others. The starting point for inculturation must surely be the recognition that the message about Jesus simply *is* good news for all people of all cultural backgrounds. If any cultural or ethnic segment of humanity is consistently hearing the message of Christ not as good news but rather as bad news, or simply as no news at all, the fault lies not with the message itself, but in some way with the institutional and ideological structures and cultural forms in which Christians have enveloped, even disguised, the message.

Ultimately more satisfactory and permanent, as Kwame Bediako has powerfully argued,[10] is the process of inculturation from inside: that is, the process of reception, appropriation, and interpretation of the Christian gospel by indigenous people. Can the outsider ever have the final word on what it means for the word of Christ to take flesh in somebody else's cultural context? Surely not, though this does not excuse the outsider from the necessity of thinking deeply and creatively about the content and forms of the message he or she presents. Theologically, the key event is the experience of Pentecost, when those of multiple linguistic and cultural backgrounds (even though they were all Jews) heard the one message about God's mighty deeds in and through Jesus of Nazareth in their own languages, and hence from the beginning responded to it in terms of their own varied cultural frameworks. At Pentecost the Spirit representatively baptised and sanctified all languages and hence in principle all cultures.

Inculturation from above or from below?

A related choice to make, or perhaps balance to maintain, is that between inculturation from above and inculturation from below. Much of the energy that is currently devoted to inculturation derives from the activities of theological or academic elites, and the fact that we are here today means that we are all part of such elites. For a whole variety of reasons, we often find ourselves abstracted from the Christian communities on whose behalf we are supposed to be labouring. Many of the most influential scholars in Asian theology, for example, write their books from New York or Chicago or the University of California rather than from their home countries. The vast majority of Christians in Asia and Africa are poor and poorly educated. They know very little of the books that we write about inculturation, and if they did

[10] See Bediako, 1995

know about them, they probably would not approve of them! But does this mean that no process of inculturation goes on at the grass-roots or bamboo-roots level? Surely not. Ordinary Asian and African people respond to the word of the gospel in the power of the Spirit just as the very first Christians did on the Day of Pentecost: they respond within the matrix of their own linguistic and cultural frameworks, and hence inculturation is to an extent inevitable. The primary task of theologians of inculturation is not to tell such ordinary Christians what they ought to be making of the gospel if they are to be culturally authentic believers. Rather it is to interpret and reflect sympathetically but critically on what they are already making of the gospel. Hence what is needed is not a choice between inculturation from above and inculturation from below but a bringing together of what are so often two disparate spheres. The process of globalization has made the whole process infinitely more complex, for it is now harder than ever to define the identity and frontiers of a particular ethnic, national or regional culture. What we have learnt to call discrete 'cultures' have always been constructed approximations to reality, in perpetual flux, and with porous boundaries: globalization has simply accentuated that trend.

How feasible is it to separate 'religion' from 'culture'?

Much of the contemporary writing on inculturation, at least at a semi-popular level, presupposes a degree of transparency about the notions of 'religion' and 'culture' and a degree of optimism about the possibility of separating the two. Evangelical Protestant missiology in the Lausanne tradition, for example, has tended to affirm the signs of divine presence in non-Christian *cultures* but to be much more sceptical about the possibility of divine presence in non-Christian *religions*. The Lausanne Covenant of 1974 insists that no culture can claim superiority over any other in the sight of God: all cultures reflect something of the beauty and goodness of God, yet are also shot through with sin and the power of evil (section 10). But the Covenant elsewhere rejects 'every kind of syncretism and dialogue which implies that Christ speaks equally through all religions and ideologies' (section 3).[11] I want to affirm both those positions, and yet as an historian I am conscious that culture and religion cannot be separated quite so easily. The supposition that they can be so separated is characteristic of western Latin thought, which has tended to operate with a simple dichotomy between religious belief and social custom, as the 1659 statement by Propaganda did. The Enlightenment made the dichotomy even more stark by systematizing the concepts of religion and culture as definable and discrete spheres of human activity. Post-Enlightenment Europe has put religion in one clearly labelled box and culture in another.

In most non-western societies, however, it is much more difficult to delineate the boundary between what may be labelled 'culture' and what may

---

[11] Stott, (ed.) 1996:39, 16

be labelled 'religion'. The Sri Lankan Catholic theologian, Aloysius Pieris, has put it in this way:

> The very word 'inculturation' which is of Catholic origin and inspiration, is based on this culture-religion dichotomy of the Latins, in that it could, and often does, mean the insertion of 'the Christian religion minus European culture' into an 'Asian culture minus non-Christian religion.' This is inconceivable in the South Asian context what seems possible and even necessary there is not just inculturation but 'enreligionization' of the Church.[12]

By that ugly word Pieris meant that the task facing Christians in Asia is to find ways of constituting the body of Christ in Asian contexts which fit naturally into the historic structures of belief and practice of Asian societies. He was arguing for ways of 'being church' that are recognizably Hindu, Buddhist, Confucian, or Islamic. I can understand and even sympathize with that aspiration, for what we have in the New Testament is an ultimately successful struggle to find ways of being church that were recognizably Gentile, despite the fears of Jewish Christians that 'religious' truth was thereby being compromised. Nevertheless, we have to ask whether Pieris takes sufficient account of the challenge which the message of the Cross issues to all human systems, whether we label them as 'religious' or 'cultural'. Brahminical Hinduism, for example, denies both the fundamental reality of material things and the intrinsic equality of all human persons. Can one be authentically Christian and deny the reality of the material creation and the equal worth and dignity of all human beings? Most Christians would say one cannot. Theological reflection on inculturation neglects at its peril what Stephen Bevans has termed the 'counter-cultural model' of contextual theology. This takes context with utmost seriousness, yet insists that it cannot be given ultimate primacy. Bevans cites Lesslie Newbigin, whom he regards as perhaps the most influential exponent of this model of contextual theology:

> If it is truly the communication of the gospel, it will call radically into question that way of understanding embodied in the language it uses. If it is truly revelation, it will involve contradiction, and call for conversion, for a radical *metanoia*, a U-turn of the mind.[13]

Conclusion

The enterprise of inculturation of Christianity into cultures that are profoundly shaped by non-Christian religious traditions is always going to be fraught with difficulty. The real challenge is for Christians to discover *together* what it might mean for particular portions of humanity to re-orient the totality of their

---

[12] Pieris, 1988:52

[13] Newbigin, 1986:5-6; cited in Bevans, 2002:117

life and thinking (including elements of life and thinking that westerners have tended to label as 'religious' rather than 'cultural') towards an acknowledgement of the Lordship of Jesus Christ, for that is surely the central strand in the DNA of the Gospel. Such reorientation can and will mean profound revolution, but it also implies continuity: what is re-oriented towards Christ is still there in some shape or form. Defining the nature and precise shape of that re-orientation is the central task of inculturation, and it is a task that is central to our response to the Christ who calls all human beings to follow Him.

This paper is indebted to the writings of Professor Andrew Walls. It began with a quotation from him, and he shall have the last word as well:

> The faith of Christ is infinitely translatable, it creates "a place to feel at home." But it must not make a place where we are so much at home that no one else can live there. Here we have no abiding city. In Christ all poor sinners meet, and in finding themselves reconciled with him, are reconciled to each other.[14]

[14] Walls, 1996:25

THE BIBLE AND CULTURE IN THE SHAPING OF ASIAN THEOLOGY[1]

Carver T. Yu

Dr. Carver T. Yu is President of the China Graduate School of Theology, Hong Kong

Preliminary Reflections

Asian theologies are as various as the perceptions of the Bible, the culture and even the theology intrinsic to them. To talk about the respective roles of the Bible and culture in the shaping of Asian theology, we need to know what actually we are talking about. To illustrate the point, let us take C.S. Song as an example.[2] His understanding of the nature of revelation in the Bible and that which is in the culture can be quite different from that of evangelicals or what Song calls traditional theology.

To Song, 'God is everywhere. God speaks out of everywhere. And God is at work everywhere.' It is the task of theology to show the presence of God. Whenever or wherever God and his work is made known, there we see theology at work. Since 'God was with the prisoners on their way to execution singing the "Song of Ariran", a folksong that has not ceased to speak to oppressed Koreans,' so 'there is theology in the Song of Ariran. Or rather there is theology in the hearts of those climbing the twelve hills of Ariran to meet their death.' With this understanding of theology, theology can no longer be restricted to the task of the church in her proclamation of the revealed truth of God. Revelation is everywhere if only we have eyes to see it. A Hindu poet can be unveiling God's presence in his work just as distinctly as Jesus' proclamation.

To further understand Song's perception of the Bible and culture in relation to theology, the term *hibiki* (the Japanese word for 'echo') is highly suggestive. For Song, 'theology is a deep resonance of God's *hibiki* echoed in the *hibiki* from the heart of nature and from the innermost recess of the human soul. Poetry, painting, and music seem to have been invented to sing and paint that *hibiki*. And theology is inherent in human beings because God has imaged

---

[1] Yu, 1998:16-20

[2] See, among others, Song, 1980, 1982, 1986, 1989, 1993, 1994

God's own self in them and enabled them to image God in creation and human community.' So the Bible can be said to be a text laden with the resonance of God's *hibiki.* It is in essence no different from any other piece of human work out of the innermost recess of the human soul. Reading the Bible can be perceived as an event when God's presence and his work are being revealed. Theology is present in the Bible. If theologians listen carefully, they will be able to hear God's *hibiki* resonated in the Bible which is at the same time echoed in the songs and the poetry of the oppressed. 'The Song of Ariran and the Song of Golgotha! Do they not echo each other? Do they not call one to the other?' It is therefore the task of theologians to identify the resonance of the echoes in the Bible with those in Asian cultures. 'Stories of Christians and stories told by persons of other faiths are not just parallel stories designed for each other to read, learn from, and admire. These stories come together, penetrate each other, and become integrated into the same stories.' However, Christian theologians very often 'mistakenly assume that God's presence is Christianity. They compare Christian faith with other faiths under the overt and covert assumption that what Christians believe is superior – not only superior but unique and absolute... To add to our problem, traditional theology has taught us that these religions are prone to revolting against God. All this points to the urgent need for us to become engaged in a theology of religions, not speculating about and comparing religions as a theoretical exercise, but feeling them, experiencing them as spiritual forces that have shaped or failed to shape the lives of peoples, the mores and ethos of societies.' With this, C.S. Song not only raises questions about the absoluteness of Christianity but also makes clear his theological approach to religion. Religion should not be assessed from the transcendent perspective of biblical revelation. Rather it can only be grasped in its being experienced as a life-shaping spiritual force in human societies. The starting point of theological reflection is human experience, and the ultimate reference is its significance and relevance to the life of the people.

C.S. Song's approach is a clear example of what is now called 'cross-textual hermeneutics'. The biblical text as a revelation of God has not been denied. However, in affirming the Bible as God's revelation, one cannot deny the fact that there are non-biblical textual traditions which are life-giving and life-sustaining in their unique contexts. What are these traditions in the eyes of God? Is it conceivable that God is absent from the historical process of these traditions which have been sustaining the life of so many peoples for so many generations? If God is not absent, as some theologians may like to assume, then can there be mutual affirmations between the biblical tradition and those other traditions as the resonance of God's compassion for humanity, or even the identification of certain events in the historical processes of both as God's providential and redemptive acts? These questions are implicit in Song's hermeneutics. To make these questions more explicit, what is the status of biblical truth among the 'truths' unfolded in non-Christian traditions? Can biblical truth be nothing more than an echo of truth among many echoes in the human symphony of spiritual quest? To reverse the question, what is the status of 'truths' (or truth-claims) in cultures in the light of biblical revelation? To what extent are they valid or do they have to be rejected?

Ecumenical theologians like Archie Lee would attack the so-called 'Christian text alone' approach. This approach, according to Lee, assumes that the gospel is static and self-sufficient. What is worse is that 'it denounces all other truth-claims in human religious traditions and holds a hostile attitude toward all non-Christian cultures that are considered basically pagan and perverted.' Lee's characterization is evidently an over-statement. It is highly doubtful that theologians who take the biblical text as authoritative would denounce all truth claims in human religions and hold a hostile attitude towards non-Christian cultures regarding them as perverted. Many evangelical theologians would acknowledge the spiritual insights in most of the religious traditions, seeing tremendous spiritual resources in them for the sustenance of a relatively holistic life as well as the quest for transcendence. However, this does not mean that there should be an unconditional affirmation and a total acceptance of the truth-claims of these traditions. The truth-claims may only be valid to a certain extent. They do not only have limitations but also oppressive elements as something implicit. A prophetic critique is, therefore, necessary for the sake of humanity. It is true that evangelical theology puts great emphasis on the significance of the Christian text, for the Christian text is the ground on which Christian theologians as Christian theologians should stand to engage in dialogue with all other religious traditions. It is a ground which they cannot abandon. Evangelical theologians would agree that we should not denounce truth claims simply because they are of other religious traditions. However, we should not affirm truth claims purely on the basis of the fact that they are of other religious traditions. Critical judgments have to be made. To evangelical theologians, the Christian text is sufficient in the sense that it is a revelation from God. It is insufficient, however, in the sense that it has to become flesh in the cultural traditions affirmed by the grace of God. Without the flesh, the Christian text cannot become the truth for humanity.

Culture and the Transcendent Perspective

It cannot be emphasized enough that the ecumenical critiques of traditional theology, particularly those with a triumphalist frame of mind, are deeply appreciated. Evangelical theologians are definitely with C. S. Song when he points out, 'The oppressed and humiliated have been speaking out of their suffering since the time of Abel, but theologians in Asia have just begun to hear them. Their groaning, their complaints, their sobs – in a word, their distress and anguish – were not in our theological textbooks.' One cannot agree with him more that there is no true theology without compassion. If there is true compassion, then theology would have to begin with silence rather than with words. It is only in silence that one can hear the groaning and yearning of human souls in extreme anguish. It is only then that one begins to know where it hurts and where liberation or healing is needed, it is only then that one begins to know where to search for relevant words with the liberating power in the gospel. It is only in silence that one can have a deep sense of wonder, marvelling at the tenacity of the human spirit, the vitality of the divine image in it, and at the depth of God's sustaining grace. Proclamation, true proclamation, has to begin in silence, in awe in the presence of God's grace even in the darkest pit of human existence. God's grace has already preceded even the liberating Word that we are to proclaim. At the same time, it is in silence that we understand what it means to be rendered speechless by the shocking cruelty of man to his fellow men. It is then that the relevant words of judgment may come roaring like thunder from the gospel. In this respect, evangelical theologians stand together with ecumenical theologians.

However, a fundamental difference between certain ecumenical and evangelical theologians in Asia remains. Ecumenical theologians like C. S. Song are quite ready to relinquish the transcendent perspective while evangelicals are adamant about it. It really boils down to this question: is Christian faith merely a cultural tradition among many? Is it merely a story born out of the womb of human consciousness, an echo of the self-same yearning and hope for liberation in many cultural traditions? Or to put it in another way, if indeed oppression or suffocation of humanity is real, then redemption and liberation is needed, but the question is, where does the Word (or Tao) of liberation come from? Does it come from within each and every culture itself out of its own self-regenerating energy, for each and every culture contains within itself the spiritual resources for self-liberation? Could the liberating Word have come from a reality which is transcendent to culture, a reality which evangelical theologians refer to as the transcendent God? To put it in yet another way, is there such a thing as transcendent revelation coming through ways and means as well as agents in accordance with the freedom of God? Or does revelation unfold itself in and through cultures as God is present in human activities? To some of the Asian ecumenical theologians, evangelical theologians are taking an absolutist position in regard to the status of the Christian faith relative to all other Asian cultural traditions. To evangelical theologians, some ecumenical theologians are too ready to forfeit the uniqueness and absoluteness of the Christian faith in order to adopt a relativist position. To engage in genuine dialogue, we need to come to terms with these issues.

As an evangelical theologian, I would like to point out certain inconsistencies in the relativistic approach to revelation and culture. There are in Asia trends of humanism which believe that humanity needs liberation and that can be achieved through human effort. There is no need of God or the revelation from God. The reality and presence of God may not be denied, but God is either so remote from human existence or so diffused in all things or so closely identified with humanity that he cannot be meaningfully identified as the distinctive source of the liberating Word. Here humanity is believed to be endowed within himself with the resources for self-regeneration. Certain trends in the Chinese cultural tradition are quite confident about that. Buddhism and Neo-Confucianism, for example, come close to this perception of liberation. Zen Buddhism and a form of Neo-Confucianism espoused by Wang Yang Ming believe in momentous liberation out of rigorous spiritual self-discipline. Revelation here means inner illumination about the true nature of human existence leading to liberation.

Some Asian ecumenical theologians are ready to adopt such a perception of liberation. They would proclaim on the one hand that the Zen Buddhist or Neo-Confucian perception of the human condition and the way to liberation is equally valid and sufficient as the Christian tradition because it is conceivable that God can be at work in and through humanity's spiritual discipline even without any awareness of his reality. Taking such an approach, there are at least two problems.

First, in insisting on maintaining the Christian God-talk, our ecumenical theologians cannot avoid being perceived as taking a condescending attitude. They can be regarded as looking at the Zen Buddhist or Neo-Confucian perception of reality from a higher plane of being aware of God's presence behind everything. In identifying the illumination in Buddhist meditation as the work of God, in effect they point to something more ultimate that our Buddhist or Confucian friends are not aware of. In insisting on holding onto the Christian theological language to validate the experience of liberation in other traditions, some of our ecumenical theologians cannot avoid imposing 'the presence of God' or 'the work of God' onto a framework that does not need them. Could our ecumenical theologians be radical enough to abandon their *theologos* so as to be truly on an equal footing with our humanist friends so that their affirmation of such an approach to liberation is genuine? If they truly believe that such an approach is equally valid and sufficient, then are they ready to abandon their Christian baggage and adopt a Zen Buddhist or Neo-Confucian frame of redemption and liberation, without having to interpret others' experience in terms of the work of God or whatever? To many of our Buddhist and Confucian friends, the so-called ecumenical dialogues are less than genuine because there is no true readiness on the part of the Christian theologians who see uniqueness and absoluteness in their Christian faith to adopt what others regard as the true and right path to salvation. The Zen Buddhist may challenge the ecumenical theologians to 'annihilate' God for the sake of total liberation, as genuine seekers of illumination should be ready to 'kill' anything (including God) that stands in the way to *nirvana*. Are we ready to do that? If indeed Asian traditions are equally valid and sufficient as the Christian traditions, and if the Christian tradition has nothing unique to say to the Asian traditions, then why should Asian Christian theologians continue to hold onto the Christian faith only to suffer the problem of identity crisis?

Secondly, to affirm an approach which has no use for the idea of the presence and the work of God as being equally valid as one that acknowledges God's involvement as vital, are we not in effect saying that belief in God or non-belief in God is culturally relative? Does this not in turn amount to acknowledging that belief in God is culturally constructed, that God is nothing but a device for certain socio-cultural functions? If God is a figment of cultural consciousness, then each God fits well only into the culture which creates it. If that is held to be true, then Christian theology would have nothing to say to Asian cultural traditions. In fact, cross-cultural hermeneutics is futile, as each and every cultural system is so unique that it is doubtful whether it is commensurable to one another. As human issues and religious quests in different cultures are so unique, why should we believe that cultural text A can illuminate and enrich cultural text B? What could we expect from cross-cultural hermeneutics as each culture has its unique way of coping with its inner problems? In fact, the only positive message out of this relativistic approach is that Asian cultural traditions have no need of the Christian tradition. That is something that Asian cultural traditions have known all along. The only service of such ecumenical theology is to remind the Christian church that the Christian faith is irrelevant in Asia, as Asia has its own cultural traditions. In fact, some would even point out that to maintain their own integrity, Asian traditions should beware of the Christian faith. In that case, 'Asian' 'Christian' theology may even be a contradiction in terms.

However, theologians like C.S. Song would be quick to point out, 'stories of Christians and stories told by persons of other faiths are not just parallel stories designed for each other to read, learn from, and admire. These stories come together, penetrate each other, and become integrated into the same stories.' Such an assertion certainly makes very good rhetoric for promoting dialogue, but the problem is, on what basis can we make such an assertion? Are they making it out of sheer conviction, or is there a theoretical justification for that claim? At the same time, what does 'come together, penetrate each other and become integrated into the same story' mean? The fundamental problem is that in proclaiming that all the traditions of faith are nothing but human stories born out of the worm of human consciousness, are these relativist theologians not in effect standing in a superior position, towering above all the traditions they interpret to announce the 'true nature' of all these traditions? While the 'insiders' of these traditions are totally committed to the truth of their traditions, these ecumenical theologians are completely free. They stand only on their transcendental reflection of human consciousness. They are 'non-foundational' so to speak.

For evangelical theologians there is a clear defining line between 'transcendent' and 'transcendental'. If all cultural traditions are nothing but systems of human ideology, and the so-called 'presence of God' or 'revelation of God' is nothing but a mythical device in the construction of such ideologies, then there is no transcendent dimension other than the 'transcendental' position of these ecumenical theologians. Without the transcendent reality, humanity is the sole agent in each and every culture to work out its own salvation. If that is the case, then humanity should decide what oppression is and what it is not. The Nazis too have their story of human liberation. Why should their story be less valid than stories of Jews who suffered in their hands, and on what grounds? Why should the caste system in India be challenged and not affirmed? In fact, at the height of the Cultural Revolution in China, there was great euphoria among ecumenical theologians about the new humanity and the kingdom of God emerging in China. There were even some who would speak of 'Christ incognito' in China under Mao. C.S. Song would give theological meaning to it in this way, 'The order that now prevails in China seems to reflect partially the order which God has brought into being out of chaos and disorder. The land which used to be torn and laid waste by natural disasters and by human brutality has begun to function again. New China seems now destined to represent the possibility of the future classless society. Is this not a picture of man come of age?' However, the so-called kingdom of God in China during the Cultural Revolution turned out to be almost like hell to many Chinese people who were subjected to the most severe kind of oppression. In the name of the benevolent totalitarianism of the proletariat, the brutal violation of human rights and lawless injustice was totally legitimized by ideological gymnastics. Many ecumenical theologians who should have been proclaiming prophetic critiques nevertheless became co-opted. Without the transcendent perspective, any society can justify its most hideous social crimes. Liu Hsiao Bo, a prominent dissident fighting for democracy in China over the years, who told his story about the Chinese people, said, "The tragedy of the Chinese people is the tragedy of a people without God".

When the light of the other (i.e. the transcendent) side has become dim, the deep darkness of our society can be made into infinite light.' The Chinese people had witnessed in the Cultural Revolution how a society can make darkness their infinite light. With the transcendent perspective, humanity is left to absolutize and divinize their own inhumanity. When the transcendent perspective is lost, theology will inevitable become ideology. That is why evangelical theology sees it as absolutely necessary to ground itself on the reality of the transcendent God. It is the uncompromising conviction of evangelicals that it is God who 'speaks' the universal Word of liberation, the Word incarnate, the Word both of affirmation and judgment. All cultures, including cultures under the shaping influence of the Christian faith, are created by human beings on the grounds of God's grace, and his mandates to preserve and promise to redeem in the face of the reality of sin and God's judgment. Humanity is to work out in his culture the divine mandates of preserving God's creation as well as the promise of redemption. The Word of God's grace is there in each and every culture.

Attempting an Evangelical Theology of Culture

The word 'culture' is derived from the Latin word *colere* which means 'to cultivate'. Cultivation of the environment is perhaps the more noticeable manifestation. Yet much more fundamental is humanity's cultivation of their own existence as a human person. Culture is that which gives form to human existence, in which human freedom assumes a concrete mode of expression, and human creativity takes a certain orientation. Culture is, therefore, the cultivated condition of human existence as well as the mode through which each person expresses his/her humanity. It is the totality of a constructed world in and through which a concrete humanity takes shape. This world includes the structure of meaning acted out ('lived out') by human beings, and through which they experience the world. It includes the emotional pattern which gives personal distinctiveness to humanity's response to the world. The structure of meaning and the emotional pattern integrate to give a personal identity to an individual. The world is to an extent an 'open' world. The 'openness' indicates the incompleteness (or 'less-than wholeness') of the world, and thus the perpetual quest for self-transcendence or to an extent self-denial (self-criticism). As a container, culture provides the boundary. Yet it also provides a transcendent horizon to transcend this boundary. Thus a culture, in its ideal state, contains in itself the possibility for continual self-renewal.

From the biblical perspective, culture is endowed as a mandate from God for humanity to act out the divine image of freedom, creativity and communion. Humanity is called to act in the world created by God. To give a name to things created by God is to communicate with them, to give human meaning and order to a world where God's meaning and order is intrinsic. By the act of naming, human meaning and order merge with divine meaning and order, and with this, God's intention for the created world may be expressed through human creativity. In Adam's act of naming, human language becomes loaded with divine intention. Through Adam's speech in naming the world God's creativity is 'spoken' through human words. In naming, Adam gives expression to the intrinsic relatedness within the world, and he also defines the way humanity is related to each and every unique creature in accordance with its particular mode of being. It is, therefore, an act of communication and communion. The 'humanized' world, i.e. the world now pregnant with human meaning, may be regarded as a co-creation of God and human beings.

Correlated to the mandated act of giving meaning is the mandate for humanity to 'rule over' the world (ASV), to bear the covenantal responsibility of taking care of the world now co-created by God and human beings. In entrusting the world to humanity, God calls them out from their own self, to go beyond their self to an actualization of being a human person. In acknowledging the actuality and integrity of the world, man is destined by God to always look beyond his subjectivity. With the mandate to create and to care, humanity can no longer regard themselves as a subject over and against the objective world from which they may choose to stand aloof or subject, but can only regard himself as an agent through which the reality of the world and the divine purpose in it may find its fullest manifestation. As an agent, humanity is a co-creator with God. Thus culture, in accordance with God's intention, is a co-creation with God through which the communion, the mutual involvement, and the integrity of those involved may be expressed in and through the human agent. In the fall, however, humanity attempts to subject God's mandate (covenant) as well as the world in accordance with their own vision for self-satisfaction or self-realization. The tree of knowledge defines humanity as subject over and against the world as object, as something to be apprehended by the grasp of human definition of good and evil. It defines the horizon of humanity's self-transcendence, viz. their own self-fulfilment. From then on, the world becomes a problem to be subdued. Culture is threatened to be turned completely into civilization in which the technological-utilitarian perspective of human creativity takes over. At the same time, humanity's horizon for self-transcendence is confined to the 'world-picture' or ideology he constructs for himself. After the fall, God's blessing is implicit in his judgment. It is a blessing in and through culture. Humanity is to face the reality of the world which has its own integrity. Humanity, who has to till the earth, ties himself to work in solidarity with the earth with a sense of dependence. Culture carries within itself certain redemptive pointers. However, culture is also dictated by human subjectivity – their subjective construction of meaning, their subjection of the world under their ideological construct, and their limited scope of transcendence for self-fulfilment. Culture is not only the arena where God's preserving and redeeming grace is played out or where the image of God is manifested, but also contains within itself a matrix of human sin. Indeed from the song of Ariran we see the irrepressible quest for justice, there we see the glory of the image of God and hear the echo of God's affirmation and promise of justice. Nevertheless we see simultaneously the other side of the reality of human culture – the perpetual institution and legitimation of injustice. Culture can become a self-legitimizing system of injustice. There is no guarantee that the singers of the song of Ariran by virtue of their aspiration and struggle for justice would become the embodiment of justice. It is in fact quite possible that they may in turn usher in by their struggle a new oppressive institution. The communist revolution has been a living testimony to such a possibility.

Here we cannot but agree with Barth in his dialectical years, though he was often represented unfairly by ecumenical theologians as the archetype of absolutism. To Barth, the world – humanity's life-world included – is a world sustained by God's love, and because of that, 'we shall be led first not to a denial but to an affirmation of the world as it is. For when we find ourselves in God, we find ourselves committed to the task of affirming him in the world as it is and not in a false transcendent world of dream. Only out of such an affirmation can come that genuine, radical denial which is manifestly the meaning of our movements of protest.' Despite the fact that the glory of God in the *regnum naturae* is veiled by the reality of human sin, the glory of God is still there. Even in the sinful world, the 'living and divine element is always there', and we have to commit ourselves to it. God's absolute commitment to the world is manifested in the incarnation and death of Jesus Christ. The world is 'created by him and for him', and 'in this "by him" and "for him", by Christ and for Christ, lies our victory over a false denial of the world and also our absolute surety against a false affirmation of the world.'

Evangelical theology, by virtue of the fact that it is theology of the good news, has the task of affirming the world as God would affirm it, as it is. We thus have the task of identifying God's preserving and redeeming grace at work in culture. Evangelical theology has to develop the spiritual apparatus to enable the church to see the image of God shining through cultural traditions. It has to be bold enough to identify mandates set by God in culture to redeem humanity from the complete sway of destructive evil forces. Even outside Eden, God had not abandoned Adam and Eve. Despite his judgment and curse, God continued to bless them, made provision and gave orientation to them so that they can overcome the total victory of evil forces. It is, therefore, the task of evangelical theology to identify the redeeming forces at work in culture and claim back what belongs to God.

Here the concept of *hibiki* may be useful. It is a genuine theological task to find *hibiki* between theological themes in the gospel and certain prime symbols (images) in Asian culture. Here a deep sense of humility is needed for the genuine attempt of a theological affirmation of aspects of value-creation in Asian cultures. These should be affirmed as spiritual resources for the attainment of human wholeness.

However, in the face of the reality of sin, affirmation is not enough. Some theologians are so eager to affirm cultural traditions that they risk becoming co-opted into systems of self-legitimization and become blind to the reality of sin in these traditions. In this sense, they have not taken culture seriously enough. To take culture seriously, one cannot avoid the critique of culture. As it was pointed out above, each culture is to a certain extent self-critical and self-transcending. Theology has to respond to such openness. It would be a theological disservice to culture if theology gave uncritical affirmation to culture for the sake of an ideology of pluralism.

The good news that evangelical theology expounds is the news that God would not sit still in the face of the reality of sin. It is a message of liberation – liberation from the oppressive bondage that human beings create for themselves. Thus prophetic proclamation of the judgment of God is intrinsic to the proclamation of the good news, and a prophetic critique of culture that cannot be avoided.

The Bible, Asian Cultures and Theological Construction

Since culture is the matrix in and through which human existence is concretized, it pervades every single human perception or action. It is the structure, the orientation as well as the raw material with which one is to build one's life. Thus there is a real danger of self-affirmation, self-perpetuation and even self-absolutization of a culture. This makes the biblical critique of culture all the more significant. Yet it also makes biblical interpretation all the more complicated. Is it possible to work out a cross-cultural hermeneutics that is at once evangelical, incarnating and transforming? Can Archie Lee's approach serve as a useful model? How can one be rooted in one's own culture and yet manage to transcend the pervasive presence of it which may distort the biblical message?

There is no denying that certain truth claims of Asian traditions have to be affirmed. However, theologians can never be blind to the oppressive elements and orientations in Asian cultures or else one betrays the prophetic character of biblical revelation. Hans Kung, for example, despite his strong affirmation of Asian traditions, does point sharply to the oppressive realities of the caste system in Hinduism.

The Biblical critique of culture may take a two-prong approach of drawing implications from the horizon of self-transcendence as well as drawing implications from the master-image (or prime symbol) of a culture.

The horizon of self-transcendence for Taoism, for example, is the perception of the fundamental nothingness of all that changes and the identification of oneself with the unchanging reality of Tao, leading to non-attachment to one's transient existence. There is thus no fear for death, no anxiety for non-being, and yet no joy, no sense of wonder to life, no celebration of the beauty of the differentiated world of distinctive identities. The biblical horizon of self-transcendence may be unfolded in juxtaposition with the Taoist horizon. Shining through the acknowledgement of the reality of human anxiety, fear, alienation, conflict and pain, there is the biblical celebration of the overcoming of alienation, of the beauty of human relations, the strength of love, the sanctification through suffering, and all things bright and beautiful that are created by God. Self-denial is the key concept for both horizons. However the orientations of self-denial are quite different. The Taoist self-denial is for the identification with the undifferentiated Tao, so as to achieve tranquility through inactivity. Christian self-denial begins with self-affirmation of one's infinite value in the eyes of the Absolute. God affirms the uniqueness of each and every living being. Each is present to complete a multifarious design of his creation. Self-denial is oriented towards self-transcendence for mutual participation and communion, for enriching one another.

In such a 'comparative' study, the vitality of a tradition may be brought out. However, evangelical theologians would have to ask themselves, are they ready to explore the possibility of reformulating their concept of revelation to acknowledge that certain spiritual insights in Taoism have their source in God's revelation? Are they bold enough to identify God's revelation even in non-biblical religious traditions, as some of our early church fathers did?

The other approach may be called the 'ontological approach'. The master-image (image or perception of reality) of a culture is uncovered through an ontological critique. That is, the symbol that gives the unity to the empirical as well as to values is unravelled. Then socio-cultural implications are worked out from those ontological foundations, thereby revealing the ontological root of the socio-cultural problems prevalent in the tradition. Likewise, relevant fundamental theological themes in the Bible are presented in response to the socio-cultural problems perceived. An ontological understanding is 'constructed' out of these themes and its socio-cultural implications drawn. The two ontological perspectives may then be compared through their respective concrete socio-cultural ideals and realities.

With this, we are in effect affirming the fact that the horizon opened up by the Bible for self-transcendence is much wider and more holistic than those of various Asian cultures. The biblical horizon may not need to reject the cultural horizons, but certainly it has much to offer to transform them so as to broaden them. Reconciliation-communion with God the Father and the outpouring love of the Father is the ultimate horizon for self-transcendence. At the same time, the master-image for human existence or the ontological understanding implicit in the gospel is affirmed to be the ground for a socio-cultural critique and transformation.

Conflicting Roles of the Bible and Culture in Shaping Asian Theology[1]

V. Devasahayam

Rt. Rev. Dr. V. Devasahayam is Bishop of C.S.I. Madras Diocese, India

Introduction

'The role of the Bible and culture in shaping Asian theology' was the original title assigned for this presentation. The present title aims to recognize and highlight the conflicting roles played by the Bible and culture in shaping Indian theology based on the variety of the Bible and culture and on the approaches, perspectives and stances adopted by different theologians. The Bible contains materials written over several centuries by several writers in different contexts; it is not a book speaking in one voice on several issues, but contains a variety of voices. Apart from the Bible's variety, the changes in the approach to the Bible and the changes in the interpretation of the Bible affect decisively the role of the Bible in shaping theology. As Moltmann remarks, 'Reading the Bible with the eyes of the poor is a different thing from reading it with a full belly;' we recognize that one's standpoint affects one's view point.

India is a land of bewildering diversity in terms of the plurality of religions and languages, the regional differences and ethnicities, and the economic and cultural differences. In spite of the bewildering diversity, the unique Indian social system, the caste system, is the most important cultural factor that is all-pervasive and affects all aspects of human life. The caste system, built on the religious foundation of Hinduism, is a hierarchical system that places people in a graded hierarchy of four *varnas* based on birth. It excludes a fourth of India's population, the Dalits, known as untouchables, who are outside the pale of the Hindu social order. The theologians' different approaches to caste resulted in varied ways of shaping Christian theology in India.

Attention is drawn in this paper to two significant theological developments in India: the emergence of classical Indian Christian theology and the emergence of Dalit theology. These represent two ways of theologizing in relation to caste reality, from an elitist or caste perspective and from an oppressed or Dalit perspective. The role of the Bible and culture is assessed in

---

[1] Devasahayam, 1998:21-27

relation to these theological developments and this paper assumes the form of a comparative study as a tale of two Indian theologies.

The Context: the Hindu scriptures and caste culture

Source of Brahminic Pride

India is a land of ancient scriptures and of ancient culture. The ancient Hindu scriptures and caste culture have been symbols of Brahminic pride. J.S.M. Hooper writes:

> It has to be remembered that India has never suffered from a dearth of religious literature, and that at one end of the scale of her vast population, there has always been a section whose religious pride has become proverbial and this arrogance has been based on the exclusive possession of an ancient sacred literature.[2]

During the nineteenth century and the early decades of the twentieth century, during the nationalist struggle for freedom from the British, this Brahminic pride became the common stock of India's new self-consciousness and self-respect. Nationalist politics were imbibed with religion and the Bhagavad Gita became the nationalist ideological rallying point during the struggle for independence, and the beginning of the process of the communalization of politics or the politicization of religion. Of course, this was done vis-à-vis the imperialism of 'Christian' Britain and the demand for a separate Islamic state, Pakistan.

The caste system, the most dominant element of Indian culture, is founded and sustained by Hindu religion and especially by Hindu scriptures. Hinduism and caste are irrevocably bound together as body and soul. Hinduism is hailed as Varna Dharma, the ethic of caste. This unique and distinctly Indian social organization is built on the principles of hierarchy, purity-pollution, segregation and is underpinned by the religious doctrine of Karma (the Hindu view of life is based on the belief in the existence of a cycle of births and holds that one's status and fortunes in the present birth is dependent on the deeds of the person in the previous birth). This was also hailed as India's unique contribution to the world and a symbol of India's caste greatness. S. Radhakrishnan, a Hindu philosopher and a former President of the Republic of India, praised the caste system. His work, *The Hindu View of Life*, is a thoroughgoing apologia for caste. He speaks not of the evils of caste but the evils of non-caste societies. He maintains that caste is a system of collaboration between races and the co-operation of cultures, and is the outcome of tolerance and trust; it insulates various groups from each other and ensures that they do not come into competition; caste transcends individualism, overcomes competitiveness and

---

[2] Hooper, 1938:6

holds work as a vocation of service for the common good.[3] The glorification of caste is not restricted to the Hindu upper-castes but is also strangely undertaken by Christians of upper-caste background. S.K. Dutta states, 'Caste has served in the past a useful service.... Caste has placed upon the community the responsibility of providing for the poor without its pale. In India accordingly there is no necessity for a poor law'.[4]

The Source of Dalit Shame

While India's ancient scriptures and caste culture have been praised as symbols of pride by upper-castes, they are perceived as the source of shame by the Dalits. The Rig Veda is one of the most important and the earliest written literary source in Hinduism. A large part of it is addressed to Lord Indra. The Aryans, the people of the three higher *varnas* are the people of the Lord Indra and the Dalits are pictured as the enemies of Lord Indra, whom the Lord Indra chases, defeats, loots and scatters, destroying their fortresses. They are described negatively as of a dark and dusky skin, faceless, nose-less, ritual-less, inhuman people, following alien laws.[5]

Manu Smrti, another important Hindu scripture, hailed as Hindu jurisprudence, codifies the rights and obligations of different *varnas* which in a way seals the fate of the Dalits. Manu prescribes segregated living for the Dalits, outside the village. The Dalits are permitted to own only a dog and a donkey and any transaction in land is forbidden. They are prescribed to wear the clothes of the dead, ornaments made of iron and to eat in broken dishes. The Hindu scriptures are out of bounds for the Dalits. Religious education was not only forbidden but was also made a punishable offence to its own adherents. Hearing the scripture is punished by pouring molten lead into the ear and the reciting of a scripture text is punished by pouring of it down the throat.

Caste culture, which is built on the principle of inequality, gives rise to the idea of superiority and inferiority among people, a sense of pride and superiority on the part of high castes and a sense of shame and inferiority on the part of the low castes and the untouchables. The psychological impact of caste culture on the Dalits is damaging: lowered self-esteem, confusion of self-identity, self-hate, the perception of the world as a hostile place, hypertension, neuroticism, etc. The caste system's cruellest form is the practice of untouchability, through which the Dalits are as treated as polluting people, unseeable, unapproachable and untouchable. The Dalits hated the caste system due to its ascending order of reverence to upper castes and descending order of contempt for low castes and outcastes.

---

[3] See chapter 8 in Forrester, 1980

[4] Forrester, 1980:180

[5] See chapter 1 in Massey, 1994

The Dalits and the non-Dalit sympathizers have condemned the caste system as deplorable as it constitutes a grave blot on our social arrangement. Gokhale, a Hindu reformer says:

> We may touch a cat, we may touch a dog, we may touch any other animals, but the touch of these human beings is pollution. And so complete is the mental degradation of these people that they themselves see nothing in such treatment to resent, that they acquiesce in it as though nothing better than that was their due.[6]

William Carey, a Christian missionary, speaking on behalf of the oppressed in the caste culture called it, 'the most cursed invention of the devil that ever existed, the masterpiece of hell'.[7]

The Advent of the Bible and Christian Theology

The modern missionary movement facilitated the advent of the Bible in India as a scripture in the midst of other scriptures and led to the search for and emergence of Indian theology as a result of the confluence of the gospel with Indian culture.

Although Christianity in India is as old as Christianity itself, the Bible was still unknown until the eighteenth century. St. Thomas, an apostle of our Lord, is said to have ministered and established churches in South India. In the ancient Syrian church, the Bible was in the Syriac *Peshitta* version, a language not spoken by the people, and there was little use made of the Bible in Syrian worship. Then came the Catholic missionaries in the sixteenth century who established churches. There was a strange silence as regards the Bible in the churches established by them. Hooper makes the following observation of the Catholic missions:

> But they have always shown themselves at best indifferent and at worst bitterly hostile, or have had a Bible without an interpreting church, so they have produced no Bible translation of value. Men of conspicuous linguistic gifts such as the Jesuit fathers Nobili and Beschi, who made other contributions to Christian literature, neglected the translation of the Bible.[8]

Protestant missions came to India at the beginning of the eighteenth century. Following the reformation tradition, the pioneering missionaries like Ziegenbalg and William Carey recognized the prime importance of the Bible and straightaway started Bible translation in all earnest. Bible translation was put at the forefront, for the Bible, as a vehicle of evangelism had the potential to cross the pollution boundary. As Hooper asserts:

---

6 Forrester, 1980:161

7 See Irudayaraj (ed.) 1990:21

8 Hooper, 1938: 8

> For him (Ziegenbalg) to put the Bible into the hands of the people was the greatest service that could be rendered to them. It was realised that the printed word can go where no human beings could go, that it remains with its message long after the human messenger has left, that through it God can and does speak in the quietness of the heart.[9]

The Bible came to be established as a scripture among other scriptures in the religiously pluralistic Indian subcontinent.

The modern missionary enterprise in India came to be associated with western colonization, though the East India Company had banned the entry of Christian missionaries until the beginning of the nineteenth century. The nineteenth century also witnessed the emergence of nationalist movements and struggles for independence from colonial rule, which left marks on Indian Christian thinkers, who raised critical questions on the appropriateness and relevance of western theology to an Indian church. It also kindled the search for an Indian theology, a search that forced them to come to terms with Indian culture, in order to facilitate its interface with the Christian gospel. The issue of caste came to the forefront also from an evangelistic strategy since caste was perceived sometimes as a help and sometimes as a hindrance. The nationalist struggle was built on the awakening and revival of Indian consciousness over and against the western colonizers. This at the same time had ripple effects in reviving ethnic identities particularly among the oppressed peoples, who extended the nationalist logic to its logical ends by saying: if one nation has no right to rule over another nation, how can one caste rule over other castes? The leaders of the nationalist movement, drawn from the elite castes who wanted to build one nation, one people and one culture, were forced to recognize the cultural diversity and the competing interests of Indian peoples. Christian theology, therefore, came to be articulated within this complex context.

Two Approaches to Theologizing

At the initial stages of attempting to construct Indian theology, two strands vis-à-vis caste are clearly discernible. One maintained that the caste system is Indian social order and hence part of Indian culture. It adopted an unethical attitude to caste and tried to relate the gospel to the dominant Brahminic tradition. In so far as this approach failed to critique and judge caste in the light of the gospel, and valued the status quo with regard to caste, it could be called caste theology. The other approach held that the caste system as a Hindu religious institution, perpetuated values that are totally inconsistent with the Christian gospel. It challenged the churches to a total break with the caste system. This approach is identified as the Dalit approach in theologizing. It is necessary to point out that the term 'Dalit' denotes an anti-caste identity,

---

[9] Hooper, 1938:8

symbolizing the aspiration of those who are committed to the dismantling of the caste system. However, it should be recognized that these two approaches are not mutually exclusive, for some thinkers who theologized from an elitist Brahminic perspective in terms of a religious philosophical tradition were critical of the caste system, though there was no clear call for a radical break with it.

The emergence of a Dalit theology is said to be of recent origin beginning in the 1980s. I would like to affirm that Dalit theology in the seminal form was already present during the last century, although neither recognized nor systematically articulated. In this paper, I am restricting it to the early attempts at theologizing from a Dalit perspective, in order that these attempts can be compared with their contemporaries. It is also intended to bring to light the contributions of the silenced and side-lined leaders of the Indian church and to bring their contributions to bear upon the ongoing theological task.

The Biographical Musings of Theologians

'That man thinks is a biological fact and what he thinks is a sociological fact' observed Thorndyke. Those who adopted a more tolerant stance towards caste were theologians who were themselves converts from an upper-caste background although there were some exceptions. A majority of these thinkers were silent on the issue of caste, thereby adopting a more status quo stance. These theologians have been accorded due recognition and are celebrated as the architects of 'Indian Christian theology'. They had limited influence on the church's life, though some of them have attempted excellent expositions of the Christian faith, drawing heavily from Brahminic traditions. These Indian thinkers found some western allies in missionaries, who are themselves from feudal societies and from aristocratic families.

Those theologians who adopted a Dalit stance in theologizing are less known, little documented and studied and are sometimes maligned as heretics, disturbers, animists, etc. They are converts to Christianity from among the Dalit communities. Some of the prominent ones are: Vedamanickam (Travancore), Periah (Andhra), Ditt (Punjab), Poiykayil Yohannan and Abel Tewathan (Kerala). They found allies from among missionaries and other Christians. Since they are little known, some biographical details would be helpful in assessing their importance and contribution to the Indian church. First, their conversions were motivated by a spiritual quest. There existed a false notion among missionaries that the conversions from among the Dalits are not genuine, as is the case with conversions among caste people. Christian Dalits were also denigrated as 'rice Christians'. A missionary remarked: 'I would rather baptise one Brahmin than a thousand Chamars (Dalit)'. Ziegenbalg stated:

> For, as for the rich and great, there are so many obstructions to hinder them from changing their faith. And so as to the poorer sort, and such as have no caste to

> value themselves upon, they are so vile a people that for a little rice, they would be of any religion, and for as small a consideration leave it again.[10]

This view was shared also by the leaders of the Indian church. The National Churches Council recommended that baptism of the Dalits should be stopped for some time.

Vedamanickam was a man of deep spirituality, who undertook a long pilgrimage to Chidambaram with the determination not to return to his village without finding the truth. He took with him Sivagurunathan, his brother's son, to perform the funeral rites in case he were to die on his long and risky travel. Vedamanickam was shocked at the crude and unspiritual worship at Chidambaram and was left disillusioned and disappointed. With his sister's family who were Christians, Vedamanickam attended Christian worship and encountered the call of the living Lord and obeyed. He recalls:

> The first time I heard the words of life, which the Lord revealed to me by his servant in Tanjore, my heart was rent asunder and the blessed news of salvation was to me as the sudden appearance of a star to one who had wandered in thick darkness without a ray of light, so that I felt reluctant to leave the place.[11]

Yerranguntala Periah, a cobbler belonging to an untouchable community, had a religious bent of mind since childhood. He had established contact with the Pothulumi Veerabrahman Saiva Sect as well as with the sects of Ramanuja and Nazar Mohammed Hasthan. Dissatisfied, Periah went to meet Dr. Jewett, a missionary at Ongole. During his meeting with Dr. Jewett, his mind was enlightened by God and he returned to the village converted, in order to work for the conversion of his family and community.[12]

Ditt was from the low and much despised Chura tribe in Punjab, lame in one leg, and accepted Christ as his saviour in the face of severe opposition from his family. He was put out of the house and curses were heaped upon him. His sister-in-law said, 'Alas, my brother, you have changed your religion without even seeking our counsel; our relationship with you is over. Henceforth you shall neither eat, drink, nor in anyway associate yourself with us. One of your legs is broken already, so may it be with the other.'

Rev. Martin, whom Ditt approached for baptism after undergoing a deep religious experience and acquiring sound Christian knowledge, although resistant in the beginning, was overwhelmed by his faith and baptized him.[13] Yohannan and Abel Thewathan too were converted to Christianity as a result of their search for truth and a casteless society.

---

10 Ziegenbalg, 1718:58

11 Gnanadason, 1994:44

12 Devasahayam (ed.) 1997:237

13 Devasahayam (ed.) 1997:185

Secondly, these leaders were charismatic personalities endowed with the gifts of preaching, prophesying and at times healing. They were the leaders of the movement of the Holy Spirit (called mass movements) and were responsible for bringing hundreds or thousands of disciples into the church. Vedamanickam was responsible for establishing the London Missionary Society work at Travancore. Periah brought into the church a large number of converts. He was visiting villages for evangelistic work along with his work as a trader. Ditt brought into the church more than 500 members within the first decade of his conversion. In the following two to three decades almost all the Dalits known as the Churas of Sialkot district had become Christians. Poiykayil Yohannan was able to attract a large crowd into his Prathyaksha Raksha Daiva Sabha. Abel Thewathan was responsible for bringing a large number of Dalits into the church. However, it is strange that these true apostles of India have been ignored and forgotten. The church needs to rediscover its authentic roots in order to equip itself for the contemporary mission.

Theological Agenda

Theologians of the caste approach are concerned with interpreting the Christian gospel within the cultural context of India. They use the Brahminic religious philosophical tools liberally in their task. The primary aim of these theologies is the promotion of Christ to non-believers i.e. non-Christians. Theology is based on an individual experience of Christ and takes the form of apologetics or boundary theology aimed at the people of other faiths.

Theologians who have consciously accepted a Dalit approach to theologizing have recognized their experience of new life in Christ as the basis. This experience is holistic with vertical and horizontal dimensions. The new life in Christ is experienced as the emancipation of from an individual and social identity to a new liberated individual and social consciousness. Equally influential on their theological task is their experience of disappointment due to the contradiction between the church's profession of equality and the practice of caste discrimination. Theology has a two-fold focus: to call the church to repentance through grounding her on the teachings of Christ and to share this new life with the wider society, particularly the Dalit community who are reduced to 'non-persons'. As regards reaching church and society, theology here seeks to contribute to the establishment of God's reign over a casteless society.

Theological Assumptions

Theologians with a caste approach have certain assumptions that have influenced their theological task. Religion is perceived primarily in individualistic and spiritual or other-worldly terms. Hence sin and salvation are also conceived of in individualistic terms as the bondage to a cycle of births and as a regeneration of the individual. Evangelism is conceived of as an aid in the process of 'born again'.

Thinkers who favour a Dalit approach to theologizing have accepted broader and more holistic assumptions. Religion is conceived of as holistic and related to the corporate social reality; its role is conceived of in spiritual as well as social and prophetic terms. Though these thinkers identify individual sin, gradually they move on to identify structural sins, and structural enslavements such as caste, class and patriarchy. Salvation is conceived of as an historical process, concerned not merely with life after death but even more with life after birth. It is inclusive of education, land, protection, etc. Salvation offered by Christ aims at the social transformation and infusion in society of the values of the reign of God such as freedom, equality, fraternity, peace and justice. The Christian life, especially corporate worship, is related to the Dalit reality. Songs are used to express the joy at the freedom gained from caste through Christ. Worship is used to help the Dalits overcome an inferiority complex, while sermons are predominantly an awakening of a hope for the future. Evangelism and mission aim at bringing forth men and women who are 'born against' the structures of sin and to motivate people to struggle for a fuller and richer human life.[14]

The Conflicting Role of Culture

Culture is a comprehensive reality that includes both a view of life and a way of life. It is expressed through the values people hold and their patterns of behaviour. Culture is the sum total of the identity and experience which has bound us as a community and forms our collective consciousness and our collective memory. It is passed on from generation to generation. India is a land of plurality of cultures and religions. In spite of the variety the predominant cultural dimension of caste cuts across religious and regional boundaries and manifests itself as the most appropriate commonality of a pan-Indian culture. Other identities based on language, region, religion, gender and class pale into insignificance in the face of this great demon of caste identity. The primary identity for almost all Indians (except the Adivasis) comes from caste and it determines almost all aspects of human life from spirituality to secular polity. Hence I would like to focus on the caste dimension of Indian culture in assessing the role of culture in shaping theology. Here two approaches are discernible.

Culture Shaping Domination Endorsing Theology

Theologians with a caste approach perceive caste as an element of culture that needs to be affirmed. They maintain that caste is not inconsistent with the gospel and hence there is no need to renounce caste as one becomes a Christian. This view permitted the building of separate churches for separate caste groups since segregation is a cardinal principle of the caste system. Robert de Nobili, a

14 Oommen

Jesuit missionary said that, 'the caste system as such is not un-Christian. It need not be an obstacle in the spread of the gospel.' He adds, 'the holy and scriptural law which holds the doctrine of mine does not make anyone lose his caste or pass into another, not does it induce anyone to do anything detrimental to the honour of his family'.[15]

For the Indian Christian theologian, Upadhyaya, the caste system is the symbol of Indian genius and a mark of self-respect of Indians and as such needs to be preserved. For him Indians' past greatness can be traced to the principle of the conservation of location by means of hereditary differentiation. He states, 'social reforms should be carried out on national lines, according to the genius of the Hindu race or otherwise self respect will be lost and all reforms will lead to our denationalization and disintegration'.[16]

This group of thinkers maintains that the Christian gospel is for all people, both high and low, the oppressor and the oppressed. They are mostly ambiguous with regard to the identity question and fail to see the relationship between the Christian gospel and the aspirations of the marginalized for self-identity and liberation. Christ is affirmed as the friend of all nations, classes and castes, without destruction, without calling people for repentance. God's option for the oppressed is ignored. De Nobili remarks:

> Whoever says that it (Christianity) is the law of the parangis, fit only for low castes, commits a very great sin.... Therefore he who wants to attain the glory of paradise must do nothing which brings dishonour to his caste, and whoever dares say the contrary deserves the punishment of hell.[17]

However, they advocated the well-being of the Dalits, who were seen as objects of compassion.

Culture Shaping Liberation Theology

Thinkers who adopt the Dalit approach in theologizing perceive caste as an oppressive cultural element that needs to be rejected by the Christian gospel. It is seen as inconsistent in its values with the gospel. Hence those who receive the gospel of Christ must renounce caste as a mark of allegiance to Christ. The Methodist Synod passed a resolution. The American Madurai Mission advocates participation in the love feast to be made obligatory for its members. The church is conceived of as a following of Christian believers cutting across caste lines. Rajagopalan states:

> If you admit caste to be true, the whole fabric of Christianity must come down for the nature of caste and its association destroy the first principle of Christianity. Caste makes distinctions among creatures where God had made none; it attaches

[15] Forrester, 1980:15

[16] Upadhyaya, 1901:8–11

[17] Forrester, 1980:15

> moral impurity where God does not make one class of men clean and another unclean in direct opposition to the word of God.[18]

Hence Bishop Daniel Wilson advocates the rejection of caste distinction in the church. He says:

> Under the name of Christianity, half the evils of paganism are retained. The distinction of caste, then, must be abandoned decidedly, immediately, finally and those who profess to belong to Christ must give proof of their having really put off the old and having put on the new man in Jesus Christ.[19]

These thinkers recognize the universality of God's reign yet the priority for the oppressed. P. Yohannan affirms incarnation as our Lord's traversing the length and breadth of the earth in search of the offspring of the slaves and in order to banish the masters of the Veda Sastras, who enslaved them. He speaks of God's boundless love for the despised and says, 'Lord, do not forget the descendents of slaves to whom you gave as a boon the heavenly wisdom'. He also pictures Dalits, not as objects of comparison, but as allies of God, a messianic people struggling to usher in God's rule.

These thinkers have evaluated the cultural elements in the light of gospel values and extended it to gauge the truth in religions. Equality and soteriological effectiveness in community life are used as criteria to judge cultures and religions. Hinduism with its principle of caste hierarchy is compared with the principle of equality. So also the experience of Christianity's power to transform the lives of people especially the oppressed, was pitted against Hinduism's status quo. Mohini Das says:

> Stop for a moment and see what is happening. In both mission schools and government schools and hospitals, the daughters of so called depressed classes, now Christians are teaching and tending the children of 'Brahmins'. Untouchables? What has happened? They are untouchables no longer, for Jesus has touched them.[20]

G.A. Oddie also remarks:

> For they see that these degraded outcastes, on becoming Christians, are trained up into educated, self respecting communities that can compete on almost equal terms with the proved Brahmin. The growth of such communities increases the influence of Christianity. And it is the proof of the superiority of Christianity that

---

[18] Forrester, 1980:127

[19] Forrester, 1980:127

[20] Jeffery, 1938:128

it can take these poor people, trampled down into mire by Hinduism and make them a community that can compete with their best.[21]

The Conflicting Role of the Bible

The Bible is authoritative for Christian life and theology. The Bible gives us an identity by showing us our beginning and a hope by showing us our end. It also provides certain norms for Christian belief and behaviour. The Bible also functions as a check on the individual's conformity to the norms. In the entire history of theology it was during the Reformation that the first serious demand to a theology based on holy scripture alone was made. This demand was made to free theology from the domination of philosophy. It was in fact a demand for reform the style and ethos of theology. Theology must be in agreement with the Bible, if it is to be Christian theology at all, for the Bible is the text that bears witness to Jesus Christ. The point in dispute within Christian theology is not the fact but the way in which the Bible is related to theology. Here we shall see the two ways in which the Bible is related as a theology in the Indian context.

The Bible and Domination

In the works of theologians who adopted a caste approach to theologizing, the following features are prominent in their use of the Bible.

i. Generally an individualistic and devotional approach is adopted, since the Bible is recognized as an authority and aid in the spiritual realm of human beings. This is similar to the Hindu view of scriptures as authoritative in the transcendental realm.

ii. A high regard for the Bible's inspiration was held due to the impact of the Hindu view of scripture as eternal. N. Goreh, a Hindu Shastri, brought his deep love for and knowledge of scripture into the Christian faith. He assigns to the Bible, the status given to the Vedas, and assigns the status of Smrti to the writings of the fathers. He maintains a high regard for the inspiration of the Bible: 'I allow that these have used their reason, the peculiarity of style, etc. Yet the Spirit of God so overruled and used their reason and all their individual peculiarities, as to accomplish his own purposes through them.'

iii. The relationship between the Bible and Hindu scriptures engage their attention considerably and the relationship is conceived in terms of continuity. Efforts are made to identify parallels between the Bible and Hindu scriptures, as evident in the volume, *Gita and the Bible*. A number of Christian thinkers began to claim that the pure Vedic religion is, in fact, closer to Christianity than to any of the Hindu traditions and claimed that Christianity was the fulfilment of Hinduism. Krishna Mohan Banerjee goes as far as to identify Indian Christians as the true

[21] Oddie, 1979:143

descendants of the Brahminical Aryans of India, the authors of the Vedas. He also states that the Bible confirms and illustrates the Vedic tradition by exhibiting the true *prajapati*, the lamb slain from the foundations of the world. This positive view of the inter-scriptural relationship led to the view that the Christians stand to benefit through the use of Hindu scriptures. Appasamy maintains that the Hindu scriptures will supplement our understanding of God and hence have assimilated ideas and taken over sections from Hindu scriptures and published *Temple Bells*.

iv. The theological construction was undertaken through the use of the inner canon and interpreted within the framework of the Vedanta. Upadhyaya's theology was based on the Johannine text: 'Father and I are one' and was interpreted within the Advaitic framework. 'The father is greater than I', was the other Johannine text, used by Appasamy in explicating his theology within the Visistadvaitic framework. Chenchiah following the Eastern tradition's concern for creation, interpreted Jesus as the new creation based on a Pauline text, 2 Cor 5:17.

v. The Bible is used as an endorsement of domination. It is maintained that Jesus came not to abolish but to fulfil the law (Mt. 5:17) and it is also claimed that Jesus did not speak against slavery or the downgrading of women. It is also pointed out that in the church's history, social customs are maintained. Paul was against Christian slaves showing contempt for their masters, it was argued. Bishop Heber states:

> God forbid that we should wink at sin, but God forbid also that we should make the narrow gate of life narrower than Christ has made it or deal less favourably with the prejudices of his people than St. Paul and the primitive church dealt with the almost similar prejudices of Jewish converts.[22]

The Bible and Liberation Theology

In the writings of theologians, who adopt a Dalit approach, the Bible is used as an instrument of liberation as can be discerned from the following features:

i. A sociological and communitarian approach to the Bible is an important aspect. The interpretative process starts from the world of the Dalits and revolves around the dialectic between God and the people. This way of reading the Bible results in the mutual illumination of the world of the Bible and the world of the Dalits. It rejects the privatization of sin and salvation and relates to structures. This reading aims at action, a performative approach aiming at motivating Christians to become collaborators with Christ in his struggle against the enslaving principalities and powers.

ii. We also notice a critical and creative use of the Bible in order to make the message relevant to the contemporary world, particularly to the Dalits. Poiykayil Yohannan dares to challenge the canonical status of the epistles in order to bring out God's message to the oppressed of all religions. He writes

[22] Forrester, 1980:36

that in the New Testament there are certain epistles by St. Paul and others. To whom did St. Paul write these epistles? To the Romans, Corinthians etc. There were none written to the Pulayas of Travancore. Therefore, there is no revelation in those epistles for you, but only for the Romans, Corinthians, etc. The revelation to you Pulayas of Travancore is through me. Although this appears a subversive approach, Yohannan bases his reasoning on his belief in the continuing revelation through the Holy Spirit. He also recognizes the evocative role of the Bible, which evokes new experiences of the divine and facilitates the challenging encounter of our story with the biblical story.

iii. An inter-scriptural relationship is conceived of in terms of a discontinuity with regard to the Brahminic tradition and in terms of a continuity with regard to Dalit history and culture. Conversion to Christianity is seen as a radical break with the oppressive Hinduism and the rejection of it. Vedamanickam, Periah and Ditt experienced Hinduism as an oppressive religion and with their experience of Christ stood for a clear break with the past religiosity. Yohannan identifies Brahminical Aryans as the oppressors and enemies of Christ. He interprets incarnation as the Lord travelling the earth in search of the slaves and in order to banish the masters of the Veda Sastras. Yet there were attempts made to build relations with Dalit history and culture. Yohannan in his religious assemblies permits Dalit cultural expressions such as singing, dancing and the use of Dalit musical instruments. He undertakes investigations to build Dalit history in order to interpret God's salvific activity in the history of the oppressed people. He laments, 'I behold the histories of many races. Every history in Keralam was searched for the story of my race. But there was none to write the story of my race'.

iv. God's concern for the oppressed became a favourite theme of Christian preaching and theology. 1 Cor. 1:26–28 became the key text during the movement of the Holy Spirit (mass movement).[23] The kingdom of God on earth, as the goal of Christ's ministry, became another important theme. Rev. John Subhan conceived of the kingdom of God as a programme of individual transformation and social reconstruction. He depended heavily on Jesus' life and sayings frequently referring to the Nazareth manifesto and the parable of the judgment of the nations (Lk. 4:18–19; Mt. 25:31–46).[24]

v. Thinkers reject the interpretation that social and racial distinctions are part of the created order and interpret them to be consequences of the fall and hence are expressions of human sinfulness. Christ overcomes all barriers (Eph. 2:13–15; Gal. 3:25) and the gospel recognizes no distinctions such as those of castes, imposed by a heathen usage as asserted by Bishop Daniel Wilson. They also affirmed the church as a community of equality and fellowship across the social divide (1 Cor. 12). Some Anglo-Saxon missionaries interpreted the Eucharist as a rite in commercialism, and a negation of non-egalitarian values and practices

[23] Webster, 1996
[24] Webster, 1992

of secular life. A new life in Christ is the basis of Christian social action, constantly inspired and encouraged by the apocalyptic vision of God's final victory over all enemies. The Bible was clearly seen and experienced as a stimulating agent for the historical struggles aimed at the establishment of God's reign.

Concluding Remarks

Theology is inseparably related to the Bible. If theology is to be specifically Christian, and not merely theistic, it must be related to, and faithful to, revelation. Of course it needs to be expressed in a meaningful human discourse. Calvin defines the theological task as the translation of the substance of scripture into the plainer language of another place and time. The same view is expressed also by Barth: 'The first requirement of dogmatics is that its investigations, formulae and demonstrations must correspond with biblical ways of speaking and thinking'. Yet the composite character of the Bible necessitates a selection and ordering process in theologizing. Hence the Protestant theology affirms the sole scripture principle while at the same time subjecting it to the principle of solemn Christian. The Bible also has an indirect bearing on theologizing through its direct impact on the life of people and communities.

We have exploded the myth of epistemological primitivism. It was noted that the interpreter's biographical context affects the interpretative process and the emergent meaning of the text. The interpreter comes with his own bias – either caste bias or anti-caste bias. There cannot be a cognitive virginity. So also there is no neutral state of a text, no neutral meaning, but only meanings as responses to particular questions asked. The meaning of the text emerges in the dynamic interplay between the text and the interpreter. We have also identified that the perspective of the oppressed is a liberative perspective.

It was adequately brought out that the gospel and culture are to be related in a theologizing endeavour. The two kinds of relationship, one where the gospel affirms caste culture and the other where the gospel rejects the caste culture have been noted. The gospel and culture relationship must be conceived of in terms of a creative tension, so that the divine and demonic elements of culture can be identified and the former affirmed while the latter are rejected. The gospel has a responsibility to expose an oppressive cultural element and help theologians and the Christian community to free themselves from a colonized consciousness, in this case colonized by Brahminic caste consciousness. The gospel on the other hand should help in the affirmation of the liberative dimensions of culture, particularly as they are discernible in the cultures of the subaltern peoples, and in the Indian context, the Dalit people. The gospel needs to be interpreted in the light of the Dalit culture.

Inculturation, we demand, should lead to the emergence of a qualitatively new kind of community. The Indian church has lost a historic opportunity during the modern missionary movement to give birth to a qualitatively different community in the midst of caste communities. In the name of indigenization or inculturation, we have been satisfied to borrow certain externals of culture such as dress, diet, gestures in worship and techniques of meditation. Soares-Prabhu's warning is timely: 'To borrow behaviour patterns without accepting the cultural and religious values they express, would not be inculturation but imposture – what Jesus would call hypocrisy' (Mt. 7:6).[25] He adds, 'inculturation, it seems to me, does not stand for any and every interaction between religion and culture, but for the specific interaction through which a new (culturally different) form of a religious tradition appears'.[26] Citing the conversion of Paul, Soares-Prabhu states that Paul has moved into a new situation, where all he had counted as gain, he now counts as loss (Phil. 3:7–11). The gospel-culture encounter should lead us to a new perception of the world, a new set of values and new life-style with a commitment for the liberation of the last and the least, which may be very different from those of the caste ideology.

---

[25] John (ed.) 1991:82

[26] John (ed.) 1991:80

Indian Contribution to Contemporary Mission Pneumatology[1]

Kirsteen Kim

Dr. Kirsteen Kim is chair of the British and Irish Association for Mission Studies in York, U.K.

In the late twentieth century, the Western churches rediscovered the truth of the creedal statements that in addition to God the Father and God the Son, there is also God the Holy Spirit. Furthermore, Western theologians began to discuss the presence and activity of the Holy Spirit not only in the church and the human heart but also in the world. The Canberra Assembly of the World Council of Churches in 1991 highlighted the controversy over the relationship between the mission of the Son and the mission of the Spirit and raised the question of how and where the Spirit is discerned. The Assembly drew attention to the importance of a further discussion on the mission of the Spirit and the potential for applying a pneumatological approach to a range of missiological questions.[2] These included: What is the source of the Spirit and the spiritual resources for mission? What is the nature of the Spirit's involvement in history? What is the locus of the Spirit – creation, a community or a human heart? Can pneumatology help to solve the "Christological impasse" in the theology of religions? What does the theology of the Spirit suggest about identity, community and the nature of Christian unity? Are we dealing with one Spirit or many spirits? What constitutes authentic mission spirituality?[3]

Many of the most interesting recent contributions to the discussion of mission pneumatology come from theologians who are reflecting on the Holy Spirit within the context of a cultural understanding of spirit and spirits that differs significantly from western frameworks. India – a land where there is deep awareness of one universal Spirit and there are also many spiritualities – offers outstanding examples of creative thinking on the Spirit from Christian theologians. The purpose of this paper is to explore Indian Christian theology from the perspective of pneumatology to highlight its contribution to the international debate.

---

1 Kim, 2006:30-36

2 Kinnamon (ed.) 1991

3 Kim, 2002

God as Spirit

In his *Introduction to Indian Christian Theology*, Robin Boyd observed that over nearly two hundred years of Indian Christian theology, pneumatology, particularly as it is expressed in John's gospel, emerges as the "corner-stone". That is, God's dealings with the world are seen primarily in terms of the Spirit.[4] This reflects the dominant cultural understanding that God is Spirit and that the earth is the embodiment of the feminine power of God. Similarly, the Catholic theologian Felix Wilfred explains to the critics of Indian theology that, in keeping with Eastern religions in general, Asian Christian theologies recognise particularly "the inexhaustible aspect of the divine mystery which St John expresses laconically: 'God is spirit' (Jn 4.24)".[5]

Spirit Christology

The Indian christology that Boyd describes tends therefore to be "Spirit Christology" rather than "Logos Christology", that is, it begins from the work of God in the world through God's Spirit since the creation and understands Jesus Christ as the fulfilment of that, rather than by justifying the claims about the person and nature of Christ. In other words, in their dialogue with the twin realities of the religious traditions of India and in awareness of the material poverty of its people, Indian theologians have been particularly concerned with the role of Jesus Christ in mediating the presence and salvation of God, rather than with the traditional Western preoccupation with matters of ontology. According to James Dunn, the New Testament record gives grounds for Spirit Christology as one of the earliest traditions, which was combined with Logos Christology in the development of the Trinity.[6]

Spirit Christology amounts to a recognition that "Jesus is not only the giver but also the *receiver* of the Spirit".[7] It is preferred by many Indian theologians, first because it shifts the focus of the question of uniqueness and universality from Christ to the Spirit, therefore providing a fresh approach to the question of exclusive claims about Jesus Christ, which appear so divisive in a pluralistic context. Secondly, Spirit Christology is also seen as a better way of justifying and affirming the presence and activity of God outside the boundaries of the church or Christendom than the earlier "cosmic Christ" theologies, which were criticised as patronising to those of other religions or ideologies by describing them as "anonymous Christians" or in other ways appearing to co-opt them into the Christian faith.

Amongst Protestants, Spirit Christology tends to be presented as an Indian framework for theology as opposed to the Greek one of Logos. However this

---

4 Boyd, 1975:241-42
5 Wilfred, 1998:890-915
6 Dunn, 1998:74-79
7 Heron, 1983:127

makes it difficult for those who wish to retain their allegiance to the historic creeds and a common Christian confession. The difference between these approaches is illustrated by the respective interpretations by Stanley Samartha and Lesslie Newbigin of John 16.13, in which it is said that the Spirit will lead "into all truth". Samartha, Indian theologian and first Director of the World Council of Churches' sub-unit on dialogue, is confident that the truth to which the Holy Spirit leads includes the truth contained in other religions,[8] whereas Newbigin, British missionary theologian and Bishop of the Church of South India, argues that, since all truth is found in him, "the Holy Spirit does not lead past, or beyond, or away from Jesus".[9] Samartha often refers to God as Mystery in order to say that God is greater than human understanding and though Jesus is the Revealer of God, there is room for other revelations. Whereas Newbigin stresses the fullness of the revelation in Jesus Christ which has made known what was unknown.[10] The two therefore reached an impasse, although both affirm that truth is one and both confess Jesus Christ as the source of truth.

However, Indian Catholic theologians, led by Jacques Dupuis, though initially criticised by the Vatican for their alleged view that "the mystery of God is not exhausted in the revelation in Jesus Christ but is also revealed in other religions",[11] have largely succeeded in establishing the legitimacy of Spirit Christology as long as it is understood that it is complementary to traditional Christology and not an alternative.[12] From their perspective, Spirit Christology is another way of saying that there is more to theology than Christology or, in other words, of stating Christian belief in the Trinity. It understands the event of Jesus Christ from the perspective of the presence and activity of the Holy Spirit of God in the world since creation, while also stressing the sending of the Spirit into the world by the risen Christ.[13] In this approach, "all truth" in John 16.13 would be understood to be as broad as the Spirit's work in the whole creation but also focussed in Jesus Christ.

The Spirit as *Atman* and *Antaryamin*

Boyd pointed out that the concept of the Holy Spirit may be rendered in Sanskrit by several different words – *atman*, *antaryamin* and *shakti* – each reflecting a different tradition and carrying different connotations.[14] The word *atman* (spirit, soul, self) and its cognates – including *paramatman* (Supreme Spirit) and *antaratman* (inner spirit) – come from *advaitic* or classical

8 Samartha, 1994:47-48
9 Newbigin, 1982:216-17
10 Newbigin, 1995
11 Mojzes & Swidler (eds.) 1990
12 Dupuis, 1997. See also Burrows, 1993.
13 Dupuis, 1997:196-98
14 Boyd, 1975:241

Hinduism. Advaita means "oneness", or more literally "not two-ness" or "non-duality". Describing the Spirit as *atman* draws attention to the interior dimension, the spirit within, and its union with the universal Spirit, *brahman*. George Gispert-Sauch finds the expression "ground of being" a better translation of the concept of *atman* than "soul" or "self".[15] The Catholic ascetic, Abhishiktananda described the Holy Spirit as "the *advaita* of God, the mystery of the non-duality of the Father and the Son".[16] In this vein Vandana, a leader of the Catholic ashram movement, presents *ashramic* spirituality as a holistic approach to life, leading to and flowing from a realisation of oneness with the One Spirit and hence a connectedness with the universe and with "spiritual" people regardless of gender, caste and religion.[17] This image of the Spirit as the unifying principle of the Godhead and, therefore, of the universe lies behind Samartha's theology of dialogue, which is foundational to the ecumenical approach to other faiths.[18] He insisted on the relevance of the philosophy of *advaita*, claiming that the universal or "unbound" Spirit or *advaita* provides the "unitive vision" that holds Indian communities together and allows for the "traffic across the borders" that is dialogue. Samartha describes dialogue itself as not so much a method or technique but "a mood, a spirit, an attitude of love and respect" for "our neighbours of other faiths". That is, dialogue takes place in the "milieu" of the Spirit.[19]

Another word used for the Holy Spirit is *antaryamin* – "Indwelling One", a term from the *bhakti* tradition of devotion to a personal deity. In the 1930s Bishop A.J. Appasamy used this concept to interpret the doctrine of the Holy Spirit in terms of "abiding" in John's Gospel, understanding this to refer to the inner life of the believer, particularly in its moral dimensions.[20] In fact, Appasamy uses *antaryamin* to refer to the indwelling of all the persons of the Trinity, as do other famous *bhaktas* such as Narayan Vaman Tilak, the Maharashtrian poet.[21] It seems the closeness of the *bhakti* relationship with the divine needs no mediation and, therefore, no explicit theology of the Holy Spirit, though the language is highly spiritual. This is clearly evident in the work of Vengal Chakkarai who regards the Holy Spirit as the continuing presence of the resurrected Jesus, the permanent *avatar* or appearance of God, and concludes that 'the Holy Spirit is Jesus himself taking his abode within us'. Chakkarai's theology starts from the reality of the experience of the Spirit, of 'faith-union' with Christ and he accuses Western theologians of obscuring this

---

[15] Gispert-Sauch, 1999:80

[16] Abhishiktananda, 1984:184

[17] Vandana (ed.) 1993

[18] Samartha was responsible for the World Council of Churches' Guidelines on Dialogue (1979), which are still in use.

[19] Samartha, 1981:75, 100

[20] Francis (ed.) 1992:22-42

[21] Jacob, 1979

fact with creeds and formulations.[22] For the *bhakta*, the union with Christ is not the result of renunciation and a process of self-realisation but an immediate experience in the midst of life from which loving devotion flows.[23] This is what gives *bhakti* its popular appeal. It is a revival or pentecostal-charismatic type of spirituality and, in this sense, many indigenous Christian movements of India, such as those described by F. Hrangkhuma,[24] could be described as *bhakti* movements.

The Spirit as *Shakti*

Believing that the Bible affirmed the presence of God in creation from the beginning, Appasamy identified the meeting place of the communities of India as a spiritual one and this paved the way for the dialogue with religion and society initiated in post-Independence India by P.D. Devanandan. In Appasamy's view, the Christian experience of the Holy Spirit was an intensification of the general presence of the Spirit that preceded it. He, therefore, disagreed strongly with P. Chenchiah, who emphasised the "new cosmic energy" of the Holy Spirit released in "an outburst or inrush into history" by the resurrection of Jesus Christ, as if it had not been present before. Chenchiah, who was the leader of a group of radical Indian theologians known in the 1930s as the Madras 'Rethinking Group', reversed *advaita* mysticism by advocating the affirmation of creation and of activity rather than withdrawal from the world. He did so on the grounds that the universal Spirit or *brahman* is manifested in the power of *shakti*, or the Spirit, which comes upon the world from outside not within and empowers a process of evolution of creation toward a better humanity – an idea that he derived from the philosophy of Aurobindo Ghose.[25]

Like Appasamy, Chenchiah found the immanence of the Spirit in the Fourth Gospel in keeping with "the intellectual and spiritual leanings of India" but he differed in that he based his theology of the Spirit on a dynamic conception of *shakti* rather than the more static *antaryamin*. Chenchiah believed "the raw fact of Christ" would lead to the establishment of a new universe by a process of unconscious change in which the Spirit, like a gas, was infused into history.[26] Rethinking Christianity in terms of *shakti*, Chenchiah insisted that the uniqueness of Christianity could not depend on its institutions or doctrines but only in its transcendence over other faiths as the religion of new birth by the Holy Spirit.[27] Appasamy believed Chenchiah's approach was more Western

---

22 Chakkarai, 1932; reproduced in Thomas. (ed.) 1981:116-31
23 Neill, 1974
24 Hrangkhuma (ed.), 1998
25 Thangasamy, 1966
26 Francis, 1992:70-81
27 Job, *et al.* 1938:47-62 & Appendix

than Indian, that it was incompatible with orthodox Christian doctrine, and that it ignored the church.[28] For his part, Chenchiah rejected Appasamy's *bhakti marga* because he saw it as a way of retreat as opposed to a dynamic way forward.[29]

The *shakti* tradition derives from the pre-Aryan concept of primal energy, the feminine power of creation. That is, it predates the rise of the Brahmins and the Hindu caste structure. It is, therefore, attractive to those who reject the hegemony of Vedic Hinduism and seek to subvert it. The late elder-statesman of Indian Christian theology, M.M. Thomas followed Chenchiah in making the new creation wrought in Christ the starting point for theology in order to interpret the gospel for modern, secular India, rather than in traditional, religious terms. Thomas recounts how Hindu reformers struggled within classical Hinduism to transform a static concept of the world as the unfolding of the Universal Spirit into a purposive one in which the Spirit is "the dynamic of cosmic evolution". Though they succeeded in so doing, in Thomas's view they still tended to lack a "realistic appreciation of the depth of evil which the Spirit of God has to contend with", as described in the New Testament by the language of Satan and evil spirits.[30] The language of non-brahminic *shakti* contains within it the "spirituality for combat" that Thomas was searching for and lays a pneumatological foundation for theologies of liberation.

In his liberation pneumatology Samuel Rayan, theologian and long-time campaigner for the rights of the *dalits* or the outcaste people of India, sees "the Holy Spirit, the Spirit of God and of Jesus Christ" as the "heart of the Christian gospel". Drawing on the *shakti* tradition, he portrays the Spirit as a "breath of fire", who comes "to enable us to re-create our earth, not to put us to sleep" and is present "not in ethereal euphoria, but in committed historical action".[31] He advocates "spiritual struggle" to overcome the forces of violence and oppression in society and bring about justice. The Spirit is the "breath" or yeast of new life that invigorates the "bread", which is the earth, and brings about a redistribution of its resources for the benefit of all.[32] This understanding of the earth as a theological and a liturgical reality has made Rayan into a leading voice in ecotheology in ecumenical circles.[33] The feminine nature of *shakti* is particularly attractive to feminist theologians, who have used the *shakti* tradition, especially its close association between the female and nature, to motivate eco-feminist commitment to the liberation of both women and creation.[34]

---

[28] Francis, 1992: 70-81

[29] Boyd, 1975:157

[30] Thomas, 1990:216-224

[31] Rayan, 1979b:vii

[32] John (ed.) 1991

[33] Rayan, 1994:130-148

[34] Gnanadason, 1993:95-105

Discerning the Spirit

A study of theologians from different strands of Indian Christian theology reveals that they discern the Spirit according to different criteria. This can be illustrated by further consideration of three of the theologians we have already mentioned, all from the late twentieth century – S. Samartha, Vandana and S. Rayan.[35] Samartha, a Methodist ecumenical, for example, looks for the Spirit of dialogue, who creates openness to others and enables 'traffic across the boundaries' of one religion and another. In order to bring communities together for the task of nation-building, he discerns the Spirit where there is co-operation and mutual respect. Vandana, the former Provincial of the Society of the Sacred Heart, seeks to build bridges between Christians and Hindus by inculturating the gospel in terms of Hindu traditions of spirituality. She sees the Spirit in the common spiritual experience which, she believes, lies at the heart of both Hinduism and Christianity: the experience of the oneness of the inner self with the Divine Self or of the unity of Son with the Father. She, therefore, looks for the Spirit of the waters of life who brings personal peace and religious harmony. As a Jesuit liberation theologian, Rayan discerns the Spirit at work in movements for the liberation of the poor and oppressed. The 'Breath of Fire' is an uncontrollable wind that consumes the unjust structures that oppress the poor and frees them to experience the good news of the kingdom where there is "bread for the breadless" and 'wine for the wineless'.

Samartha's spirit of truth, Vandana's spirit of abiding in God and Rayan's transforming Spirit of fire are all recognisably biblical models of the Spirit – Samartha and Vandana drawing mainly on John's Gospel and Rayan primarily on Luke. None of them alone is a full interpretation of the biblical witness to the Spirit and this suggests that all three aspects of the Spirit's work need to be taken together. Other aspects could also be added such as witness and charismatic power.[36]

Spirituality

India not only has an awareness of God as Spirit, but also is a land of many spiritualities, of which *advaitic* Hinduism, *bhakti* devotion and *shaktism* are three major types. 'Spirituality' is a very difficult term to define but it is used to distinguish religious approaches or attitudes from religions themselves and thus it crosses the boundaries of religious communities. So Samartha identified and utilised a spirituality of dialogue found in all religious traditions. As we have seen above, the term need not apply only to a 'passive self-interiority or transcendentalism' – though it is most used by this camp – but also to an active

---

[35] See Kim, 2003

[36] See e.g. Moltmann, 1992:272

response to the world that issues from a relationship with the Divine.[37] Nevertheless, the awareness of God as Spirit explains why Asian (as illustrated by Indian) theology gives much more importance than Western theology to the categories of interiority, experience and mystery. In other words, there is a close relationship between theology and spirituality and between the mode of theologising and the religio-cultural traditions of India.[38] This enables Vandana to define spirituality as 'life lived according to the Spirit'.[39] Rayan's awareness of the Spirit's activity in the world as Liberator and presence as Creator brings together action for human welfare with aesthetic and mystical concerns. Rayan has developed a theology of 'mission in the Spirit' that is also a comprehensive approach to the whole of life in which contemplation serves to motivate historical action.[40]

In the awareness that God is Spirit, Indian theology is not only propositional but also sometimes mystical, analogical and creative in its imagery.[41] Though Indian theology may be very rational, Indian theologians of many persuasions insist that theology should be interpreted more broadly than the systematic formulation of doctrine. Theology is enriched by the use of symbols and myths and expressed in varied cultural forms; in other words, it is an art-form as well as a science.[42] In the visual arts, Jyoti Sahi has reflected deeply on his work and the significance of art as a mediator of the gospel and a form of theologising. A Catholic with a Protestant and Reformed Hindu background, he aims to bridge *advaita*, *bhakti* and *shakti* frameworks through his work by expressing the "theology of Indian Christian culture" through its diverse traditions.[43] The heritage of *bhakti* leads many theologians to express themselves in poetry and song. Thomas Thangaraj advocates a "singable theology" as a way of changing the heart as well as educating the mind[44] and, similarly, Rayan describes the Spirit as a poet who "sees and senses symbolism, relationships, and meanings..." and points them out in order to inspire action for liberation.[45] Dance is also an immensely popular art-form in India and so Vandana creatively interprets the role of the Spirit in John's gospel as the "dance of the waters", moving gracefully in and between contemporary movements in India under the direction of the Master Choreographer.[46] Thus Indian theology reflects awareness of the creativity and boundlessness of the Spirit of God.

---

37 Selvanayagam, 1998:418-38
38 Wilfred, 1998:890-915
39 Vandana, 1993:103
40 John (ed.) 1991
41 Wilfred, 1998
42 Samartha, 1991:89-91; Rayan, 1979b:77-90
43 Sahi, 1986
44 Thangaraj, 1992:163-72
45 Rayan, 1979a:110
46 Vandana, 1989:9-24

Conclusion: mission in the Spirit

The interaction between Indian theologians on the theme of the Spirit addresses and sheds light on many of the questions raised in the international debate at the Canberra Assembly referred to earlier. This short paper does not allow for a detailed answer to each question from an Indian perspective; this I have attempted elsewhere.[47] However, some brief concluding remarks can be made to address them.

Indian Christian theologians have drawn attention to the mission of the Spirit that everywhere precedes that of the church. Christian mission is then defined as recognising and co-operating with the Spirit. If so, then discerning the Spirit becomes a matter of crucial significance because it determines the nature of the mission.[48] It is clear that the Christian criteria for discernment will be derived from the life and teaching of Jesus Christ and, therefore, be distinct (though not necessarily different) from Hindu criteria for spiritual discernment. On the other hand, the varied interpretation of the Spirit as *atman*, *antaryamin* and *shakti* highlights the problem of discernment and raises the question of whether the one Spirit appealed to by religious leaders (both Hindu and Christian) is always legitimately identified with the Spirit of God. This diversity calls into question categorical claims that a particular tradition or spirituality or movement represents the work of the Spirit. It implies that the Spirit is associated with contemplation *and* devotion *and* acts of liberation rather than exclusively with one kind of religious expression over against another, and points towards the combination of the three – in Indian terms *jnana*, *bhakti* and *karma* – as the true evidence of the Spirit's work.[49]

Spirit Christology suggests an openness of approach to people of other faiths and a willingness to affirm what is good and true in other faiths on the grounds that the mission of the Spirit precedes and goes beyond the incarnation. However, the use of *atman* and *antaryamin*, which lead to theologies of the Spirit of peace who promotes co-operation and mutual respect and who brings personal and religious harmony, contrast in India with theologies of non-Brahminic *shakti*, the Spirit of fire who refines and humanises society. They reflect the conflict in Indian Christian theology between an emphasis on the inculturation of the gospel in Vedic terms that will be appreciated by caste Hindus educated in their philosophical traditions and a concern for a theology of liberation for the poor, whose indigenous spirituality is of a folk tradition and who see the Hindu caste system as a major cause of their poverty. Taken together they imply that the Spirit of mission is a way of peace with justice in the knowledge that the Spirit of Jesus Christ both inspires whatever is good and true and also empowers challenge and change.

---

[47] Kim, 2002

[48] Dunn, 1998:72

[49] Painadath, 1993:12-14

The Indian spiritual tradition also brings a distinctive contribution to the understanding of mission: the sense that mission, however it is done, should be "in the Spirit" and therefore the need to consider mission spirituality to ensure that the means of mission are consistent with its end. It implies that mission should be understood not as a task but as a spirit – the Spirit breathed into the disciples by Jesus Christ. Mission is a way of being in Christ that orients us to share the gospel. 'Mission in the Spirit' calls into question some traditional models of mission and opens up the way to missionary activity that is sensitive and appreciative of the cultural and spiritual heritage of others. An awareness that the Spirit of peace is also the Spirit of fire is a reminder of the need for both presence and prophecy, affirmation as well as discernment in mission. The Spirit that is both the breath within us and also the wind that comes from outside is the medium in which true mission takes place.

The Creation of Afro-Caribbean Religions and their Incorporation of Christian Elements: A Critique against Syncretism

Bettina E. Schmidt

Dr. Bettina E. Schmidt is a former lecturer in the Study of Religions at the University of Oxford, U.K., who is now at the University of Wales, Bangor

Introduction

Afro-Caribbean religions are an excellent example for the conjoining of different religious traditions and the rebirth of newer forms. One main example in Christianity (both popular Catholicism and Protestant) is baptism. The term *santería,* for instance, derives from the Spanish word, *santos* (saints). *Santería,* literally meaning, devotion of (Catholic) saints (also called, *la religión de los orichas* or the religion of the Orishas), indicates that *santería* means more: it is an Afro-Caribbean religion rather than a Catholic cult. *Orishas* is the name of deities in the traditional Yoruba religion in West African Nigeria and Benin; Afro-Caribbean religions such as Santería have incorporated various different traditions from Africa, Europe and Native American (indigenous) tribes. Hence, even though these are American religions, they incorporate religious inputs from both Africa and Europe.

Can these Afro-Caribbean religions traditions be called syncretistic? The word syncretism has negative connotations; it is also too simple to embody the full meaning of the creation process.[1] The idea of syncretism would indicate that these religions were formed by mixing the dominant Catholicism with suppressed African traditions during the time of slavery. Hence, using the term syncretism would give a pejorative undertone to African traditions which does not appear to be true to reality. Why, for instance, do Caribbean believers still use Catholic symbols when they worship African deities? Why do they still use Christian iconography, more than hundreds of years after the end of slavery? If they used Christianity just as a cover-up during the period of slavery, why not stop it now? These questions indicate already, as I shall argue, against this

---

[1] See Leopold/Jensen, 2004 for an overview about the syncretism debate in religious studies

cover-thesis. It is for this reason that the term syncretism will not be used in this paper. The process of creating new religious belief systems is very complex and is based on more levels than the superficial similarity of iconography.

I will start with some background information about the historical and cultural frame in which the religions were initiated, and will then present the elements which lead to the creation of autonomous religious systems. Most of the data I present will refer to the Afro-Cuban religion, Santería. Following this, the Christian framework of the Afro-Caribbean religions will be discussed with reference to another religious example, Haitian Voodou. It will then lead to the argument that religions can be seen as a location of memory (*lieux de mémoire*) in order to conserve information about Africa in new surroundings. Here I will also explain my concept of polyphonic *bricolage* as an alternative to the term syncretism.

This paper is based on my research among religious communities of Afro-Cuban Santería, Puerto Rican Espiritismo, Haitian Voodou, and Shango from Trinidad and Tobago though some of the data apply to most Afro-Caribbean religions. Whilst I discuss data from other scholars, my own experience as the participant-observer is based mainly on fieldwork done in Puerto Rico and in New York City and among the immigrants from Cuba, Puerto Rico, Haiti, and Trinidad and Tobago.

Historical and Social Context

The creation of Afro-Caribbean religions is connected with the transatlantic slave trade. Nearly from the beginning of the European conquest, slaves were transported to the colonies, in the first years, from Europe and, then, directly from the African coast. In the beginning of the 16th century (1518), the Spanish king allowed slave traders the direct transport of human goods from West Africa to the Spanish colonies. During these voyages, people from various ethnic (and religious) backgrounds were put together in the ships. Some believed in Allah, others in ancestor spirits and deities; some were patrilineal, others matrilineal; some spoke a Yoruba dialect, others Hausa, Ewe, Fon, or various other languages including the Bantu languages. Hence, from the time of their capture, people had to find a common language, a new social network, and a new common cultural structure in order to survive. Until 1850 when Brazil condemned the (official) slave trade, nearly 10 million people were forced from Africa to European colonies in the Americas.

On arrival in the Caribbean the human cargo was sold and men became slaves. They were treated as non-human goods. To prevent the start of any ideas of uprising everything that could potentially remind the slaves of Africa was prohibited, including their religions, languages and customs. The European slave holders were in particular afraid of African drums and so-called 'magic' because they believed that drums were a mode of communication. This was thought to be a magical way in which slaves could harm their masters.

All slaves had to be baptized, often directly on board the slave ships. This practice was later even used to defend the slave system because the slave holders argued that it was better to live as a Christian slave than as a non-Christian (but free) savage. Whilst this attitude was common among all slave-holding societies, there was one difference between the slave-holder countries in the Caribbean: the relationship between state and church. France, Spain and Portugal were Catholic countries. The Spanish king saw himself as the only true representative of the Pope in the Americas. Therefore, the Spanish colonies were ruled as Catholic units, and the Catholic Church was the only religion allowed in the Catholic colonies. But this also led to the rule that on Sunday and on the main Christian days the slaves would be allowed to go to Church. They were also allowed to organize small festivals in honour of a Catholic saint. All meetings of more than three slaves outside the work process were prohibited, but the Catholic Church enabled slaves to create their own social space through the Catholic festivals.

The Protestant colonies also allowed slaves some kind of religious freedom, in particular, when the Anti-slavery Movement gained more recognition in Europe. In these colonies separate slave churches (for instance, Baptist Churches) were founded only for slaves. Hence, the separation at the beginning was based on social status – being a slave or a free man: later it became based on skin colour. But even in Protestant colonies, there were some Catholic elements who continued their former Catholic heritage. They too influenced the Caribbean religions.

Christianity in the Caribbean was based mainly on 16th century popular Spanish Catholicism, which was already mixed with popular beliefs of the rural Spanish. In America, religion became even more personalized: Jesus became an important figure in the popular cult of imaging the deity; the devotion to saints and of the Virgin Mary increased. On the organizational level, the Spanish *cofradias*, lay organizations for religious purposes, became central to Spanish America. They were associations of people – free and bonded – joining together to organize religious festivals and performing social activities. In particular, in the new towns throughout the Spanish colonies they became very popular. In some places they became the base of local identity, replacing all traditional social institutions. Social positions and prestige were gained through peoples' commitments expressed in these organizations.

During the seventeenth-century the number of slaves grew greatly in the American colonies. The Caribbean became the producer of sugar cane – a product valued much by Europeans. During the eighteenth and nineteenth centuries large numbers of Yoruba were imported as slaves to the Americas. The reason was probably a civil war in the area of the Yoruba Kingdoms in Nigeria and Benin. The result was that a large number of people speaking the same language and having the same customs arrived in the countries which still imported slaves, in particular, the Spanish and Portuguese colonies such as Cuba and Brazil. Shortly afterwards the transatlantic slave trade was prohibited.

Hence the Yoruba formed the last and largest group of slaves arriving in the Caribbean. Because of the civil war scholars assume that a large number of religious and political leaders were sold as slaves; hence with them a wide range of specialized knowledge of ritual was brought from Africa to America. Although the slave-holders usually had tried to separate slaves from their original ethnic group, this practice was no longer possible to sustain at the end of the slave trade. On nearly every sugar cane plantation in Cuba, for instance, Yoruba were forced to work. The Yoruba culture had, therefore, an important impact on African Cuban culture. This eighteenth and nineteenth century Yoruba culture continues to have an impact on the people here until today.[2]

Despite cultural differences, African religions arriving in the Caribbean had some common elements, e.g. the belief in a Creator God who remained outside the world after its creation; the belief in African deities as 'intermediaries'; and the worship of ancestor spirits. The kinship lineage was also very important in West Africa at that time but the slave trade brutally interrupted the lineage.

Out of this ensemble, several Caribbean religions were created. As mentioned, the practice of African customs was prohibited, but the worship of Christian saints was allowed. Hence African slaves started to use Christian iconography and symbols in order to hide their beliefs and practices. Under the shield of Catholic saints, African deities were able to survive the long period of oppression. Religious organizations, such as *cofradias* and *cabildos,* have helped rescue many of the Yoruba elements in Cuba. Based on these associations, a sense of common identity, of the so-called 'Lucumi-ship' (the Cuban name for Yoruba ethnicity) flourished. After slavery these *cabildos* founded houses or temples, so-called 'Casas de Santos' (Houses of the Saints) which became important support networks for former slaves. When, for instance, former slaves left the plantations and arrived in a town, they looked for a *casa de santos* for help, in particular for a house of the saint they already worshipped on the plantation. Hence they became even more important after the end of slavery.

Though it started as an ensemble of isolated worship of Catholic saints and African deities, the Caribbean religions became highly differentiated systems of beliefs and practices with a complex hierarchy, rituals and legends. Although their belief in the existence of God as creator of mankind, the former African deities and spirits are at the centre of the rituals with the ancestor spirits below them. The African spirits or deities are connected with nature (thunder, sea, rivers, spectress etc.) as well as with human activities and human characteristics: Yemaya is the Orisha of maternity, Oshun the Orisha of love, Ogun the Orisha of war and violence and so on. Every human being is born with a special connection to the one spirit worthy of worship. The third category is the ancestor spirits. Though the African lineages were interrupted

---

[2] See on the development of Santería, Brandon, 1993

by the slave trade, former slaves, runaway slaves and maroons who fought against the slave system, became the founders of a new form of lineage.

At the centre of the religious practice is divination, the communication between human beings and God and – even more often – the spirits as messengers of God. Priests normally use specific oracular techniques for this communication. But more popular is the manifestation of the spirits inside a human body, often called possession. This practice allows the direct communication with the spirits while they are incorporated in a human body. This practice is at the centre of the collective reunions and celebrations which often attract outsiders to the religions. In combination with music and dance the religious manifestations are one of the main characteristics of Afro-Caribbean religions.

All Caribbean religions developed in more or less similar ways though they included different influences. Voodou, for instance, has integrated other ethnic traditions apart from the Yoruba, in particular, Ewe and Fon; Santería has incorporated influences from French Spiritism, and Shango from Trinidad and Tobago incorporates influences from Kabbalah. However, the Christian framework predominates.

Afro-Caribbean Religions and their Christian element

As this point I will come to the central question of this article: Why are Caribbean religions still connected to Christianity? As African Americans (Black U.S.A., often with a Protestant education) were attracted by Cuban Santería they rejected the Catholic framework and renamed it after their Yoruba-religion. This was to sanitize their religion of every Christian influence. However, they did not succeed in removing the Catholic iconography. One possible explanation could be, of course, the ongoing prejudice against African customs. But on the other side, we also notice a growing political awareness, in particular, in the second part of the twentieth century. In the U.S.A. some religious communities even started to institutionalize their religions in order to integrate into the American way of life. All the ornamental elements had to go. However, this process of purging was not easy, as Joan Dayan explains.

Joan Dayan, an anthropologist, describes the mixture of Catholicism and African beliefs in Haitian Vodou as an uneven reciprocity between the New World deities and the Old World saints. The experiences of the saints have been minimized in Catholic hagiography and later translated into Caribbean experiences. Dayan explains the procedure with reference to Dambala, the master of waters, who presided over rivers, springs and marshes. In the Yoruba mythology he is represented as a snake. When possessed by Dambala the human believers hisses, slithers, and crawls through the temple. Yet he is also identified with St. Patrick, the evangelizer of Ireland, who is represented with serpents under his feet and by his sides. But how can it be that Dambala is represented by a saint who drove the snakes out of Ireland? The translation from one religious system to another does not mean a perfect analogy between the saint and an African deity as Dayan explains. Instead, the uneven, rough mixture adds another narrative meaning to the original one. It is not only a decorative icon because the analogy is more than a visual aspect. St. Patrick, of mixed Romano-British origin, was carried off by Irish pirates in 406 to become a slave among the still pagan inhabitants of Ireland. "Legends abound concerning the bodily hardships of bondage, his sea journey to an unknown and wild land, his escape by ship to the Continent and his return to Ireland to preach after being called to service in a dream".[3] His history tells us, therefore, a story of slavery; hence he has a lot in common with the Caribbean slaves and their deities. Joan Dayan writes that "in St. Patrick's dual sea crossings, back and forth from bondage to escape, from one kind of freedom to another, Haitians remembered how their ancestors died into life, saved by descending into the waters and arriving reborn in Guinea" (2003: 47). Dambala is born anew.

Hence, it is not only a superficial Catholic image to hide authentic African belief. The correspondence makes explicit the deep meaning of an intimacy. Danbala signifies both the snake and the spirit rising up from the waters. He materialises the abstract precepts of colonial law in an incarnation that destroys the imperial dichotomy of the master and the slave, the victimizer and the victimized, the colonizer and the colonized. When we look at the other Caribbean religions, we can discover a similar process. During the creation process, under the oppression of slavery, the slaves did not just hide their African beliefs underneath a Christian cover. They created something new, in a dynamic and creative process which allows even today the inclusion or rejection of elements. Such a system which I call, religious *bricolage,* is always open and ongoing. The results are dynamic mixtures of diverse elements with creative actors as members who make their own decisions and form their own systems. It is a combination of reaction and action, in particular in reference to the influences of society and always the local context and the specific situation are important. Although all religions were created under similar historical circumstances (slavery, colonization, and suppression of the religion) they have developed different systems that incorporated the influences in different ways. But the main attraction is the use of all the senses, in particular the combination of music, movement and ornament, and sometimes even smell. Together they create a religious artifact, which is central for the believers confronted by surroundings they regard as hostile, cold and senseless.

Even baptism served as such a frame for the development of Shango Baptism, also called Spiritual Baptists, or Shango or Orisha religion in Trinidad and Tobago. Whilst the Orisha religion and the Baptist religion can be distinguished theoretically,[4] the worshippers in Trinidad and Tobago often do not distinguish between them. It depends on the church and its leader whether

---

[3] Dayan, 2003:47

[4] Glazier, 1983

they conduct Baptist, Shango or even Kabbalah ceremonies. In distinction to other Caribbean religions, Shango Baptists became at the beginning of the 19th century an organized church lead by a reverend and a queen mother who were not necessarily blood-related. By the late nineteenth century the religion already spread throughout the island. In distinction to the Baptists, the Orisha religion focuses more on the African gods such as Shango. He comes into being as a Yoruba *orisha.* His appearance is often accompanied by thunder and lightning (hence in Santeria represented as Santa Barbara). He is also deemed to be the legendary fourth king of the ancient kingdom of Oyo. Today, he is a very popular spirit, worshiped in Brazil, Cuba, Haiti, and Trinidad and Tobago.[5]

Afro-Caribbean religions as realms of memory

In order to explain this process of interface at a theoretical level one needs to understand the concept of 'the realms of memory' *(lieux de mémoire)* developed by Pierre Nora. Nora, in his voluminous book, speaks of 'the sites of memory' of different types - from concrete locations, such as, castles and museums to imagined sites, such as novels, songs and ideas. The latter meaning is in use here. The realms of memory are, therefore, not concrete places but are memories of a bygone Africa. I argue that religious beliefs and practises serve as the sites of collective memories. Caribbean religions have integrated the memory of Africa in the Caribbean and pass on their knowledge of Africa. With Africa, of course, I do not mean the continent of Africa or even the African people of today, but an image of Africa that perhaps never existed apart from imagination. As Paul Gilroy states in his book *The Black Atlantic* "Blacks are urged [...] to replace [the slave experience] at the centre of our thinking with a mystical and ruthlessly positive potion of Africa that is indifferent to interracial variation and is frozen at the point where blacks boarded the ships that would carry them into the woes and horrors of the middle passage".[6] This is the idea of Africa that exists within Caribbean religions. The Christian components of these religions served to support this process.

The idea that religions or rituals serve as realms of memory is not new. The French sociologist, Roger Bastide,[7] demonstrated more than 30 years ago how Brazilian religions conserve old memories despite their oppression and slavery. The Afro-American societies sought for new images to fill the gaps produced by slavery, not through adaptation, but through a creative process that construes out of a disparate collection something new: a new meaning without changing the significance of the various elements.

---

[5] Houk, 1995
[6] Gilroy, 1993:189
[7] Bastide, 1970

Bastide's concept of collective memory was inspired by Maurice Halbwachs who in his book, *Les cadres sociaux de la mémoire* (1925, published in English under the title, *On collective memory*), illustrates that individual memories do not last long, whilst the memory of a social group can preserve memories of a former life. Bastide applies Halbwachs' concept of collective memory to Afro-American societies, but stresses the importance of local influences. He explains that the process of conserving memory is not mechanical but depends on the situation, time and environment and, therefore, constantly renews itself. The process of creating memory, which he calls *bricolage*, arises in a permanent movement, ends and begins again, without losing its verve. The process also includes a view of society which can manipulate the group and has an important influence on the composition of the product.

Though the term *bricolage* was originally created by the French anthropologist, Claude Lévi-Strauss, Bastide changes the significance of the term. Lévi-Strauss introduced the term *bricolage* into the anthropological debate about 40 years ago as a metaphor for the mythical thinking of traditional societies. In myths and rites Lévi-Strauss discovered "the remains of methods of observation and reflection which were (and no doubt still are) precisely adapted to discoveries of a certain type: those which nature authorized from the starting point of a speculative organization and exploitation of the sensible world in sensible terms."[8] This science of the concrete (*science du concret*) is no less scientific than the natural sciences and its results no less real. Lévi-Strauss compares this way of thinking with technical handicraft. The term, *bricoleur,* represents a person "who works with his hands and uses devious means compared to those of a craftsman".[9] This method can also be seen in mythical thinking:

> The characteristic feature of mythical thought is that it expresses itself by means of a heterogeneous repertoire which, even if extensive, is nevertheless limited. It has to use this repertoire, however, whatever the task in hand because it has nothing else at its disposal. Mythical thought is therefore a kind of intellectual 'bricolage' – which explains the relation which can be perceived between the two.[10]

Mythical thinking uses a limited number of means to find a solution to a problem. The creation process is limited in a continuously new arrangement of elements that were used in other situations, albeit, with a different function.

---

[8] Lévi-Strauss, 1966:16

[9] Lévi-Strauss, 1966:16-17. As the translator of Lévi-Strauss' book wrote there is no precise equivalent of the term 'bricoleur' in English. "He is a man who undertakes odd jobs and is a Jack of all trades or a kind of professional do-it-yourself man, but, as the text makes clear, he is of a different standing from, for instance, the English 'handyman." (trans. note in footnote, Lévi-Strauss 1966:17).

[10] Lévi-Strauss, 1966:17

Lévi-Strauss who regarded himself as a handyman (in *The Jealous Potter*) did not think of the mythical and the (natural) scientific ways of thinking as contradictory. He thought of these in evolutionary terms, as some of his critics argue. Although, the science of the concrete was developed ten thousand years ago and was valued by Lévi-Strauss as the basis for our civilization, he argues against the idea that mythical thinking is primitive. He illustrates this with the argument that even in modern society mythical thinking exists, in particular, in art and architecture. Lévi-Strauss stresses the creativity of mythical thinking, the creative energy of human beings that in the end breaks through structuralism.

Referring to Marcel Mauss, Bastide adopts another another approach. According to Bastide, Mauss (indirectly) described the process of *bricolage* long before Lévi-Strauss though without using the term; for instance, when he analyzed religious rituals that have been transferred to Brazil where they continued until today in a rearranged form.[11] In order to describe this rearrangement Bastide uses the term *bricolage* because – as he argues – the term helps to understand the transplantation, the opposition and the adaptation of Africans in America. *Bricolage* does not signify only the specific kind of invention, the *logique de l'imaginaire* (logic of the imagination), but it is more in line with Bastide's view. Bricolage is the refurbishment of an existent object such as a chair with a missing leg. Hence, Bastide argues that the significance of the existent object remains even after replacing the missing leg with totally different elements such as, another piece of wood joined with an iron strap (Bastide 1970: 100). In this process local influences are important because the bricoleur uses elements at hand. Hence, expanding on Lévi-Strauss, Bastide focuses on the operating subject, whether it is a group of human beings or an individual. Society influences the process too, through the situation that produces the changes. In the end, *bricolage* can be understood only in relationship to the *bricoleur*, the operating subject. *Bricolage* cannot be compared with a mosaic of colourful stones because it includes a never-ending process. As the handyman is never satisfied with the result of his work and always tries to alter and improve things he produces, the product always changes. Hence, the meaning once developed is not static or fixed for eternity but is flexible and dynamic.

This point leads back to my critique of syncretism. The inclusion of Christian elements was not just a replacement of the missing or suppressed religious icons but refers to a complex process of memory. The gaps caused by the slave trade and the time of slavery were filled with elements at hand, and, in the case of religion, with Christian elements. But they did not remain being Christian elements: they became central parts of the Afro-Caribbean religions. My critique of the concept of syncretism reflects also Gilroy's critique of normative categories, for instance, the 'notion of purity'. He argues that it is

[11] Bastide, 1970:97

important to "embrace the fragmentation of self (doubling and splitting) which modernity seems to promote",[12] hence one should re-define tradition, underscoring the former obsession of origin and continuity. His cultural concept of a Black Atlantic is meant as a counter-concept of modernity. He defines the Black Atlantic as "a non-traditional tradition, an irreducibly modern, ex-centric, unstable, and asymmetrical cultural ensemble that cannot be apprehended through the manichean logic of binary coding".[13] Though he criticises bipolar and static oppositions, he positions his own cultural concept in opposition to (the white Atlantic) modernity and, therefore, argues too in a bipolar schema. I follow a different approach. My concept is not a counter-concept of modernity but a concept beyond the ongoing opposition of tradition and modernity. Instead of keeping the bipolar schema, I have argued for a re-definition of culture that includes every cultural concept, tradition as well as modernity (Schmidt 2002). This concept of culture as a polyphonic *bricolage* defines culture as a dynamic process. As Bastide before, I use the Lévi-Strauss' term *bricolage* with an extended meaning. *Bricolage* becomes the base of a polyphonic cultural concept, a dynamic cultural concept with more than one voice.

I was inspired by the concept of polyphony of Mikhail Bakhtin and his literary studies.[14] Bakhtin was interested in transgression, the crossing of barriers between languages. He describes the European renaissance as a period of two languages, a time when the popular languages began to gain acceptance in opposition to Latin. The existence of a frontier does not only implicate the co-existence of two languages, but indicates also the growing feeling of the language's frontier. Bakhtin characterizes the renaissance as actively multi-lingual, with the ability to regard one's own language from the perspective of the other language.[15] The crossing of frontiers, transgression, leads Bakhtin to his interest in the 'carnivalization' of popular culture and the culture of laughter which was common during the renaissance, but exists also today, though, only in literary works. In the works of Dostoevsky, Bakhtin discovered such 'carnivalistic' elements and the disrupter of the 'monological' unity of the artificial world. Dostoevsky does not create polyphony through different languages, but through relationships and a specific characterization of the figures. By including foreign perspectives in his novels Dostoevsky represents for Bakhtin, therefore, an excellent creator of dialogue and laughter. Recently, Montoya[16] has transferred Bakhtin's concept of 'carnivalization' in her study of Colombian carnival by introducing the term polyvalence. Based on Bakhtin, Montoya defines polyvalence as the demonstration of different possibilities to

[12] Gilroy, 1993:188
[13] Gilroy, 1993:198
[14] See in particular, Bakhtin, 1968 and 1984
[15] In Bakhtin, 1984
[16] Montoya, 2000

understand and handle a situation, an event or a person. Instead of solutions, polyvalence presents only the possibilities of solutions.

Here one finds the answer to the question about the incorporation of Christian elements in Afro-Caribbean religions. The correspondence between African elements and Christian elements within the Afro-Caribbean religions symbolizes a deep intimacy between the two categories but not a power relationship. The experiences of the saints have been minimized in Catholic hagiography and later translated into Caribbean experiences. It is not only a superficial Catholic image to hide authentic African belief; it is, as Pierre Pluchon writes, a dialogue between saints and deities that can be regarded as a Creole practice,[17] or, as I would say, an example of polyphonic bricolage. Afro-Caribbean religions are neither created out of the mixture of two entities, nor frozen in a static moment. They are based on a constant re-arrangement of elements whose meaning can change according to the need of the believers – who in the end often speak with different voices and make contradictory, ambivalent statements about their own religions. Cuban and Puerto Rican santeros speak about the power of the saints, African American believers of the Orisha religion of the power of the orishas. But it does not matter which label the divine is given, both categories are the same but just focus on different aspects. Some scholars neglect this ambivalence in order to create a harmonious image of the religion they want to describe but this approach does not reflect reality. Instead of creating a false image of the religion, one should focus on the diversity within one religion.

Conclusion

The Caribbean religions demonstrate the dynamism of polyphonic bricolage that is difficult to describe. Religions cannot be regarded as homogenous entities; they include various ways to practice and believe. In the same way as Gilroy describes the Black Atlantic as "not specifically African, American, Caribbean, or British, but all of these at once" (cover text) Caribbean religions are also everything at once. Hence it has no value to distinguish between the origins of the various elements because even the meaning of a singular element has changed in the process of incorporation. My observations among Caribbean religious communities have led me to the construction of the concept 'polyphonic bricolage' in order to illustrate that every culture and every religion is in an ongoing state of change and includes different expressions, depending on the situation, time and people. Hence I argue against the existence of static entities; every religion changes continuously and incorporates new influences according to the believers. The expression "syncretism" is, therefore, not an adequate term to describe the flexibility and dynamism of a religion.

---

[17] Quoted by Dayan, 2003:49

PART TWO

CHRISTIAN POLITICAL THINKING IN CONTEXT

Christian Reflections on Indian Political Developments[1]

M.M. Thomas

M.M. Thomas was founder of the Christian Institute for the Study of Religion and Society, Moderator of the Central Committee of the World Council of Churches and Governor of Nagaland, India

There have been several new developments in the Indian political scenario, but I comment on two of them: 1. The emergence of the BJP (the Bharatiya Janata Party), with its ideology of Hindutva (Hindu nationalism and state), as the single party in the multi-party democratic system of Indian politics, as shown by the results of the General Election of May 1996. 2. The economic reforms of globalization adopted by the earlier Congress government and followed by the present government in a modified form. India by its constitution is a secular nation-state following a multi-party democratic form of government and committed to the promotion of economic development aimed at a socialist pattern of society.

The two developments referred to indicate an ideological shift by the Indian middle class which forms the political community from their profession of secularism and socialism in the Nehru era of Indian politics. Therefore, they also point to an ideological crisis requiring radical rethinking about the future.

A Basic Theological Framework

First, I would like to say a word about the basic theological framework for my 'Christian reflections' on politics, so that you may know what meaning I give to the word 'Christian' when talking about politics.

Hinduism speaks of God's three-fold action in the world as *shriti, sthithi* and *layana,* as creation, preservation and redemption. Biblical anthropology is derived from this. The Bible starts with the three covenants of God, with Adam, Noah and Abraham, the first made with all humanity and the others with Israel for the sake of all humanity (Gen.1-12). They symbolize God's creating,

---

[1] Thomas, 1997:17-22. This article was originally delivered as a lecture at the Oxford Centre for Mission Studies co-sponsored by the Theology Faculty of the University of Oxford in July 1996

preserving and redeeming activity in the world. At the same time, they symbolize three aspects of the universal vocation of humanity. These are the human vocation to share responsibility with God in the continuing creation and re-creation of the world, in the preservation of the fallen world from chaos through the promotion of legal justice based on reverence for all life and especially human life, and to share the history of the work of God mediating the grace that redeems creation. Thus human beings are called by God to responsible personal existence in a community of all humanity in the context of the community of all life on earth, as fellow-workers of God. In the Colossian Christology (Col. 1: 15-20), all those covenants and the accompanying human vocations and responsibilities are seen as fulfilled in the divine humanity of Jesus Christ. Through him all the creation comes into being and develops, and in him all creation today remains united, in spite of the force of human self-alienation and disintegration. By his Cross he redeems, renews and perfects all humanity into a new community of persons in the context of the community of life and all creation. I find H. Berkhof's combination of continuing development with continuing redemption of creation (combining the insights of T. de Chardin and K. Barth) illuminating. He defines the Gospel as 'a great movement from lower to higher, going through estrangement and crises, but also through atonement and salvation, and so directed, towards this ultimate goal, a glorified humanity in full communion with God, of which goal the risen Christ is the guarantee and first fruits.'

It is from these biblical truths that Christian anthropology and its various insights about the human situation are derived. What are some of the more important insights which are relevant to our current political situation? I list a few.

Spiritual Transcendence of Selfhood

Faith and its opposite unbelief presuppose a universal spiritual dimension of human selfhood in which the self sees itself as poised between the world and God, i.e. at once as an integral part of the world of matter and the community of life governed by the mechanical and organic laws of development respectively on the one hand, and having a limited power to transcend these laws through its spiritual relation to the transcendent realm of God's purpose on the other. This human self-transcendence provides the self with its power of self-determination to choose its own path of self-fulfilment and to bring the world process into its service. Since in the insecurity arising out of its awareness of its finite freedom, the self tends to absolutise itself and put itself in opposition to its own nature as given by God in creation and redemption, self-alienation is an ever-present aspect of human reality.

Therefore, no human situation can be analysed in its totality purely as the working out of a mechanical or organic necessity, or for that matter, purely as a relation solely between divine spirit and human souls. No doubt, scientific analyses have their relative validity and help understanding, provided they are recognized as partial. But a full analysis requires that we interpret the situation in the light of a theological anthropology which takes seriously the dimension of the human spirit's orientation and disorientation to God's purpose in its interaction with and taking hold of the mechanical dynamics of matter and the organic processes of life in the world of nature.

Moral Realism

The interpretation of the nature of human beings in any situation as 'made in the image of God' and as 'brothers for whom Christ died' should be as persons-in-relation and destined to become persons-in-loving-community with each other in the context of the community of life on earth through the responsible exercise of the finite human freedom reconciled to God. Since the Christian faith holds that as a law or an ideal, it is impossible of realization because of the human alienation from God and that when it is realized even partially in history, it is realized as the result of the divine forgiveness freely given in Christ who provides the motivation for mutual forgiveness among persons and peoples in their historical setting. 'Forgive one another as the Lord forgave you.'

This leads Christian anthropology to a moral realism which recognizes that the human community in the ultimate sense, like the human experience of friendship and love, is a gift of Divine Grace, and that, therefore, there is no final path towards it through technological, political or legal organizations. What such organizations can do is to make the structures of our corporate life more just, that is to say, check the forces of exploitation, corruption, tyranny and war to minimize their threat to human life and maximize the space for mutual responsibility so as to re-give the spiritual gift of communion. Moral realism inherent in this approach is to avoid two absolutist positions of utopianism: one, the approach of political religions which seek to bring a perfect community on earth through political action, which ends in tyranny because it asks the impossible from power-politics; the other, a withdrawal from politics because it cannot bring perfect community on earth, which ends by tolerating the worst tyranny and oppression without resistance. Utopianism is based on the conviction that human beings can justify themselves before God without God's saving grace. This, to Christian anthropology, is also quite unrealistic.

We human beings are called to be involved with imperfect men to realize the less-than-perfect ends of justice which are all that history offers. God's covenant with Noah required fallen humanity to establish a society based on the reverence for life and a legal justice system that protected innocent human beings. Furthermore, God permitted a monarchy, with new perils of oligarchy, to liberate the Israelites from the technically superior Philistines in Palestine. Likewise Paul's doctrine that the Roman state, which he knew had its role in crucifying Jesus, was ordained by God and given the 'sword' to punish the evil and promote the good in society (Rom. 13). All these cases point out that the politics of law and justice has a positive role in a sinful world in relation to the ultimate human destiny.

The state is indeed the reflection of human imperfection. Though a stateless society is the ultimate goal of human community, it is never put forth by Christian anthropology as a realistic possibility. But since the state tends to become the beast that makes war on the saints (Rev. 13), i.e. to become totalitarian, it needs the checks of tradition and law as well as opposition and revolution, to keep it as a servant of justice.

In fact, one has the feeling that the New Testament sees the realms of society and state as both capable of being transformed by the ferment of the church, the community of divine forgiveness and the hope of the coming kingdom to become communities of justice and thus be foretastes and signs of ultimate human destiny, namely the kingdom of God. Of course the Church is the sign and foretaste of the kingdom as God's minister of redemption.

The Person in Interaction with Others

Christian anthropology's emphasis on the human person fulfilling itself in interaction with persons, leads it to give priority to preserve and develop small-scale social institutions which enable face-to-face relations to develop personal values and humanize people. A papal encyclical calls it 'human ecology'. Hannah Arendt, writing on the human condition speaks of three elements which make the lives of people truly human: social life in its plurality, relationship with the earth and a relationship with time; i.e., a sense of participation in contributing to a meaningful historical future. Only social institutions like the family, the village and the neighbourhood community and the decentralization of modern big functional organizations like the state and trade unions can provide them. This has been the emphasis of Gandhi's principle of *swadeshi.* It means that politics and economics should be seen as means to *social* development without making them ends as modern politics and economics tend to do. Now, how do these anthropological insights apply to our Indian political situation, with its crisis of secular democracy which has been the basis of religious freedom and the rights of minority cultures and communities; and to globalized economics, which is geared solely to economic growth?

The Crisis of Secularism

In the course of the Indian national struggle for independence, the concept of secular nationalism had to fight both Hindu nationalism and Islamic nationalism. The Hindu nationalism with its goal of a Hindu state of *akhanda* (undivided) Hindustan which draws its strength from Hindu revivalism and the Muslim two-nation theory that India consists of the Hindu and the Islamic nations which are to be separated at independence, were quite militant in their opposition to the liberal, Gandhian and left-wing ideologies of nationalism which wanted a state which would give equal rights of citizenship to all, irrespective of their religion. The idea of secular nationalism became dominant under the leadership of Mahatma Gandhi and Jawaharlal Nehru. It provided an ideological framework within which the many religious communities of India as well as the plurality of linguistic, caste and ethnic cultures could participate together on the basis of secular ideologies like democracy and socialism. With its weakening in the Congress, it found organized expression in the Hindu Mahasabha and later in the Rashtriya Swayamsevak Sangh (RSS). The partition of India and the Hindu-Muslim riots at independence gave them strength. But the assassination of Gandhi coupled with Nehru's leadership helped Indian politics to stabilize on the secular democratic path.

Thus India's secular nationalism was a dialogic integration between renascent religion and secular ideologies. The middle class who gave leadership to the national movement was the bearer of this idea of secular nationalism. When India became independent it was this middle class committed to secularism that drew up the constitution of the Indian nation-state. They imposed the idea of a secular democratic nation-state on the Indian peoples because they were convinced that it was the basis for the unity of pluralistic India and the best path towards building a new society based on the values of liberty, equality and justice. They also hoped that the reform of religions and cultures from within as well as through legislation and economic development in general would weaken religious communalism.

Now how do we account for the emergence of RSS, VHP (Viswha Hindu Parishad) and BJP and their Hindu ideology after four decades of Indian secularism, to the extent that they are threatening the secular pluralistic basis of Indian polity? Their new strength is clear in the electoral success of the BJP, the political wing of Hindu nationalism. The BJP is governing Bombay and Gujarat. From a mere two MPs in the parliament its number within a decade has risen to a third of the parliament. It has been invited to form the government though it could not get the majority in the parliament because its electoral success was largely confined to Hindi speakers. The regional parties were unwilling to support the government of a party which plays on India's uni-cultural character and suppresses cultural diversity. So the new government is a coalition of parties whose ideological stance is opposed to Hindutva and is critical of a total shift to a market economy as supported by the Congress.

The debate in the parliament on the BJP motion of confidence was of course on the ideology of Hindutva. A report by A. Bhattacharjea clarifies this and, therefore, I have included part of it here to acquaint those who are not informed about the specific issue of secularism and Hindutva in India:[2]

> One of the most powerful pronouncements of the regional viewpoint, for instance, was made by the DMK member, Murasoli Maran ... If the BJP strategists are still wondering why none of the regional parties was willing to support it, they should

---

[2] Bhattacharjea, 1996

> read his speech. It reflects the pent-up fears and anxieties aroused in non- Indo-Aryan peoples by the "one nation, one people, one culture" thesis of BJP ideologies. He agreed that India was one nation, but resented any attempt to impose uniformity. An MP from the North East G.G. Swell was even more apprehensive of the 'cow belt' approach ... Since Veer Savarkar defended Hindutva, culture and religion have been intertwined by those accepting his thesis. As a reaction to cultural domination bolstered opposition to religious exclusivism ... Inderjit Gupta exploited these fears to the full. He quoted a passage written in 1947 by the then RSS supremo, M.S. Golwalkar, that 'non-Hindu peoples of Hindustan must either adopt the Hindu culture on language, must learn to respect and hold in reverence Hindu religion, must entertain no idea but that of glorification of the Hindu race and culture ... or they must stay in this country wholly subordinated to the Indian nation, claiming nothing, deserving no privileges far less any preferential treatment-not even citizens' rights…'

The most striking feature of the two-day debate was its ideological character. Secularism was reaffirmed as a commitment that no party could openly oppose, despite the contradictions between them and Congress' concessions to communal forces in the past.

Some Reasons for the Success of Hindutva

The BJP government had to quit. But it is their new vitality and popular support in the country of Gandhi and Nehru that needs interpretation. There are, no doubt, many reasons for a complex phenomenon like this. Here I mention a few.

The Legacy of Colonialism

Hindutva is a product of the continued impact of colonialism on Hinduism. Historians feel that the colonial interpretation of Indian history, accepted generally by Indian national historians, has strengthened religious communalism and a militant Hindu state ideology in India. S. Gopal, in a talk at Bangalore on *A Historical Perspective of Secularism in India* (1993) has pointed out how a communalist interpretation of Indian history was introduced by colonialism. He said that whether we take popular culture or the culture of the rulers, 'what you had in India was not a sectarian Hindu culture or a Muslim culture but a composite Indian culture.'

The British who colonized India had accepted the European concept of nationhood as constituted by a unity in blood and language, 'ethnic purity and a single language'; therefore, they said that:

> India is not and can never be a nation ... India is a collection of religious communities ... But the unfortunate tragic element was that this British interpretation of Indian history was also accepted by many of our national leaders ... So British interpretation plus the shortsightedness of our own leaders, not

excluding the Mahatma, together resulted in this dreadful phenomenon of communalism.

R. Thapar writes:

> The widely used periodization which has been current in historical writings since the early 19th century is that of dividing Indian history into the Hindu, Muslim and British periods. This is a reflection of a British perception of Indian history and has its genesis in the writing of James Mill who in his *History* of *British India* periodised Indian history in terms of the Hindu civilization, the Muslim civilization and the British period. This periodization was based on a very superficial knowledge of Indian history.

Thapar goes on to point out that the Indian national historians of the twentieth century saw the communal danger in it, but what they did was only to 'change the nomenclature to Ancient, Medieval and Modern' with medieval beginning with the coming of Muslims and the modem with that of the British: 'It came in very useful to communal ideologies arguing that this separation was innate to Indian society and that it began with the coming of the Muslims to India, terminating the "glorious earlier period of Hindu rule".'[3]

The Hindu nationalist movement has in recent years intensified its propaganda in terms of the necessity to regain the glory and honour of the Hindu rule. The destruction of the Ayodhya mosque and the Ram temple movement were justified before and after the event in this manner. For Ashish Nandy, the sociologist, Hindutva is 'blatantly non-Indian and recognizably an illegitimate child of colonialism', which introduced the idea of the priority of state over religion against the Indian concept of building the state on the basis of a 'secondary allegiance' as in the case of Ashoka and Akbar and, in modern India, Mahatma Gandhi. It is the semitisation of Hinduism in the nineteenth century that now 'reaches its form in political Hinduism', which desacralises the world like western secularism itself and uses faith instrumentally as an ideology. 'Hinduism is a Faith; Hindutva an Ideology'. It is 'Secularism's double, the poor man's 'Statism'.[4] Therefore, the tradition of Hindu tolerance practised within a world assumed to be the realm of the sacred, has no relevance for Hindutva as for secularism. Therefore, it attacked 'the plural patriotism on which the most important strand of the freedom movement was based, and is now culturally orphan', presumably meaning Gandhism.

S. Kappen thinks that Hindutva can be understood only as a kind of semiticization of a mystically oriented Hinduism taking into it the theocratic model of medieval Christianity and Islam. He speaks of Hindutva 'taking over from Semitic religions precisely those elements which at least emergent radical Christianity is calling in question.' Here Hindutva is a reaction against

---

[3] Thapar, 1990

[4] Nandy, 1990

colonialism in which it finds the ego-ideal in the very people who colonized them and utilizes the technocratic and political power means in colonialism to defend the Hindu traditions. Savarkar, who was the author of the word Hindutva, asked for the 'Hinduisation of Indian politics and militarization of Hinduism'.

A Spiritual Vacuum

To many the vitality of Hindutva is a reaction against the spiritual vacuum created by secularism and, therefore, the way to fight it is to encourage renascent religion which accepts an open secularism sensitive to religious pluralism and recognises the spiritual dimension of being human. It is part of a worldwide phenomenon. In most countries of the world where secularization and the privatization of religion have gone to the extent of denying religion any role in public life, there is a revival of religion in fundamentalist and political ideological forms. As K. Raiser said in his speech at the Geneva celebration of the fiftieth anniversary of the United Nations:

> Today there is a worldwide reawakening of religion, in part as a reaction to the recent past. Because this resurgence of religious feeling has sometimes taken radical, even aggressive forms, it has engendered fears in many quarters. But we must not lose sight of the fact that the widespread return to religion is also an affirmation that spirituality is essential to human existence.[5]

R. Bharucha[6] raises the question of the relation of Indian secularism to religion as a faith. The editor in the preface says that the tract 'polemises against a form of narrow sectarian secularism which refuses to be sensitive to tradition and faith' and argues that secularism needs to be rethought taking religious faith seriously, that 'only then can Secularism reclaim the ideological space which Fundamentalists are threatening to take over, only then can Secularists capture the minds of the people' (p. vi). Bharucha explains:

> If by Secularism we mean a total avoidance of religious matters, the secular weapons may not be enough' to fight religious fundamentalism and communalism. He adds that encountering fundamentalism on rigidly political lines is not enough; 'alternatives have to be explored within the larger secular drives of neo-religious forms and philosophies' (p. 92).

In this connection he speaks of the significance of the liberation theology movements in all religions and notes the significance of the radical religious movements. N. Koshy, former Director of the CCIA of the WCC, recently

---

[5] Raiser, 1993

[6] Bharucha, 1993

made the statement that 'secularism in India has to be a secularism that takes religions and religious traditions seriously.'[7]

We have already seen that the tradition of neo-Hindu movements represented by Gandhi has been a force behind Indian secularism. Nehru could re-codify Hindu personal law only because the neo-Hindu movements had prepared the Hindu religious mind for it. Nehru saw no such new-Muslim movement in Islam to touch the Muslim personal law. But Indian secularism in recent years has been too closed to take any real interest in religious movements of renewal. It denied religious spirituality or spiritually based morality any role in 'public' life. Alternatively, it has made 'secularism' mean keeping as vote-banks, a federation of fundamentalist conservative religious communities each resisting any social change towards equality in its traditionally sanctioned social structure and showing indifference to the reforming liberal elements working in these communities.

Fundamentalist Hindu opposition to change the traditional Hindu social order had played a large part in the creation and strengthening of the RSS ideology of opposition to other religions and to movements of Hindu reformation. This is clear from what Golwalkar, the former RSS ideologist, says in his writings on Hindutva. He says that Hindutva is hostile to Islam because 'Islam was the first religion to interfere with our social organization of Chaturvarna ... Islam in India challenged our scheme of class-caste organization. All post-Islamic (Hindu) sects sought to counter Islam by seeking to take the wind out of Islamic sails by themselves making the same challenge. That is why these sects have now become a source of national division and weakness'. Here the RSS chief's opposition to Islam, the Sufi and Bhakti sects and Gandhism and, by extension, to Christianity, liberalism and socialism, are all one piece. This led Golwalkar to characterize those 'who advocated Hindu-Muslim unity as necessary to fight for swaraj' as the perpetrators of the 'greatest treason in our society'.[8] Lohia, writing on the motivation behind Gandhi's assassination, couples Hindutva hostility to Islam and to the democratic transformation of Hindu society. He wrote: 'No Hindu can be generally tolerant to Muslims unless he acts at the same time actively against caste and property and for women.' To Lohia, the assassination of Mahatma Gandhi was not so much an episode of Hindu-Muslim conflict as of the war between the Liberal and the Fanatical in Hinduism.[9] This struggle is of crucial importance for the future of secularism in India.

---

[7] Koshy, 1995
[8] Sikand, 1992
[9] Lohia, 1950

The Issue of Conversion

The question of conversion, especially group conversion of tribals and depressed castes, continues to be an issue not only to the Hindu nationalists but also to the more liberal Gandhians. In a paper presented at the Nehru Centenary Seminar at Trivandrum, N.V. Krishna Warrier opposed the freedom of religious conversion given as a fundamental right to citizens.[10] His argument was the large-scale conversion from Hinduism to other religions has been a serious cause of Hindu communalism. He says:

> Hinduism as such does not favour the idea of proselytisation ... Hinduism did not object to this so long as political power depended not on numbers but on other factors. Now that democracy has come to stay, Hindus have belatedly realized that numbers do count and only numbers do count ultimately.

Further, they see that there is 'high concentration of non-Hindu communities in several states of India many of them on the borders', which places the national security of India at risk. Therefore, he asks whether it is not time that the law stops the movement of proselytization which is 'a form of aggression', and takes a decision that 'propagating one's own religion is different from proselytization and that while the former is every Indian's birthright, the latter is a punishable offence'. Here there is a mixture of religious and political motivations and the assumption that the security of the Indian nation lies primarily with Hindus on the border, because others are supposed to have extra-territorial loyalties. This is, of course, the Hindutva approach.

The Gandhian Krishna Kanth, the Governor of Andhra Pradesh, in his address to the Assembly of the National Council of Churches in 1991 and following it in a press interview with N. Choudhury[11] 'called for an end to religious conversion in the country, not by law but by a voluntary consensus of religious leaders', because in his opinion, communal strife is closely linked to conversion. His main argument was that the word Hindu which had essentially geographic and cultural meaning began to acquire religious connotations and communal overtones when missionary religions began converting the untouchables and lower castes of Hindu society with a promise of their liberation from caste indignities. But conversion did not bring liberation to the converted people from caste, because caste is not just a Hindu phenomenon but an Indian reality and is practised by all religions in India. So, the 'social logic' of conversion is no more there. But it is with conversion that the 'false concept of majority and minority emerged making Hinduism a religion and caste a Hindu phenomenon'. Only the stopping of conversion will be 'a starting point for harmony in society and for lessening mental insecurity, fanaticism and the prevalent climate of confrontation.

---

[10] Warrier, 1991:223-9

[11] Choudhury, 1991

There is certainly need to discuss the difference between mystic and prophetic religions on this question, and to come to a common understanding on the permissible parameters of the practice of religious freedom, including propagation and conversion. Of course, religious freedom is the condition and guardian of all other freedoms and, therefore, we have to watch that the attack on it does not become the thin end of a wedge of state totalitarianism.

Globalization: A universal ideology

Firstly, the market economy has made its contribution to economic growth in the world. Its contribution to economic creativity and dynamism cannot be denied. Christian anthropology, as I have defined it, does not allow us to oppose it for its utilization of self-interest and profit motive. That would be succumbing to utopianism which I have rejected in the name of Christian realism. In fact, it is the resurgence in the contemporary globalization of the utopianism associated with the traditional *laisiez-faire* capitalism we have to oppose as idolatrous.

No doubt the market economy has become the universal ideology after the disappearance of the socialist regimes of Eastern Europe. However, from its very beginning in A. Smith, the free market was set within the framework of an idolatrous utopianism, individualism and a mechanistic worldview which were characteristic of the ideology of humanism that informed the political and economic movements of that period. According to Goudzwaard and H. de Lange 'the fine working of the market is close to the heart of western society's self-definition' and they speak about its underlying presuppositions thus:[12]

> Indeed for Smith, the market played a role in all forms of human progress. It stimulated industrial growth and a desire to save. Moreover, the market itself, led as if by an Invisible Hand the participation of the poor in the expanding wealth. ...these premisess...are misleading in content, displaying the colours of the enlightenment's naïve belief in human progress and a Deistic vision of society. They have in their undertone the worldview that suggests that a good society must function like a machine whose operation is controlled by the laws of nature'

R. Preston who argues that the market is an efficient mechanism for the limited purpose of economic growth, and should be used as such by the Third World countries also, agreed that the original and continuing premises of the market that 'if each pursued his own advantage through the automatic device of the market, an Invisible Hand would ensure that the result was the promotion of the common good' was an illusion.

Further, Preston adds that it is bound to a 'possessive individualism' which is clearly false. Preston comments: 'It is important to separate [the premisess]

---

[12] Goudzwaard and Lange, 1995:44-5

from the concept of the market as a useful mechanism for solving some economic problems if it was set within a different value commitment and an extensive structural framework.'[13] The capacity of the market to maximize the productivity of relatively scarce resources 'above any other consideration' makes it useful if it is limited to that function and made to serve other considerations through state control. 'The institution of the market needs to be put into a fine political framework. Left to itself it is cruel and callous.' Preston continues:

> In short, the market is a human device set up to serve human purposes, to be servant and not master. We must not bow down to the idol we ourselves have created. It is a political decision as to which areas of economic life we let the impersonal verdict of the market [decide] and which to be decided by public discussion, as it also is to decide the broad parameters of economic guidelines within which the economy has to operate. No government however devoted to *laissez-faire* can escape that responsibility.[14]

J. Dreze and A. Sen, in their comparative study of the patterns of rapid economic development through the market mechanism in Third World countries especially Brazil, China and South Korea, have shown that social development is an essential prerequisite for what is called, *participatory* economic expansion.[15] They point out that 'it would be quite bizarre to read the East Asian success stories as simple results of liberalization and of freeing of markets'.[16] China and South Korea effected land reform, and realized a fairly high level of literacy, women's education, rural development and other aspects of social development before starting the economic reforms of globalization which made it possible for people to take part in the new opportunities offered. In Brazil this social preparation did not take place, and, therefore, the 'Brazilian economy grew very fast but achieved rather little reduction of poverty, particularly in terms of social backwardness and sectional deprivation ... India stands in some danger of going the Brazilian way rather than South Korea's.'[17] It is further said that:

> The cage that keeps the Indian economy well tamed is not only that of bureaucracy and government over-activity but also that of illiteracy, undernourishment, ill health and social inequalities, and their causal antecedents: 'government neglect and public apathy.... We have tried to argue for a broader view of economic development which has to be seen in terms of expanding social opportunities. With nearly half the people and close to two-thirds of the women

[13] Preston, 1983:42; 114-5
[14] Preston, 1983:42; 114-5
[15] Dreze and Sen, 1995
[16] Dreze and Sen, 1995:42
[17] Dreze and Sen, 1995:183

illiterate, the transformation of the Indian economy is no easy task. We have particularly emphasized the need for participatory economic expansion.[18]

In fact in this context they highlight the Kerala model of giving priority to improving the quality of social life as an investment for economic development.

State Initiative as an Organ of the Whole Community

All this calls at least for a return to J. Nehru's economic policy with more state initiative for the liquidation of poverty and for social development. But the policy of globalization and liberalization adopted by the Congress government of N. Rao, no doubt under pressure from the IMF and the World Bank was for the state to make the climate safe for the market and withdraw almost completely from the realm of social goals leaving the market alone to determine them. This means that goals like the liquidation of poverty and unemployment, the distribution of welfare, the narrowing of the gulf between the rich and the poor, the people's participation in the economic process, the accountability of economic centres to the people, economic self-sufficiency and similar other economic purposes are jeopardized because the market is not concerned with them. M.A. Oommen says, 'Globalization achieves with economic growth, globalization of Poverty.' More importantly, issues of ecological justice and justice to the weaker sections of society and specifically the development of social institutions cannot be taken by the directed only by the market profit mechanism.

As R. Kothari points out, high-tech industrialism under the market system (one should add, within the framework of an individualist and mechanistic ideology) not only globalizes the pollution of the soil, air and water but especially it:

> Leads to a wanton exploitation of the natural resource base of the country, especially based on the forest and the sea. In human terms, this has a disastrous consequence for certain groups of people like the tribals, scheduled castes, traditional fishermen and such other groups who depend on them to eke out a living. ... They would also be tom away from their natural roots as well as from their community and cultural ties producing in them a sense of isolation.[19]

The social objectives of the people are destroyed for the sake of economic growth. In this context the newly organized National Alliance of People's Movements which includes movements of the Dalit, tribal, fisher-folk and women who are victims of modern development are of some significance. Its leaders are M. Patkar of the movement for those evicted from their habitation

---

18 Dreze and Sen, 1995:181-182

19 Kothari, 1994

by the Narmada dam project, T. Kocheri of the national movement of fisher-folk fighting to defend their fishing rights against the government which permits foreign boats to fish in the coastal waters and others. Of course until the organized trade unions come to their support it has little political strength, but it may grow. The Alliance's approach is to search for a more humane alternative to development among Gandhian-Sarvodaya lines. But alternatives can grow only out of the forces which are active in the current system.

It is here that the state as the organ of the whole national community has to intervene rather than withdraw. As C.T. Kurien has written, the state has to discipline capital, both domestic and international, if capital is not to discipline the state to serve its purposes; and for it the state needs not only political power but also some economic power derived from public corporations. But the Congress government of N. Rao surrendered the state to the ideology of the free market with the backing of the Indian middle class (which includes also the upper layer of the organized working class) who find that the policy enhances their interests. Perhaps the rejection of the Congress by the electorate in the May 1996 General Elections is in part due to the lower sections' protest against the policy. The present government seems to accept the policy of economic growth with greater state intervention in the name of social welfare and justice like the left-wing parties participating in the government.

The Church always has had groups which followed two different models of Christian witness in relation to economics and politics. One is that of critical participation in morally ambiguous structures which currently operate to transform them as far as possible from within in the direction of a better alternative, and pursue the path of a total confessional resistance only when the situation is seen as institutional idolatry. The other is to withdraw to build ideal alternative models in the midst of the current more or less inhuman structures as the base of a counter-culture movement hoping for the moment of a radical irruption of the new. I suppose both are valid. Recently J. Habgood, the former Archbishop of York, said:

> The counter-culture model has its attractions. It provides a basis for prophetic ministry, and there is widespread longing for clear prophetic utterance even if such prophecy is over-simplified. But there are losses as well. I am not thinking about the loss of status and privilege, but about losing the intimate sense of belonging within a society where Christ is still at work, despite the apparent secularity, and which still needs reminding that its creative energies can and must find their true source in the creative Spirit of God.[20]

[20] Habgood, 1995

Rights, Law and Political Community: A Theological and Historical Perspective[1]

Joan L. O'Donovan

Dr. Joan L. O'Donovan is honorary fellow the School of Divinity, the University of Edinburgh, U.K.

Most citizens of this country and of other advanced western and westernizing nations approve of human rights, some more guardedly than others; and most perceive rights to belong to the moral, political and legal fabric of modern liberal democracy. By rights, I mean rights attributable to subjects, to persons, whether individual or collective 'persons'. To suggest that rights, freedom, and democracy go together (as does the United Nations Universal Declaration of Human Rights of 1948, which has been the template for subsequent generations of declarations) is a modern truism, which, like most truisms, is largely true.

Less clearly perceived, I think, is the extent to which human rights and democracy are bound up with liberal economics and free-market capitalism. Approval for free-market capitalism, even with a kinder face, is more equivocal in most advanced western societies, particularly, it would seem to me, among serious-minded Christians. Indeed, in today's thinking circles, anxieties are rife about the threats posed by unrestrained market forces to social, economic and democratic rights in the developed and developing world, quite apart from environmental considerations. It is widely perceived that excessive corporate profit and inflated managerial salaries flout the democratic ethos of social equality, that the coercive features of market exchange diminish individual economic freedom, and that the influence on governmental policy of powerful financial and commercial interests threatens the commanding role of the democratic majority. Indeed, there is a mounting sense among democratic populations that the global flow of investment capital seeking larger profit margins, favourable tax benefits and speculative gains is robbing the majority of the world's citizens of effective political controls over their economic and social futures.

While this raft of anxieties are well-placed at the practical level, they somewhat cloud the deeper issue of how rights, democracy and liberal economic principles are related. To grasp this relationship, it is necessary to

[1] O'Donovan, 2003: 30-38

become acquainted with the liberal contractarian political tradition: the tradition of Hobbes, Locke, Rousseau, Kant, the apologists of the American and French Revolutions, and still vigorous, with utilitarian accretions, in the work of such contemporary contractarians as John Rawls and Robert Nozick. This, I would suggest, is the majoritarian tradition of *liberal natural rights* in the modern world.

In this tradition, which has supplied much of the ideological glue of contemporary liberal democracy, the equality of individuals is economic before it is political: behind the multitude of naturally self-governing individuals, whose sovereign collective will government serves, is a multitude of naturally self-owning individuals, each with a proprietary right over his/her spiritual and corporeal capabilities and acts, to dispose of them in whatever way he/she chooses. Although individuals are (obviously) not equal in their physical and spiritual resources, they are equal (so it is asserted) in their ownership of them: they are equal as proprietors. Self-proprietors are interested in maximizing their powers of self-disposal or self-determination, their freedom of choice; and they participate in political society as a contractual creation to achieve maximum freedom through the protection of and provision for their rights. Believing in the equality of self-proprietors, individuals are not adverse to honouring the rights of others, but only as far as their prudential calculations allow, or the political contract which authorizes governmental action requires.

Given the strength of the liberal 'rights' tradition in advanced technological societies, churchmen and theologians are, at best, naive in their facile appropriation of 'rights' talk. Across denominational boundaries there is quite a predictable argument from the creation of human-kind in God's image to the unique dignity of persons in community to their universal possession of rights. Albeit different denominations bring different theological nuances to the argument; nevertheless, there appears to be a consensus about the unproblematic nature of the move from human dignity to human rights, once the theological 'foundation' or 'analogy' is prepared. 'Rights' is accepted by all as expressing moral attributes of a theologically conceived humanity.

Having said this, the Roman Catholic tradition of social teaching over the last century stands out as more theologically and philosophically astute in regard to rights. The concept of 'natural rights' came into contemporary Catholic teaching with the pontificate of Leo XIII at the end of the nineteenth century, and his famous encyclical *Rerum Novarum* put its stamp on the subsequent integration of 'rights' into Catholic social and political thought. As many of you will know, Leo XIII was responding simultaneously to two aspects of the contemporary malaise: on the one hand, to the industrial degradation of the labouring class in a *laissez-faire* environment, and on the other, to the seductive appeal for the downtrodden of atheistic socialism. His alternative Catholic social vision and campaign of action placed in the foreground the right of the labourer, as well as the entrepreneur, to property, and the right of the family to fulfil its natural purpose of mutual love and provision.

In plotting his Catholic alternative, Leo turned principally, as in other matters, to the thought of Thomas Aquinas. But his sources were varied (possibly more than he realized), and included later neo-scholastic theologians and even a dash of John Locke. In fact, Leo's encyclical tapped into two (let us say) *early-modern* sources of 'rights': firstly, a late medieval theological tradition of 'natural rights', and secondly, a tradition of civic corporatism, powerful in northern Italian, Flemish and German cities from the thirteenth century onward. Forty years later, Pope Pius XI would develop more extensively this corporatist 'rights' tradition. Subsequent Catholic social teaching, it should be said, has increasingly (but by no means wholly) aligned itself with the majoritarian liberal tradition, under the influence of such 'modern' Thomists as Etienne Gilson and Jacques Maritain.

Today I wish to look with a critical theological gaze at these three streams of 'rights' development, the two early-modern and the modern streams, in the hope of clarifying our understanding of how we, in advanced liberal democracies, have come to be where we are, and also of how we should proceed. At the outset, I wish to situate these streams in the larger historical landscape of Christian political thought with a few very general (and possibly reckless) remarks.

Up until the fourteenth century, Christian political thought functioned virtually without any concept of subjective natural rights – I say virtually, because the concept made a few scattered appearances before the fourteenth century, but was not theoretically developed. In earlier patristic and medieval political theology, God's right established a matrix of divine, natural and human rights or objective obligations that determined the ordering justice of political community. Justice (*iustitia*) was synonymous with objective right (*ius*) – i.e. the objectively right action in any situation – and objective right was what accorded to law, to legal right (*lex, ius*). Political authority or government was primarily a matter of divine institution, appointment and authorization; and the central moral-political act on the part of ruler and ruled alike was to consent to the obligations inhering in communal life according to divine intention and rationally articulated as laws. The ruler commanded, gave laws, issued binding judgments, but he was to command obediently; his judgments were to conform to the binding revelation of God's will in Scripture. The subject was obligated to obey the ruler's commands, not only because of his rightful authority, but because of their intrinsic conformity to the requirements of justice. And there were, of course, unjust commands that the subject was obligated by God's law never to obey.

In the fourteenth century there was a turn to the moral subject and his capacity for right action, and, from the start, this subjective capacity (i.e. subjective right) was associated with man's created freedom and lordship over the rest of creation. In this newer orientation to natural right, the active individual will occupied a central position, the emphasis being on the subject's control and ownership of his own acts, and increasingly, on his control over his moral and physical environment. Nevertheless, the late medieval development of subjective rights took place on the basis of 'objective right', of natural and divine law; only in the 'rights' theories of the seventeenth and eighteenth centuries was this basis superseded. Moreover, throughout the early-modern period, the older, 'rights'-free political theology continued to be represented in both Augustinian and Thomistic circles, and was revived in the sixteenth century by continental and English reformers.

The Theological Tradition of Natural Rights

In the late 1320s and early 1330s, Marsiglio of Padua and William of Ockham produced early, influential, formulations of the concept of subjective right. They produced these formulations in the course of defending the Franciscan order (to which Ockham belonged) from papal attacks on its practice of poverty. This context is significant for the theological issues surrounding subjective right. Briefly, the Franciscan practice of extreme poverty came out of a 'theology of the Cross' that dwelt on Christ's earthly sufferings and destitution; for the brothers, the most perfect discipleship meant participation in Christ's earthly poverty. The brothers' renunciation of wealth came in time to include renunciation of all legal ownership of goods, individual and collective. This allowed them to sustain themselves and their ministries with a range of goods that were owned by others and donated for their use.

While the practice of absolute legal poverty was not, I think, without theological (as well as practical) problems, its theological justification contained a profound truth: namely, that the most perfect love of God and neighbour leaves no room for claiming earthly goods *for oneself and against one's neighbour*. Because property-right creates the possibility of *defending one's claim to something in court*, it is disruptive of the human response to divine love. The great Franciscan theologian, Bonaventure, understood that the legal proprietor of something, in seeking to impose obligation on others regarding it, is involved in a degree of self-possession, separation from other wills, and self-referential attachment to the thing that approaches selfishness and covetousness. Thus, the status of legal poverty was to remove the brothers from the temptation inhering in *property as such*. Now, it is easy to see how Franciscan poverty threatened a church endowed with vast property. And not only that, it threatened the late_medieval claim of the Roman pope, as Christ's earthly vicar, to have universal *ownership* of temporal goods – a claim that reflected, among other things, the inseparability of 'ownership' and 'jurisdiction' in medieval feudal organization, which forms the backdrop to the appearance of 'natural rights'. In attacking Franciscan poverty, Pope John XXII argued that universal ownership (*dominium*) of temporal goods belonged to Christ's human perfection and lordship (*dominium*), and as well, to Adam's earthly lordship (*dominium*); and that no one could use material things without having, minimally, a legal right of use (*ius utendi*) and in the case of consumable goods (such as food or drink), full ownership of them. Here, in the Pope's protracted vindication of property-right, we already have the theological model that the seventeenth century 'natural right' thinkers would inherit – which, no doubt, explains why the Catholic Church had to wait over 600 years for Pope John XXIII! (Actually, John XXII was condemned for – what one can only describe as – his Barthian eschatology.)

Replying to the Pope's arguments, Marsiglio and Ockham attributed to Christ and his disciples a 'natural right' to use goods necessary for their sustenance, in the absence of any positive legal right. Moreover, Ockham proposed that Adam and Eve's lordship (*dominium*) over the nonhuman creation was not ownership in any sense, but a power (*potestas*) of rationally ruling (*regendi*) and managing (*gubernandi*) the non-human creation, which included the power of using the earth's resources for human sustenance and comfort. Apart from his relatively novel concept of a subjective moral power or 'right', Ockham was merely endorsing the mainstream patristic and medieval view of Adamic society before the Fall as a community of sharing in the earth's abundance according to individual need, with no claims of 'mine' and 'thine'. In addition, Marsiglio precisely distinguished the 'objective' and 'subjective' meanings of 'right'. In the primary or objective sense, he explained in *Defensor pacis* 2.12, 'right' meant a dictate of law, whether divine or human; in the subjective sense, 'right' denoted 'a human act, power, or acquired habit' conforming to law (i.e. to objective 'right'). For both thinkers, then, subjective right was the power of a person to perform a lawful action: in other words, it was a 'lawful' or 'licit' power. In a more voluntarist move, Marsiglio described human freedom – that is, the relation of the person's will to his acts – as a form of ownership. Both thinkers also attributed natural rights to collective as well as individual subjects, but we shall reserve collective rights for later discussion.

The next important figure for the theory of subjective right was the late fourteenth/ early fifteenth century Paris theologian, Jean Gerson, a follower of Ockhamist nominalism, but also steeped in Aristotelian and Thomistic thought. While his theological interest was more with corporate than individual rights, he and his mentor, Pierre D'Ailly, inspired a Sorbonnist tradition of theorizing about individual right which continued into the sixteenth century, with far-reaching influence on humanist, Catholic neo-scholastic, and Protestant legal and political thought, well into the seventeenth century. Gerson's legacy included, firstly, his definition of individual right as a 'proximate faculty (*facultas*) or power' conforming to the dictate of 'right reason' or 'primary justice'; secondly, his assimilation of the *facultas* of individual freedom to Adam's natural *dominium*; and thirdly, his proposal that a theory of 'primary justice would assign to everything it proper 'right', in the sense of 'title' or 'possession' (*De potestate ecclesiastica* 13).

Some of Gerson's followers carried the 'faculty' concept of right further in a voluntaristic, subjectivist, and proprietary direction. As property-right or ownership (*dominium* in the civil-legal sense) increasingly eclipsed non-proprietary use (Adamic *dominium*) as fundamental natural right, it shaped subjective right in a twofold way. In the first place, rights were conceived as immanent spiritual capabilities possessed or owned by individuals, so that their relation to divine command and authorization was not as immediate or transparent. One consequence was that individual freedom was considered by certain late scholastic thinkers to be a property alienable by agreement or contract (as when someone sells himself into slavery). In the second place, the relation of individuals to the external objects of their rights (even objects which they did not own) took on a proprietary character, so that the individual's claim-right *to something* was construed as a form of *dominium*. Thus, the individual was a moral proprietor (*dominus*) not only of what he actually possessed but also of what he demanded as an entitlement.

It is hardly surprising, then, that social and economic relationships took on an increasingly covenantal and contractual character, and that, from the mid-fifteenth century onward, political society itself was quite regularly viewed as formed by a compact among rights-bearing individuals. Nevertheless, it must be observed that neither the objects of individual rights nor the terms of compacts entered into by individuals were severed from objective right as determined by divine and natural law (even if the moral content of the latter was attenuated at times). Limited contracts of social or economic exchange and even the compact establishing political society itself recognized divinely established social-moral bonds transcending them. All the major late scholastic thinkers affirmed the natural sociability of individuals and natural patterns of human fellowship. Moreover, the majority did not proceed from the civil compact to endorse principles of popular sovereignty and republican self-government, for this reason: that they were concerned to harmonize their more voluntarist and individualist perspective with the older biblical theological tradition. At their best, they conceived theories of constitutional Christian monarchy – as, for example, did Richard Hooker in his *Laws of Ecclesiastical Polity*; at their worst, they constructed more statist and absolutist monarchical polities on the basis of a total transference of political right from the civil community to its ruler.

Finally, we cannot fully understand this late scholastic tradition of natural rights and political contract apart from the polemical pressures of the times to repudiate the associated 'heresies' of John Wyclif and Martin Luther. Both Wyclif and Luther gave moral centrality to gospel freedom and divine right – indeed, they viewed all right as God's in Christ and refused to develop an independent concept of natural law and subjective rights. Of course, it was Wyclif and Luther's use of this evangelical perspective to attack the proprietary and jurisdictional powers (spiritual and temporal) of the papal church that called forth such polemical resistance from Parisian and other late scholastic thinkers.

Our next task is to see what the late medieval theologians accepted, as well as what they rejected, in the other early-modern tradition of 'rights': that of civic corporatism.

The Civic Corporatist Tradition of Rights

The twelfth and thirteenth centuries saw the proliferation over western Europe of cities enjoying a large measure of political independence and sharing many communal, corporate and republican features: legal structures defined by charters; guaranteed equal freedoms and equal civic obligations for their citizens; participation of citizens in municipal administration, either directly or through representative bodies (chiefly guilds); and local churches under some degree of municipal control. The single most important *institutional* source of urban republican developments, whether incipient or full-blown, was the corporation as a juridical, social and economic reality. Loosely definable as a 'sworn fellowship in pursuit of common aims', the medieval corporation comprised a collective 'legal' (sometimes called 'fictive') subject to which legal rights and obligations were attached, both collectively and distributively, i.e, to its individual members. The self-governing and property-owning corporation typically had a head (*syndic*, *rector*, *tutor*) elected by the whole body (*universitas*) and a representative at law (proctor) authorized to act for it in various transactions, frequently to carry out its express will. Certain prerogatives such as corporate rule-making remained with the assembled members. Urban communities and corporations interpenetrated in various ways. Not infrequently, towns and cities developed out of mercantile guilds which already exercised wide-ranging legislative and judicial control over local trade and commerce. Towns and cities were themselves established as comprehensive corporations with jurisdiction over lesser guilds. In the course of the fourteenth century, municipal corporations absorbed leading guilds into their political structure, resulting in popular representation or in power-sharing between the patrician and artisan classes. Thus medieval urban society was politically homogenized along corporative principles; and, moreover, integrated through a more embracing civic ethos in which natural loyalties and social virtues blended with popular Christian devotion and cultic piety. In mercantile, professional and craft guilds, concerns of economic justice and self-interest, social reciprocity and mutuality, and works of love and piety were deeply intertwined. Correspondingly, the urban churches took on not just congregational but civic features, as church fellowship merged with guild solidarity and the culture of corporate rights and obligations.

While most theologians and philosophers of the period viewed the republican and populist features of urban corporatism with suspicion, many were, nevertheless, drawn to corporative principles and ideas. Construing political society as a natural corporation, they attached to it the rights belonging to other corporate subjects in positive law: rights to make corporate rules and to elect, advise, correct and even to remove corporate administrators. While a theologian like Ockham was clear that all communal political rights were *divinely imparted, post-lapsarian rights*, a theologian like Marsiglio of Padua neither made the distinction of pre-and post-lapsarian nor mentioned God's authorship of them.

In his *defensor pacis*, Marsiglio carried through most consistently the theoretical project of republicanism, combining urban corporatism and Aristotelianism in the starkest defiance of the older theological tradition. He laid down the power (right) to make laws as the principal political power, and then set up the political community (*universitas*, *populus*) as the primary, permanent *legislator* that either acts immediately, or mediately, through the (secondary) agency of a chosen ruler. He granted to the communal *legislator* an ongoing right of political judgment, to be exercised in the periodic election, correction, and (if need be) deposition of rulers, either immediately or through representatives.

Ockham, by comparison, avoided the full-blown republican project of Marsiglio in the following respects. He did not make law-making the pre-eminent political act, nor invest the people as *legislator* with the ongoing, inalienable right of political judgment. Rather he proposed that, in electing a ruler (or a dynasty), the people conferred on him jurisdiction over itself, so that the ruler ruled under God and under law (divine, natural, and communal), but not under the people. In other words, political authority was acquired from the people, but held from God. Moreover, he admitted forms of communal consent other than election in the establishment of political rule; and he justified the forcible removal of rulers by the natural law of necessity, i.e. the necessity of preserving the common good under dire threat, rather than by an inalienable right of corporate self-government.

Of vital importance to the cautious undertaking of Ockham and later theologians to integrate corporative ideas into the theological tradition, was the centrality of the ruler's judicial function: his function of judging and punishing wrong-doing, of vindicating and rewarding right-doing. In the light of the biblical testimony, this function seemed to require the immediate dependence of human on divine political authority, whatever the community's original and continuing powers. But even with this limitation on communal powers, the project of harmonizing communal rights and God's right was fraught with tensions, the thorniest problem being how to relate the divinely bestowed form of political authority to the constitutional form dependent on communal choice. The coolness of many Protestant reformers (both continental and English) to the Aristotelian legacy, to juristic corporatism and to urban republicanism cannot be put down entirely to the political needs and pressures of church reform. Not only the problem of judicial authority but also that of political wisdom – how political judgments may be grounded in a secure knowledge of divine and human law – made them wary of egalitarian rights of political participation.

The Roman church, by comparison, was concerned less with the threat posed by urban corporatism to civil government than with its threat to ecclesiastical government. While the church was by far the most corporatively developed of late medieval polities, having integrated many popular devotional, charitable, and monastic corporations, still the central core of its corporative structure was the clerical hierarchy; and the corporative rights – administrative and jurisdictional – of the clerical hierarchy were attached to their sacerdotal powers. As the fundamental corporate constitution of the Roman church was, therefore, episcopal and monarchical, collisions with the congregational and corporative ethos of civic churches were plentiful.

The Modern Libertarian Rights Tradition

With the political writings of Hobbes and Locke, and the Leveller manifestos of the seventeenth century, arrived the full flowering of the proprietary paradigm of subjective right. Hobbes's chief contribution to this paradigm in *Leviathan* was his redefinition of natural right, over against the scholastic mainstream, as each individual's *unrestrained liberty* 'to use his own power' and to act for his self-preservation , so asserting both the radical priority of natural right to natural law and the radical separation of natural right from social obligation. In their natural condition, Hobbes's individuals have an unlimited right to use everything, including one another's bodies, unbounded by obligations of natural justice. Only the intolerable insecurity of right in this condition necessitates the prudential stratagems for peace known as 'laws of nature'; which include the 'mutual transferring of right' by individuals to a recognized civil power (excepting the right in life and its defence), with the object of securing a sphere of limited (civil) rights.

If Hobbes's emphasis on the appetitive and unlimited content of natural right projected a model of social relationships as essentially acquisitive, atomistic, and competitive, the Levellers' and Locke's concentration on property right projected a market model. The following passage from a tract of Richard Overton indicates how complete was the Levellers' assimilation of subjective right to property:

> To every Individuall in nature is given an individual property by nature, not to be invaded or usurped by any: for every one as he is himselfe, so he hath a selfe propriety, else could he not be himself, and on this no second may presume to deprive any of, without manifest violation and affront to the very principles of nature, and of the Rules of equity and justice between man and man; mine and thine cannot be, except this be; No man hath power over my rights and liberties, and I over no mans, …and as we are delivered of God by the hand of nature into

> this world, every one with a naturall, innate freedome and propriety… even so are we to live, every one equally and alike to enjoy his Birthright priviledge...[2]

Not only does Overton conceive the individual's property in himself and in his energies and capacities as full ownership – an exclusive power of disposal effective against the whole world, but, as C.B. Macpherson astutely observed, he identifies his total self-possession, his 'freedom from other men', with his essential humanity. This identification underpinned the entire Levellers' claims for specific civil, religious, economic, and political rights and freedoms.

The principle advance of Locke beyond the Levellers was his elaboration of the relationship between the individual's ownership of his capacity to labour and his ownership of the produce of his labour. On analogy with God's exclusive proprietary right over his creation, the individual has exclusive proprietary right over the objects created by his work, within the broad rational constraints of natural law, that place virtually no obstacles in the way of wealth accumulation through enterprise in a money economy. The individual's control of his labour is merely one aspect of his autonomous freedom – his right of unrestrained disposal of his actions *apart from* the obligations belonging to the natural law. Locke's labour theory of private property also focused attention on the consequences of alienating one's labour in a wage contract, and so, on the quality of labour as an exchangeable commodity in the economic market.

A century later, the project of reconstructing the political contract along the lines of a market exchange of rights would occupy the forefront of American Revolutionary thought, revealing the outer limit of libertarian individualism. Addressing the question of which natural rights are alienable in the civil contract and which inalienable, Thomas Paine in *The Rights of Man* proposed that each individual retains those natural rights 'in which the power to execute is as perfect in the individual as the right itself' (e.g., 'right of mind') and 'deposits… in the common stock of society' those in which 'though the right is perfect in the individual, the power to execute them is defective' (e.g. the individual's 'right to judge in his own cause'). Paine's analogy of the joint stock company in which 'Every man is a proprietor in society, and draws on the capital as a matter of right', has the effect of accentuating the superior bargaining position and adjudicating power of the contracting individuals and the dominant role of calculative rationality in setting the terms of the civil contract.

The continuing predominance of property right within the negative libertarian tradition is hardly surprising; for it sustains the individual's primary right of freedom as a power of acting that he possesses, and which entails an obligation of non-interference on the part of all other subjects, and especially, of government. The influence of property right on the more recent tradition of positive or welfare rights is less obvious. For welfare rights are 'entitlements'

---

[2] Macpherson, 1962

of subjects to goods or opportunities that others alone or in part can provide – e.g. medical care, housing, employment, voting opportunity etc. If the language of entitlement signifies no more than the moral obligations that certain others are under to provide these benefits, as far as is possible, then it does not express property right. In this case, I would suggest, the language is superfluous. If, however, these entitlements constitute obligation imposing demands on others made by potential recipients on the basis of their active powers, then they remain within the ambit of property rights. The strongest evidence for the latter is the historical sequence of rights theory in which negative freedoms have preceded positive welfare claims and supplied the framework for their conceptualization. The logic of the transition is this: that individuals are impeded in using fully their personal property (their freedom, and their powers or capacities), owing to the unavailability of the necessary means: their property in these capacities implies their claim-right to these means. In advanced liberal democracies, these claims are regularly held against the government, which, consequently, has the duty to provide the relevant means. That this is so reflects the assumed terms of the political contract in which definite civil/social rights are universally acquired by contracting individuals in exchange for their natural rights.

In a political climate in which communal obligations are derived from contractual exchange, it is hardly surprising that political authority and action should succumb to the logic and principles of market economics. Not merely have contemporary political theorists, enamoured of neo-classical economics, conceived the state as a 'business run by entrepreneurs', political parties as 'firms trying to maximize votes', and voting preferences as 'utility functions', but politicians themselves, as Ian Shapiro observes (in *The Evolution of Rights in Liberal Theory*), 'sell a commodity as entrepreneurs, employ agencies to 'package' their products for advertising, and gear those products to what they believe the market demands'. Correspondingly, citizens, in their dealings with politicians and government, are increasingly consumer-conscious, seeking the most advantageous political exchange, the best possible protection and provision for their indefinitely expanding range of personal rights in return for their surrender of some freedom and material property. On the basis of their ever more explicit contractual relations with the state, as formalized in bills and charters of rights, citizens have growing incentives and opportunities to demand legal redress of the failures of governmental and public agencies to furnish the expected goods and services. Such political contractualism spells the reduction of public law and the common good it enforces to private law and private good.

In a wholly secularized liberal democratic polity, where the only coherent public moral language is that of subjective rights, the only universally respected right will be that of freedom, understood as the sovereignty of the subject over his/her physical and moral world, that is, the subject's emancipation from all externally imposed material and spiritual constraints on his/her freedom of choice. In such a polity, rights claims are only limited by two horizons: the expanding horizon of technological ingenuity and the shrinking horizon of the public purse. Both have already become causes of popular unease, as the gathering clouds of ecological disaster reveal the Faustian character of technological hubris to ever-more people; and ever-more taxpayers are coming to realize that their political investment is subject to the law of diminishing returns, given the inflationary logic of rights.

In addition, liberal democratic polity is inexorably blighted by the tension between the freedom and the equality of rights-bearers, particularly in the economic sphere, where the maximizing of proprietary freedom in market exchange continues to generate extreme economic inequality. But even more corrosive of political community is the denial of a *common moral universe* in which shared spiritual as well as shared material goods mediate and determine the self-transcending of individual wills in their mutual relationships.

Conclusion: The Way Forward?

Does my historical and theological perspective on rights project a way forward for secular liberal democratic- rights polity? The answer must be 'no' for this reason: that the principles peculiar to modern liberal democracy are two: the maximization of individual and collective freedom, and the equality of individuals in respect of freedom, and these principles, my analysis suggests, necessarily entail the modern liberal conceptualization of rights. There are, as I trust I have shown, other rights traditions, but neither of the early-modern traditions manifests the united aspiration to freedom and equality that marks liberal democratic rights culture.

The theological tradition of *natural rights at its liberal best* underpinned Christian constitutional government: it underpinned the rule of law – the principle that government is not its own law but governs according to laws publicly enacted by recognized authorities and consented to by the governed; it underpinned the principle of participation of the governed in legislative and judicial processes, either directly or representatively; it underpinned protection of the lives and property of the governed from unjustified governmental interference. At its worst, it underpinned political absolutism, all rights ending up on the side of government through the mechanism of the civil contract. At any rate, the understanding of the divinely revealed purpose and the requirements of government and commonwealth in this tradition precluded the idea of a self-governing, egalitarian rights polity.

The urban corporatist tradition of rights, while more egalitarian, was, if anything, *less liberal* than the theological constitutional tradition. In the first place, its egalitarianism was limited by the commercial foundations of the corporatist culture, which meant that civic rights were, for the most part, tied into economic status, citizenship being a function of guild membership. More significantly, the corporatist culture of *common property and common freedom* was a highly regulative one at the level of guild and of city council –

oppressively so, we might decide. Most significant of all, its merging of commercial, civic and ecclesial identity tended toward an immanentist, local cult-piety, insufficiently attuned to the universal church and the distance between the city of God and the city of man. In brief, urban corporatism demonstrated what astute political thinkers have from time to time observed, and what has been proved over and over in history: that radical participatory democracy requires a high degree of intellectual, spiritual, and ethical integration – inward and outward conformity, if it is not to dissolve into anarchy and license.

The secular liberal-democratic rights culture of today, in seeking to combine radical spiritual and moral individualism with political and social egalitarianism, is in danger of collapsing into legal and political incoherence. It is largely the remnants of Christian political thought and practice in advanced western polities, in their legal and public traditions, and in the social and moral sentiments of at least some of the population and politicians, that keeps collapse at bay. People vaguely sense such a collapse lurking in the tyranny of an increasingly bizarre 'political correctness'; but the very term, typical of journalistic triteness, invites disapproval without serious analysis. If liberal democratic polities are to retain any semblance of legal coherence, they will have to ensure that the concept of rights is a secondary language of justice, subordinate to and continuous with that of law, in the sense of objective right and duty, as expressing a community of political judgment. But even this achievement, I suspect, will require a more self-conscious recovery of the theological foundations of western legal and political institutions; and such a recovery is bound, sooner or later, to transform the fabric of contemporary political societies. For the theological tradition has understood that the work of civil justice, made necessary by the moral failings of a sinful human community, exists for the sake of, and in dependence on, the communion of self-giving love that is the body of Christ; and that the true relationship between Christological love and civil justice is spoken in the language of goodness, and right and law, of obligation and obedience, rather than in the language of subjective rights.

CHURCH AND POLITICS IN KENYA[1]

David M. Gitari

Rt. Rev. Dr. David M. Gitari was the third African Archbishop of Kenya and bishop of the diocese of Nairobi in the Anglican Church of Kenya

Preamble

In Kenya I am not merely an observer but an active participant in the unfolding drama of the church-state relationship. The experience of faithful Christians in Kenya in their struggle to be true witnesses of the Gospel could also be a help to Christians in other parts of Africa who are being confronted with similar challenges.

For many years Kenya had been a British Colony but we fought for and gained our independence in 1963. Ever since, Kenya has for a long time been known as one of the very few African countries which has enjoyed true freedom and democracy. Kenya has also often been quoted among the few African countries which are not under military rule. It is true that except for a short-lived air force coup d'état on 1 August 1982, Kenya has not experienced a violent military takeover. Seen from that perspective Kenya has been exemplary in terms of political and economic growth. At the same time Kenya might be one of the few countries outside Southern Africa where church leaders have boldly taken issue with those in authority and as a result Kenya may provide a very fertile ground in the study of church-state relations.

The Great Debate

Key church leaders in Kenya have been longing for an opportunity to meet the Kenyan politicians to debate on recurrent issues pertaining to the welfare of our nation. The debate mainly revolves around this question, 'Should the church be involved in politics?' Every time a church leader makes a statement that appears political, politicians rush at him warning him to stick to the pulpit and leave politics to politicians.

The Sunday sermons of some church leaders receive good coverage in the Monday newspapers. One can always be certain that the following day the daily

---

1 Gitari, 1991:7-17

papers will carry statements by politicians rebuking the church leaders for daring to comment on current political issues from the pulpit. Many times church leaders have been challenged to resign their positions and stand for political party elections if they want to involve themselves in politics instead of hiding behind the pulpit and turning it into a political platform in the guise of preaching.

These threats have made some church leaders develop a kind of fear that leads them to turn against their fellow church leaders whom they condemn and accuse of abandoning the mission of the church 'to save souls from sin'. With the same breath of condemnation, they feel duty-bound to praise the state for giving the church 'freedom of worship'. The church leaders who adopt this position are by far the majority but their impact in society is negligible. This stand is faulty and is based on a misunderstanding of the mission of the church as well as on a misunderstanding of what political involvement really means. To condemn anyone for political involvement is by its very nature political involvement; likewise to praise politicians for whatever reason is also political involvement.

To give politicians credit for giving 'freedom of worship' to the church, is to give them credit where credit is not in the least deserved. It is God our creator who has given us freedom to worship him and no one else can take that freedom from us. Politicians tried to deny Daniel freedom to worship his God by casting him in the lions' den. But in that den Daniel continued to exercise his freedom of worship, (Daniel 6). The least that those in authority can do is not to give freedom of worship but rather to guarantee the same.

Church leaders who have adopted the attitude that politics and religion cannot be mixed may have come to the conclusion that there is nothing to be debated as the line of demarcation between church and politics is very clear. It may be more correct to say that such church leaders have joined the debate on the side of politicians and have themselves taken a political stand without realising that that is the case.

On the other hand, there are a few church leaders whom the Kenyan Press prefers to call "controversial" because they have refused to be intimidated. They have consistently continued to proclaim the wholistic gospel, applying the same to the contemporary situation. I happen to be one of those few and for that reason I may be allowed to speak using the first-person plural.

We have often pleaded with the politicians including party leaders and parliamentarians etc. to agree that we hold a conference to discuss church-state relations. But our request has always been turned down. As a result the great debate continues from the pulpit or political platform but without a chance for personal encounters between the protagonists. In that case it is no wonder the press has been extravagantly used as a meeting-point between the "controversial church leaders" and politicians. Yet one might pause and ask whether this press encounter helps to heal the growing rift in any way. However, we believe that in the final analysis the truth will be triumphant.

Given the opportunity to meet the politicians whose opinions on the church-state relation verge on political fanaticism, we would present our case from our biblical and theological convictions.

The Doctrines of Creation and Humanity

The story of creation recorded in the book of Genesis chapter 1 portrays God as the one who 'lets be' And God said 'let there be light, and there was light', (Genesis 1:3). God is the one who says, 'let there be' and whatever he wishes to be comes into being. God the creator can therefore be called, He who lets be. In this 'letting be' God confers 'being' on what he creates. This 'letting be' is both his creativity and his love. God did not create the universe and then abandon it. He continues to sustain his creation by letting be. The creatures which God has made are in turn called upon to participate in God's creativity. As John Macquarrie has put it:

> Thus the fullest imitation of or participation in God comes about when the creature in turn 'lets be'... living beings which reproduce themselves participate in letting be more than do the inanimate things; but on a far higher level is man who, with his capacity - however limited – for creativity and love brings the 'imitation' of God on to an altogether new level, that of free co-operation in 'letting be'.[2]

The climax of God's creation was the creation of human beings. Then God said, 'Let us make man in our image... and let them have dominion over the birds of the sea, and over the birds of the air, and over the cattle. And over all the earth, and over ever creeping thing that creeps upon the earth' (Genesis 1:26). In this passage we have the doctrine of *imago dei* being closely connected with the doctrine of dominion. The doctrine of *imago dei* shows that humanity is created in the image of God and the doctrine of humanity is supposedly to have dominion over all creation. When the image is obscured, then the dominion is impaired, when the image, is restored, the dominion is fulfilled. Humankind was created in God's image so that they could co-operate with God not only in 'letting be' but also in caring for what God has created.

It should be noted that God did not say the dominion over all creation was reserved only to certain sections of humanity. It was not the 'male' who was told to have dominion over the earth – it was both the male and the female. It was not "politicians" alone who were given dominion over creation; this dominion belongs to all human beings. Politicians left on their own have sometimes made decisions which have devastated creation and their actions have demonstrated the reality of the doctrine of the fall.

---

[2] Macquarrie, 1967:208

Politicians and those who rule must be reminded that though humanity is the Lord's creation and the ruler of' nature, this must not be taken as a personal right. Rather he should see himself' as God's viceregent, responsible to God for his stewardship. Otherwise as Alan Richardson says, 'his science and industry will bring not a blessing but a curse, they will make the earth not a paradise but a dust-bowl or a Hiroshima.'[3] Human history is full of sad spectacles of humanity's age-long effort to subdue the earth to its own ends and not to God's glory. Indeed the *imago dei* though not completely obliterated is indeed defaced.

With this understanding church leaders have every right to remind decision-makers that the earth belongs to God (Ps. 24: 1). God has appointed human beings (not just politicians) to be the stewards of creation and to exercise proper accountability of their stewardship. After all, it is not to fallen humanity that the promise contained in Genesis 1:27-28 will be fulfilled; it will be to the redeemed humanity of the last Adam, the church of Christ: "whom he foreknew, he also foreordained to be conformed to the image of his Son". (Rom 8:29).

The creation story clearly shows that God's purpose in creating man was not to leave him as a lonely creature, but to make him a social being. Thus when God says, 'I will make him a helper fit for him' (Genesis 2: 18) it is because God himself is social and the decision to create man in Genesis 1:26 is introduced with the plural words, 'let us make man in our image, in our likeness.' As C.J.H. Wright puts it:

> The first fact about this 'image of God' is sexuality, that complementary duality in unity, from which flows the rest of man's social nature: marriage, parenthood, family, kinship, and outward in widening circles… God himself, therefore, in the mystery of Trinity, subsists in the harmonious relations of equal Persons. Each of whom possesses his proper function and authority. Man, his image, was created to live in the harmony of personal equality but with social organisation that required functional structures of authority. The ordering of social relationships and structures, locally, nationally and globally, is of direct concern to our creator God, then. But that is precisely the stuff of politics. Hence, while the Bible makes no unnatural separation between 'politics' and 'religion', it does not portray them as identical. Both are essential dimensions of what it is to be human. Man the worshipper is also man the political animal, for God made him so.[4]

To 'let be' may also be understood as 'enabling'. Human beings have a duty before God to assist each individual or a community to make full use of their potential. God did not make Eve for Adam so that Adam could exploit her and hinder her from being a fulfilled creature. She was made to be a helper with the full potential to explore and create. Cain and Abel were both born with the full

---

[3] Richardson, 1953:56

[4] Wright, 1983:104-105

potential to let be. Abel had the talents of a shepherd and Cain has talents of a farmer. As a result of jealousy, Cain, the older and stronger brother, killed Abel the younger and the weaker brother. In other words, Cain will not let his brother be. He will not permit him to continue looking after the sheep and making his economic contribution.

To this day those stronger brothers who have found their way to positions of power and authority will keep an eye on their weaker brothers and will not allow them to exercise their full potential as God's chosen stewards of creation. Cain would rather have his brother dead, than see him rising as a political leader to become the minister for livestock development.

The doctrine of creation and the doctrine of humanity convinces us that the affairs of this world cannot be left to politicians alone. The welfare of human beings is so important an issue that it cannot be left to a few politicians alone.

The Doctrine of Incarnation

Our understanding of the doctrine of incarnation gives us a further mandate to be deeply involved in the social, economic and political affairs of our country. The prologue to the gospel according to St. John declares that: '…and the Word became flesh and dwelt among us, full of grace and truth, and we beheld his glory, glory as of the only Son from the Father' (John 1: 14).

The Logos which had existed before the world was created and which participated with God the Father in the creation of all things now becomes flesh without losing the qualities of Logos in any way. The Word does not only become flesh but also dwells among human beings. The clause "and dwelt among us" emphasizes that the Logos really shared our human lot by taking residence in our midst.

As Ezekiel had prophesied to the exiles who had been deprived of the temple which symbolized God's presence among his people, 'my tabernacle shall be with them, and I will be their God and they shall be my people' (Ezekiel 37:27). John in his prologue now suggests this prophecy is fulfilled, not in a restored temple but in the incarnate logos who is the true temple. The Gospel of John presents the Word which became flesh as Jesus, a truly human being who mingled with people, and felt such human emotions as hunger, sorrow, anger, pity etc. John's prologue suggests that this incarnate Logos revealed his divinity not so much in mighty acts, though these were important, but in his revelation of divine glory through loving and humble service, 'It is moral attributes which matter, grace and faith come through Jesus Christ.'

The way the early church may have formulated its faith in the incarnate Christ is recorded by Paul in Philippians 2:5-8.

> Have this mind among yourselves, which you have in Christ Jesus, who though he was in the form of God, did not count equality with God as a thing to be grasped, but emptied himself, taking a form of a servant, being born in the likeness of man

and being formed in the human form, he humbled himself and became obedient unto death, even death on the cross…

The key phrase in this *Kenosis* passage is that (he) 'emptied *himself*.' Unlike Adam who was tempted by the devil to be like God, the second Adam did not commit this 'robbery' and, therefore, remained faithful to the divine destiny to be the image of God. Therefore, he emptied himself; i.e. he became a man in order to enter into the world of humanity which had lost the likeness of God. In order to become like a man he had to empty himself and abandon 'the glorious and Lordly prerogatives which go along with equality with God in order to take on the humble form of a servant and to die.'[5] Salvation history clearly shows that God wanted to redeem fallen humanity and to reconcile it to himself. To do this, God had to become a human being and to dwell in our midst with all the risks which this self-emptying implies - even death on the cross.

Billy Graham told a crusade rally in Nairobi that he once stepped on an ant-hill by mistake and it crumbled. Then he noticed how busy the ants were trying to rebuild their city. Being a man of God he very much wanted to assist in the rebuilding of the hill. Then he realized that to be able to assist the ants in this task he had to become an ant himself otherwise he could offer no help. Similarly, for God to be able to redeem humanity, he had to empty himself, take the form of a servant and be born in the likeness of man. The writer of Hebrews begins his letter by introducing his own form of incarnational theology:

> In many and various ways God spoke of old to our fathers by the prophets; but in these last days he has spoken to us by a son, whom he appointed the heir of all things, through whom he created the world. He reflects the glory of God and bears the very stamp of his nature, upholding the universe by his word of power (Heb. 1:l-3).

In days gone by, God spoke to people in many and various ways, through the prophets using different modes such as visions, angelic revelations, prophetic words and events. The prophets were men raised by God to challenge the injustices and other evils of their time. Their mandate to prophesy was their unshakeable conviction that they spoke from God. Their ability to say, 'God says', gave their words a unique authority. Though ill-treated they persisted with their message. As Donald Guthrie says, 'Their stories make heroic reading, but what they said was incomplete. The writer knows that it needed a better method of communication, and he recognises that this has come in Jesus Christ.' The essence of Christian revelation is that God himself has now spoken in his Son because Jesus Christ perfectly shows all that is knowable about the Father.

---

[5] Cullman, 1959:178

In days gone by God was speaking through the mouth of agents. But in these last days God has spoken in a much more superior way through his own Son. To see the Son and to hear him is to see God and to hear God: '...he who has seen me has seen the Father...' (John 14:9). By the coming of Jesus into this world, God himself has come on stage of human history not to be a spectator but to be deeply involved in the affairs of men and women. Jesus has come onto the stage of human history to confront men and women with the very message of God himself with a challenge to accept or reject it.

Involvement

When politicians call upon leaders to confine themselves to spiritual matters one cannot help feeling that they would prefer the Logos to remain where he was from the beginning; that the heavenly Christ should not empty himself; and God should not send his son to speak from the platform of human history. To tell us not to be involved in the welfare of our country is virtually to tell us not to follow the example of Jesus Christ. Jesus assumed human form and took up residence in this world prepared to take part as a perfect human being in every sphere of life with the hope of bringing salvation to the world. In his earthly life Jesus did not live in an ivory tower of meditative asceticism like the Qumran community or the early Christian monks. He went out into every city and every village as Matthew tells us: 'And Jesus went about all cities and villages, teaching in the synagogues and preaching the gospel of the Kingdom, and healing every disease and every infirmity' (Matt. 9:35).

By going where people were, he was able to see with his own eyes the plight of the people and to make statements which the politicians of the day would have considered highly political and provocative. 'When he saw the crowds, he had compassion on them, because they were harassed and helpless, like sheep without a shepherd' (Matt. 9:36). The crowds he saw were harassed politically as they were under Roman colonialists, harassed economically as the rich were making themselves richer at the expense of the poor, and harassed religiously as the Pharisees were putting unbearable burdens on the people, '...They bind heavy burdens, hard to bear, and lay them on men's shoulders, but they themselves will not move them by their finger' (Matt. 23:4).

The incarnate Lord seeing all this harassment could not help being moved by compassionate pity - the kind of pity that touches the core of one's inner being. He could not but be moved by such compassion and remain the same. He had to take the necessary action to help the helpless - to feed the hungry, heal the sick, cast out demons and challenge the status quo:

> Woe to you, Scribes and Pharisees hypocrites! for you tithe mint and dill and cummin and have neglected weightier matters of the love, justice and mercy and faith; these you ought to have done without neglecting the others, you blind guides, straining out a gnat and swallowing a camel (Matt. 23:23-24).

The Pharisees and Sadducees of the day had been so concerned 'to apply the tithing law in respect of every garden herb that justice, mercy and faith have been ignored.'[6] The doctrine of incarnation expresses the perception that Jesus 'emptied himself' and chose to 'become flesh and to live among us,' thus identifying himself with humanity. This demands our Christian presence in the world so that we may be able not only to evangelize but also to be involved in every aspect of human life. The incarnational model invites us to proclaim the Gospel not from a distance but rather by penetrating communities and cultures, cities and villages so that we can see for ourselves the harassment and helplessness of God's people and then stand in solidarity with them even if that means taking a political stand which brings hope to humanity.

The Doctrine of the Kingdom of God

The doctrine of the Kingdom of God demonstrates how the incarnate Son of God became deeply involved in the affairs of the world be they economic, political, social or spiritual. The Synoptic Gospels are all agreed that the main theme of the preaching of Jesus was the Kingdom of God. The Gospel according to St. Mark tells us that after the arrest of John the Baptist, Jesus went into Galilee preaching the Gospel of God and saying "The time is fulfilled and the Kingdom of God is at hand, repent and believe in the Gospel" (Mark 1:15).

Jesus was convinced that he had an obligation to preach the Kingdom of God because it was for that purpose that he came to this world (see Luke 4: 43). Scholars have vigorously debated on whether Jesus thought the Kingdom he was preaching about was entirely in the future or entirely in the present. As Ron Sider has put it:

> [T]here is a growing consensus that, in striking contrast to contemporary Jewish thought, Jesus viewed the Kingdom as both present and future. Jewish eschatology looked forward to a supernatural convulsion when the Messiah would come to destroy Israel's natural enemies in bloody battle and initiate a new age of Messianic peace. In Jewish expectation there was a radical, almost total break, between the old age and the new Messianic age. Jesus on the other hand, taught at the Messianic age had actually broken into the old age. Its powers were already at work in this old age in his person and work, even though the Kingdom would come in its fullness at the end of history.[7]

Rene Padilla goes further to emphasize that the central theme of the preaching of Jesus:

---

[6] France, 1985:328

[7] Sider, 1989a127-128

> [I]s not hope of the coming of the Kingdom at some predictable date in the future, but the fact that in his own person and work the Kingdom is already present among men and women in great power, ...the Kingdom of God's dynamic power made visible through concrete signs pointing to him as Messiah: 'the blind receive sight, the lame walk, those who have leprosy are cured and the good news is preached to the poor' (Luke 7:22). In other words, God in Christ is showing his passionate concern for the Door. A new eschatological reality is present in human history affecting human life not only morally and spiritually but also physically and psychologically, materially and socially.... The completion of God's purpose still lies in the future but the foretaste of the eschaton is already possible.[8]

East African Revival

Our Evangelical tradition in East Africa has put more emphasis on preaching the Second Advent of our Lord Jesus who will come to take the saved ones to heaven and punish the sinners. The East African Revival Movement which began in the early thirties in Rwanda and spread to Burundi, Uganda, Kenya and Tanzania has for six decades challenged sinners to accept Christ Jesus as their personal saviour in preparation for his coming again. A person who accepts Christ is received in the fellowship of the brethren where he or she has to walk in the "light" by confessing any sins he/she might have committed since the last meeting of the fellowship. In the fellowship meeting one will often hear, "since our last meeting, I fell into a sin of jealousy and if Jesus came, I would have been left behind. But now I have repented and am ready to go with Jesus to heaven". The repentant brother or sister is restored back to the fellowship by the whole group singing the *tukutendereza* (Glory) song.

The revival movement has had a great impact in the life of the Church in East Africa. During the time of persecution e.g. during the time of the Mau Mau rebellion in Kenya and Idi Amin's reign of terror in Uganda, it was those who belonged to the Revival Movement who were prepared to stand up and be counted as followers of Jesus Christ even if it meant death. However, the Revival Movement has been more of an inward looking spiritual movement, concerned more about the Kingdom to come rather than participating in the Kingdom which Jesus came to inaugurate here on earth. The brethren are so concerned about their own individual souls that they show little concern for the corrupt and sinful world around them except to invite sinners to come out of the "sinking ship" and join the "life boat" of the brethren. At the time of the struggle for independence, the brethren kept aloof from the politics of the day.

After independence, the brethren took little interest in joining political parties and involvement in active politics. If a 'brother in the Lord' stood for elections he was seen like a brother who had become spiritually lukewarm or who had been guilty of backsliding. The advent of Idi Amin as the ruler of

---

8 Padilla, 1989:185-186.

Uganda did not worry the brethren at first. But when he killed Archbishop Luwum, many Ugandan brethren who ran away to neighbouring countries were compelled to revise their theology of the Kingdom from a perspective of refugees and exiles. Uganda is 75% Christian. It gave a murderous Muslim dictator a chance to rule the country. The regime affected even the "brethren" in the safety of their revivalist ivory towers.

Conversion

When Kenyan politicians tell us to leave politics to politicians and to confine ourselves to the pulpit, they seem to take for granted that the purpose of religion is to prepare people for the future not the present; it is a concept of a passive religion that tells citizens to accept decisions without a question; to obey those in authority for the sake of the peace of the nation; to prepare souls for the life to come. But such a concept of religion contradicts the very teaching of Jesus Christ as far as the Kingdom of God is concerned. But it may be that politicians see what they assume is true religion in the lives of those who are "converted or born again Christians and who understand "conversion" to mean aloofness; they are not of this world. Politicians have an easy time with such religion because it poses no threat. Yet as J. Wallis puts it:

> Conversion in the Bible is always firmly grounded in history, it is always addressed to the actual situation in which people find themselves... People are never called to conversion in an historical vacuum. They turn to God in the midst of concrete historical events, dilemmas and choices. That turning is always deeply personal, but it is never private. It is never an abstract or theoretical concern; conversion is always a practical issue. Any idea of conversion that is removed from the social and political realities of the day is simply not biblical.[9]

Conversion in the New Testament makes sense only from the perspective of the Kingdom of God. To be converted to Christ means to give one's allegiance to the Kingdom, to enter into God's purpose for the world expressed in the language of the Kingdom. Thus when the disciples responded to Jesus' invitation, they joined him, followed him, transferred their allegiance to him, and as a result they became a community of the new order. Again Wallis puts it thus:

> Our conversion then cannot be an end in itself; it is the first step of entry into the Kingdom. Conversion marks the birth of the movement out of the merely private existence into a public consciousness. Conversion is the beginning of a true solidarity with the purpose of the Kingdom of God in the world. No longer preoccupied with our private lives, we are engaged in a vocation for the world.... Turning from ourselves to Jesus identifies us with him in the world. Conversion

---

[9] Wallis, 1981:5

> therefore is to public responsibility - as defined by the Kingdom of God, not by the state. Our own salvation, which began with a personal decision about Jesus Chris becomes intimately linked with the fulfilment of the Kingdom of God.[10]

Our politicians will wonder what exactly we mean by the Kingdom of God. Our Lord gave us a definition of the Kingdom when he taught disciples how to pray The Lord's Prayer includes the petition 'Your Kingdom Come, Your will be done on earth as it is in heaven' (Matt. 6:l0-11)

Let Your Kingdom Come

In other words, the Kingdom of God "is the society upon earth where God's will is as perfectly done as it is in Heaven".[11] As S. Nababan told the CWME Conference on the theme "Your Kingdom Come" held in Melbourne, Australia in May 1980:

> [t]o pray 'Your Kingdom Come', is to pray for the impossible from a human point of view, both in our personal as well as public life. In our personal sphere, to pray 'Your Kingdom Come' means to ask and therefore work out the end of the reign of one's own will, riches, power, welfare, honour.. . It is to give up inherited cultural identity for a totally new, transformed identity which is neither western nor eastern. Neither Asian nor African nor Latin American, but in fact - a Christ-like identity... In public life to pray, 'Your Kingdom Come' is to ask the full revelation of what Christ did: 'He disarmed principalities and powers and made a public example of them, triumphing over them in him' (Col. 2: 15). It is to ask therefore to work for the end of the Dowers which are the ordered structures of society and the spiritual powers which lie behind them and undergird religious structures, intellectual structures, moral structures, political structures etc.[12]

In Matthew chapter 25, Jesus said that at the end of the time those who will possess the Kingdom of God are those who on this earth feed the hungry, give a drink to the thirsty, give hospitality to strangers, clothe the naked, care for the sick and visit those in prison (Matt. 25:42f.). When God's will is done in response to the needs of the poor, then they themselves have a taste of the Kingdom and those who respond to their needs qualify to be received in the Kingdom to come. But note the cries of' the present-day poor:

> I was hungry and you appointed a commission to enquire into my hunger; I was thirsty and you made Coca Cola to exploit my thirst; I was a stranger and you put a sign 'Mbwa Kali' (Beware fierce dog) at the entrance to your home; I was naked and you smuggled second hand clothes from a neighbouring country and sold them to me at an exorbitant price; I was sick with AIDS and you said you cannot

---

[10] Wallis, 1981:9

[11] Barclay, 1975:212

[12] *Your Kingdom Come,* 1980:3

> visit a sinner; I was in detention without trial and you feared to visit me in case you lose your political position.
>
> Because of your failure to respond to the needy around you, the Lord will say to you:
>
> Away from me, you that are under God's curse! Away to the eternal fire which has been prepared for the devil and his angels! I was hungry but you would not feed me, thirsty but you would not give me a drink, I was a stranger but you would not welcome me in your home, naked but YOU would not clothe me, I was sick and in prison but you would not take care of me (Matt. 25:41-43).

Church and Political Life

The church has a vital role to play in the politics of a nation. To this end I have tried as much as possible to be actively involved in the politics of my country although I have often been warned by politicians to 'leave politics to politicians,' I have never personally called a political rally in order to give a political address. Rather, I have always confined myself to the Word of God, expounding it faithfully and systematically and applying the same to the prevailing political situation. As is commonly said, 'truth hurts' and indeed it should because the Word of God is like a double-edged sword. For this reason, in spite of the hard times I and my diocese have undergone, we have not stopped declaring God's will for our nation. The struggle to uphold and to work for justice and peace must continue. The following then is a brief summary of my experiences in the religio-political life of my country Kenya.

Personal Encounter with Authorities

Joseph Mwangi Kariuki Assassinated

On 2 March 1975 the Hon. J.M. Kariuki, a member of parliament from Nyandarua North constituency was brutally murdered in the Ngong Hills just outside the city of Nairobi. Kariuki had fallen out of favour with the government of Kenyatta. But he had become extremely popular among the masses as every time he spoke in parliament, he spoke on behalf of the poor and the exploited. During election campaigns he was often barred from addressing his constituency. But nevertheless he always won the elections. He was so famous that the news of his death stunned the county and sent university students rioting and demonstrating in the city streets.

A parliamentary commission was appointed to look into the circumstances which led to his death. After several months the report of the commission was published and implicated some key personalities in the government. The government noted the report but to this day no one has ever been arrested or prosecuted for the murder.

At this time of tension, the Christian Council of Kenya requested me to give public talks on the national radio on the sanctity of human life. I gave six five minutes' talks based on Kenya's national anthem: 'O God of all creation; bless this our land and nation; justice be our shield and defender; may we dwell in unity, peace and liberty; plenty be found within our borders.' After giving the fourth talk, I was summoned by the officials of the Ministry of Information and Broadcasting. In the room 1 found seven gloomy gentlemen. I greeted them with ''Good afternoon' and only one of them responded. The chairman told me that the ministry was concerned about my daily talks and, especially, the reference I had made to Gen. 4:10: "After Cain killed his brother Abel, then the Lord said, 'Why have you done this terrible thing? Your brother's blood is crying to me from the ground, like a voice calling for revenge'."

The chairman said this reference was very disturbing as people might think I was referring to the death of Karuiki. In response, I told the chairman if what I had said was disturbing, then the message had served its purpose because the gospel of Jesus is very disturbing, especially to sinners! Kariuki's killer should indeed be disturbed. I said all human beings are made in the image of God and, therefore, every person, regardless of' their race, religion, colour, culture, class, sex or age has an intrinsic dignity for which he should be respected and served, not exploited (or eliminated).[13] Indeed the blood of Kariuki is crying out to God from the ground like a voice calling for revenge.

I reminded each of the seven gentlemen in the panel that he was made in the image of God and no one has the right to take the life of any one of them. Then the chairman told me, 'If that is what you've been saying, then continue.' So, on an issue of life and death, I refused to be put in the dock. After some warning to tone down my talks, I was permitted to leave. On Sunday 20 April 1975, I gave a summary of the six talks I had given in a live broadcast service at Nairobi Baptist Church which was heard all over the country.

On Monday 2lst April 1975, a message came from state house, Mombasa that my manuscript was wanted by the President's aides for scrutiny. The manuscript was typed at Bible House, Nairobi where I served as the general secretary of the Bible Society of Kenya. By 8.00 p.m. that day, the typed sample was ready and was delivered to state house, Mombasa. I spent two anxious weeks to hear the reaction of state house, but nothing was forthcoming. It was during this time of waiting that I received a message from Archbishop Festo Olang', informing me that I had been elected the Bishop of the new diocese of Mt. Kenya East.

I was consecrated at Emmanuel Church Kigari on 20 July 1975 in a service that was witnessed by about 20,000 people but which received very little newspaper coverage.

---

[13] See the Lausanne Covenant, Paragraph 5

June 1987 Controversies

Twelve years later I became involved in another major controversy with the authorities. Sunday after Sunday I had been preaching my usual sermons but I had never thought of inviting the press to cover the occasions or even bothered to issue press statements like some of my other brother bishops. However, in June 1987, the press, for some reason attended and covered each of the four functions I had that month.

7 June 1987

On 7 June 1987, at Emmanuel Church, Mutira, I preached a sermon entitled 'Harassed and Helpless' from Matthew 9:35-38. The newspaper headline on the following day was: 'Bishop Under Fire' for involving himself in the affairs of coffee farmers. The following day the President himself attacked me in a public rally at Bukhungu stadium, Kakamega, alleging that I had prayed for 'oppressors' in the Kenya Planters Co-operative Union. I had not prayed for 'oppressors'. Rather I had urged the clergy of my Diocese 'to mingle with coffee farmers and listen to their uncertainties as they ponder the implication of the dissolution of KPCU and the creation of NCCU. Many may appear harassed and helpless. It is our prayer that this matter may come to a satisfactory conclusion so that there can be stability in the coffee industry.' This was one among many other points that I raised in the sermon, the full text of which was reproduced in my book, 'Let the Bishop Speak.'[14]

14 June 1987

The following Sunday 14 June 1987, I preached at Kabare on the theme "Idols of our times". A local politician had recruited about 300 Youth Wingers to come and disrupt the service if the member of parliament of the area Hon. Nahashon Njuno was allowed to greet the congregation. A lorry full of a contingent of riot police was stationed at the bottom of the hill. During the service I prayed that the 300 Youth Wingers may follow the Nyayo (footsteps) of President Moi who preaches peace, love and unity. After that prayer, the youth wingers seem to have been disarmed and the service continued without any bad incident.

21 June 1987

On Sunday 21 June 1987, I was a guest preacher at an annual civic service held at St. Peters Church, Nyeri in the neighbouring diocese of Mt. Kenya Central. The service was attended by the district commissioner, the mayor of Nyeri, the party chairman and other senior civil leaders in the district. Some of the leaders warned me not to preach about politics; little did they know that I was going to preach from Daniel 6, one of the very explicit passages on matters of religion

---

[14] Gitari, 1988

and state. In my sermon I expounded the passage verse by verse informing the audience how Daniel, a very loyal and efficient civil servant in the Persian empire, was thrown into a lions' den through the conspiracy of other civil servants who were jealous of his abilities. Daniel was, however, rescued from the den by the power of God whom he worshipped. In turn King Darius ordered that those who had falsely accused Daniel be thrown into the den. It could be said that for Daniel, the truth had prevailed. I applied this message of Daniel 6 to the Kenya of today.

At the end of the service several civil leaders shook hands with me including the district commissioner who termed the sermon as "the best I have ever listened to". The following Monday all the three daily newspapers carried the banner headlines of the sermon while the Voice of Kenya Radio gave a summary of it in their press review programme that morning. The man who prepared that press review was suspended the same day and eventually sacked. During the 1.00 p.m. news bulletin, it was announced that the Nyeri district Commissioner had disassociated himself from the bishop, charging that the bishop's sermon had 'bordered on sedition.' Debates on the sermon continued for a whole week with politicians being highly critical. Only the Nyeri Party chairman, I. Mathenge, had the courage to support me amidst the tumult - he termed the sermon as having been 'intellectually stimulating and spiritually uplifting.' The application of Daniel 6 to the affairs of the state seemed to have touched the very core of the national leadership thereby causing a tremor; the national party chairman had the guts to caution church leaders against preaching from 'irrelevant' passages such as Daniel 6, and that they should only preach when it is appropriate. I was asked to apologise to the state for the 'offence.'

28 June 1987

A few days later I had the occasion to answer my critics in a sermon I preached during the dedication of one of the churches in my diocese. '*All* scripture is inspired by God,' was the theme of the sermon which was based on 2 Timothy 3:14-4:7. We wished to remind the party secretary general that 'all scripture' including Daniel 6, is inspired by God and is profitable (to the Kenyans), for teaching the truth, for reproof, for correction and for training in righteousness, that the man of God may be complete, and equipped for every good work. The party chairman had further asserted that 'the government welcomes constructive criticisms and suggestions from any quarters including the church, provided the time is appropriate.' In the same breath he had asked me to apologise to the nation for the sermon.

We had to choose between two authorities: the party chairman who suggests that we 'preach only when it is appropriate,' and St Paul the apostle who tells us to 'preach in season and out of season.' I declared before the massive congregation of about 5000 that if I were to choose between the chairman and the apostle, I would choose the apostle, 'whatever the chairman says.' I concluded the sermon in the words of Martin Luther: 'Unless I am convicted by Scriptures and plain reason, my conscience is captive to the Word of God. I cannot and will not recant anything for to go against my conscience is neither right nor safe. Here I stand, God help me.'

The following day the newspapers carried banner headlines saying I had no apologies to make. The then minister for local government, the late M. Mudavadi came to the rescue of the party chairman, warning me to 'keep politics out of the church and instead guide church members on social-economic activities rather than cause trouble and misuse the freedom of worship.' Around the same time, the late R. Ouko, addressing a public meeting in Kisumu, reportedly told the bishop not to 'turn the church into an arena where he can freely criticise the political ideologies….' He called on the clergymen to stop interfering with the affairs of the elected leaders and instead 'make the churches 'pure' and attract more worshippers'.[15] By the 1st July the controversy over my June sermons was getting out of hand. On that day, the President told the directors and employees of the Kenya Post and Telecommunications who had visited him at Nairobi state house that Bishop Gitari should be allowed to speak his mind as Kenya was a democratic country. The President, however, said that the Bishop was wrong to criticise his motherland in the presence of visitors - among the congregation were a number of Anglican Bishops from West Africa, who had been with me during the whole month of June attending a course which I was directing. However, the President's statement, 'let Bishop Gitari speak,' brought to an end the one month controversy and gave me the title of a booklet, *Let the Bishop Speak,* which was published by Uzima Press in February 1988 just in time for the first national elections by queuing.

The *Kenya Weekly Review* of 12 June 1987 put my portrait on the front cover with a caption, 'Bishop under Fire.' In its conclusion of the story *the Review* said, 'While Gitari has led a relatively quiet life as a bishop, at least in comparison to Alexander Muge and Henry Okullu, he may now find that every word he says in public will be carefully noted.'

The Queueing and Rigging Controversy

KANU and Queueing

In June 1985 the ruling party, Kenya African National Union - KANU - held their elections from the grassroots to the national level. KANU headquarters issued guidelines concerning grassroots elections which were to be by the newly elected method of lining up behind the candidate of one's choice. In Kirinyaga district the provincial administration which supervised the elections seemed to favour some candidates. At one of the polling stations we witnessed

[15] Ouko, 1987

daylight rigging when a candidate who had only five people behind was declared the winner against his opponent who had six hundred and sixteen people behind him. Such rigging was witnessed in a number of other polling stations and was influenced by the top KANU leadership in the district. On 28 July 1985, the Diocese of Mt Kenya East held a special service of thanks giving in celebration of ten great years of the existence of the diocese, an occasion which was attended by among others, members of the Africa Theological Fraternity who were attending a conference at St Andrew's Institute. Preaching on the theme: 'Justice and Righteousness - the way of peace,' based on Phil. 4:1-9, I made the following remark:

> The KANU grassroots elections done by lining up enabled the ordinary people to see and to judge for themselves whether there was justice or no justice. By and large justice was done, but those advocates of injustice may have given some people leadership without the authority of the people. It is possible to have power but without authority. This is not justice and it is not the way of peace.

Rigging became the order of the day as several leaders were rigged in and out of parliament and the party ranks. At first the message I was trying to put across fell on deaf ears. But after the 1988 general elections during which massive rigging was witnessed the message began to ring alarm bells and my opponents accepted that I was fighting for a true principle.

Queueing in Preliminary Elections

During the 3rd week of August 1986, 1200 pastors from all over Kenya gathered in the premises of Kenyatta University for a pastors' conference of which I was privileged to be the chairman. At the same time KANU was holding the annual delegates' conference at the Kenyatta Conference Centre during which they debated and thereafter adopted the queuing method of election for all future (preliminary) parliamentary and civil elections. The queuing system, it was said, would eliminate the unpopular candidates who score less than 30% of votes. Those who scored 70% and above would automatically be declared the M.P. If no candidate scores 70% then those with 30% and more would go into secret balloting to determine the winner. On 21 August the newspapers published the KANU resolution on queuing.

The 1200 pastors suspended all other business and debated the new regulation after which they concluded that church leaders could not participate in any election where voters were to queue behind a candidate. The church leaders in a statement to the press appealed to KANU and parliament to find an alternative method in which church leaders could participate in preliminary elections so that they could exercise their democratic rights as citizens. The statement, which I personally drafted, was signed by the general secretary of the National Christian Council of Churches and given to the press. The following day the newspapers carried the story in banner headlines and it was read all over the country. Immediately after that there was a barrage of attacks from political quarters. The attacks by politicians became so severe that some NCCK member churches withdrew their membership from the council, notably the Africa Inland Church, and the Baptist Convention of Kenya. However, this did not affect the council adversely as it still had the adherence of thirty member churches. The attacks lasted for three weeks and the president closed the chapter by declaring that church leaders, the armed forces and the senior cadre of civil servants were exempted from queuing and would in future vote by proxy. Up until now we have not been told how the proxy would work. As usual the Roman Catholic bishops did not involve themselves in the debate immediately. They took time to study the situation and on 13 November 1986 they sent an open memorandum to the president signed by all the 19 bishops.

The queuing system was put into practice in the preliminary elections for the first time in February 1988. To confirm the fears expressed by church leaders, there were complaints of a massive rigging of elections in various parts of the country. In the Ndia constituency of Kirinyaga district the administration allowed only "one queue" of the allegedly government candidate. Voters determined to vote for J.M. Keriri were scared away and beaten up. It was later to be announced that J. Njiru, the unpopular candidate, had won the election by 82% of the votes. He was declared the M.P. for the area to the disappointment of many.

I wrote a letter to his Excellency informing him how unfairly the elections in the district were conducted. The staff of NCCK'S leadership magazine *Beyond* did a thorough data collection of how elections were conducted in a cross section of constituencies all over the country. The revelations were that elections were massively rigged. That particular issue of *Beyond* sold like hot cakes in Nairobi streets and all over the country. The magazine which had a regular circulation of 20,000 had to be reprinted four times. On 14 March 1988 the magazine was proscribed. Its editor, B. Mbugua, was later arrested and taken into custody to face a long trial although the government eventually withdrew the case. Owing to the massive rigging of elections, it is alleged that 75% of the present parliamentarians were not popularly elected, and as Bishop Henry Okullu put it "they are in parliament by selection not election". Throughout 1988, 1989 and 1990, church leaders have time and again criticised the queuing system. In my diocese, I regularly revisited the issue and often reminded the people that we fought for our independence so that we can choose our own leaders by 'One person one vote.' But now what we witness is the imposition of unpopular leaders upon the people. It is interesting that some of the leaders who had publicly supported the queuing system were themselves created by the same method.

Death of Queuing: Answer to prayers?

On 3 and 4 December 1990 KANU held the annual delegates conference at Kasarani sports centre in Nairobi to discuss some of the issues arising from the Saitoti report on the Kanu Review Commission which had just finished its task. It seems that the main agenda had to do with the suitability of queuing as a method of election. A majority of the speakers vigorously defended the system as they always do but at the close of the day and to their great dismay, the president advised the delegates to bring queuing to an end because it had proved divisive. The delegates reacted with mixed feelings but all the same they clapped for the president. In effect, except in party elections, future national and civil preliminary elections would be by secret ballot. It took the state three years and six months to decide against queuing while the same took the church only hours. Even now, it is our hope and prayers that even the remaining traces of queuing will be wiped out.

On 9 December 1990 we held a diocesan service of thanks giving to mark the end of queuing and I preached on the theme, 'Ask and it shall be given you, seek and you shall find, Knock and the door shall be opened for you' (Matt. 7:7). We had been persistently seeking for justice in elections for almost four years and we can now hope that with an end to queuing, rigging will be largely minimised. It may be that the end of injustices in elections is the way of peace in Kenya. Our involvement in seeking such justice is not motivated by political ambition but faithfulness to the gospel of Christ and his Kingdom. To this end our struggle has not been without serious risks.

Tribulations

9 April 1989 I was shamelessly heckled by some KANU youth wingers in the middle of a sermon I was delivering on the title, "Blessed are the peace-makers for they shall be called sons of God." Then the church stewards were quickly in action to throw the evil men out of the church and the service was restored to order. Although the matter was reported to the police, no action was taken. A few days later one of those youth-wingers accosted me in a Kerugoya street in the presence of the local administration. A week later a large gang raided my house at midnight in an effort to kill me. I sought safety on the roof of my house from where I called neighbours to come to my rescue. As this raid received wide and international publicity, the president appointed a commission of enquiry to study the circumstances surrounding the attacks on the bishop. The country was promised that the report of the commission would be made public as soon as it was ready. It is now two years since the commission was appointed, yet the results are still concealed.

Condemnation by Leaders from Central Province

'Province's leaders condemn Gitari' was the big headline on Tuesday the 9th of May 1989 following the previous day's meeting of Central Province leaders at the Kerugoya stadium to condemn me. The day of condemnation was an *id ul fitr* (Id), a day when Muslims celebrate the end of the holy month of Ramadan. The Muslims assembled in a brotherly and joyful atmosphere to offer gratitude to God for helping them fulfil their spiritual obligation prior to the Id. On that day, the Central Province elders at the invitation of the member of parliament for the area, J. Njiru, gathered to condemn me, charging me with the following:

1. Having visited Canada in October 1988 and for having allegedly had a meeting with Kenyan dissidents called 'Mwakenya' and for not having reported this encounter to the authorities back home like Bishop Muge.
2. For fighting KANU and the government.
3. For reminding people about the 1988 elections.
4. Involvement in questionable activities likely to undermine Kenya.
5. For preaching perturbing sermons.
6. For having his sole aim shedding blood in Kenya.
7. For working with dissidents outside the country etc.

Two days later the Church of the Province of Kenya clergy working in Kirinyaga district issued a statement in support of their bishop. A newspaper report of the statement recorded that five cabinet ministers had accused me in the rally of undermining the government and had asked that I be investigated. The clergy claimed that the 2000 people at the Monday rally had been persuaded by their chiefs and ferried in from other places; businessmen had also been forced to close their shops to attend the meetings. They claimed that I had fully briefed the government on my recent trip to Canada and they called for those with evidence of this subversion to report the matter to the police. They criticized the speakers at the Monday rally for pre-empting the report of the committee investigating the recent crimes against me; for acting on hearsay rather than first hand knowledge of my recent statements; for being selected by rigged elections and being without grassroots support; and for not having condemned the recent raid on my house.

More attacks came later that year when I issued a statement expressing concern that 3600 Kanu delegates had passed twelve resolutions without any debate. Hence the delegates were used as a rubber stamp. This caused a nasty stir in political circles and parliament had to suspend its business for two and a half hours in order to discuss my case. Yet instead of dwelling on the issues I had raised, one member after another threw abuse and condemnations at me. It cannot be truer, that when leaders are bankrupt of ideas they revert to threats and abuse. These tribulations have not lessened my prophetic ministry in any way. I staunchly believe that in the final analysis, truth will be triumphant. In the meantime we can only hope that the political leadership in Kenya will be willing to be challenged and moulded by this truth because no amount of falsehood can ever prevail over a grain of truth.[16]

[16] See also Gitari, 1988:12-20

EVANGELICALISM AND POLITICS: A COMPARISON BETWEEN AFRICA AND LATIN AMERICA[1]

Paul C. Freston

Dr. Paul C. Freston is Professor of Sociology at Calvin College, U.S.A.

Introduction: The importance and difficulty of the comparison

This paper is based on my own doctoral thesis and subsequent articles and books on Brazil; field research in Chile, Colombia and Peru and bibliographical research on the rest of Latin America; fairly extensive reading on Africa; and interviews with leaders of the Evangelical Fellowships of Zambia and Zimbabwe and with one of the outspoken Kenyan Anglican bishops.

Because of the size of the topic, I will speak of politics mostly at the institutional level of elections, parliaments and governments, though recognizing that that far from exhausts the possible treatments of the relationship between evangelical religion and politics in Latin America and Africa.

Evangelicalism has grown very rapidly throughout Latin America, in large parts of sub-Saharan Africa and in certain countries of East Asia and the Pacific. Evangelical presidents have been elected in Guatemala, Zambia and South Korea, and in many other countries the political importance of evangelical religion has become evident. At a moment when, at the world level, the great Christian political ideologies of the twentieth century (liberation theology and Christian democracy, Dutch neo-Calvinism and Catholic integrism) have faded, and Protestant fundamentalism, though subject to conflicting analyses of its fate in the U.S.A. is being generally shown to have less influence on Third World evangelical politics than was once thought, there is clearly great need of a debate which can incorporate the two major continents which constitute the new heartland of Protestant political militancy. This debate has scarcely begun. It is made somewhat more difficult by linguistics (a lot of the best literature on Latin America is produced in Spanish and Portuguese) and

[1] Freston, 1997:23-29. This article was originally given as a paper at the annual conference of the African Studies Association of the United Kingdom, held at the University of Bristol in September 1996. See the author's earlier article, Freston, 1992: 26-32

by geography (many scholars of Latin American evangelicalism live in Latin America and have little access to literature on Africa). Yet it is clearly of vital importance, along with the extremely difficult to study case of Korea, for an understanding of major trends in global religion and, obviously, in evangelical religion, now overwhelmingly a Third World phenomenon and less and less comprehensible in classical European and North American terms.

Latin America: Key cases of evangelical politicization

One can make a conservative estimate of about 45 to 50 million Protestants in Latin America, constituting just over 10 per cent. of the population. The number of Pentecostals is probably around 30 million, or 60 per cent. of all Protestants. The degree of the Pentecostalization of each country's Protestantism is far from uniform, varying from perhaps 30 per cent in some Andean countries to almost 80 per cent in Chile.

Brazil now has probably the second largest community of evangelicals in the world. The social characteristics are illustrated in a recent survey of Protestant institutions in Greater Rio de Janeiro (Femandes, 1992): the rapid growth (a new church per day) is largely among the poor (the needier the district, the more churches per capita) and is popular (independent of the initiative of social elites). Of the 52 largest denominations in Greater Rio, 37 are of Brazilian origin and nearly all the rest have long been autonomous. Denominational creation is definitively nationalized; no newly-arrived foreign church has established a significant presence in over forty years. The Protestant religion is a national, popular and rapidly expanding phenomenon.

Between late 1989 and early 1991, evangelicals played a significant role in electing three Latin American presidents: Collor, Fujimori and Serrano. The parallels are evident. The non-Protestants Collor and Fujimori both ignored the *evangelicos* once elected. All three carried out basically neo-liberal policies. None of them were models of democratic government: Collor was impeached for corruption, Fujimori made an 'auto-coup' and governed undemocratically and Serrano, in attempting the same, was deposed.

Peru: A united Protestant world

However there are important differences in these three key cases of Protestant politics of Latin America so far. In Peru, one notes the relative strength of adventism and holiness groups; Pentecostals are less than a third of all Protestants. In addition, elite charismatic communities are not prominent. The Protestant world is relatively united through a National Evangelical Council (CONEP). Protestantism, no more than 7 per cent. of the population, is quite strongly indigenous; the Catholic Church is largely conservative; and the social context is of guerrilla warfare and acute impoverishment.

The abrupt entry of Protestants into politics in 1990 was in response to a clear initiative from a secular political source, the Fujimori campaign. The main interest seems to have been access to the indigenous vote through the *evangelico* network. In the Andes and Central America, the extraordinary growth of indigenous Protestantism is a key factor in politics. With their presence in areas where state, parties and priests are conspicuous by their presence, Protestants offer an alternative route to mass politics. In 1990, nineteen Protestants were elected to Congress, all but one on Fujimori's Cambio 90 ticket, mostly from historical churches, especially Baptists. There were very few Pentecostals, none from the AG. The existence of CONEP was vital for a concerted Protestant action stimulated by secular politicians. Its role as an intermediary was rewarded with the second vice-presidency for CONEP's president, a Baptist pastor. The fact that a pastor without any previous political participation could become vice-president of the republic testifies to the degree of disintegration of public life in Peru. His complete marginalization by Fujimori, without any significant reaction, shows how dependent on outside forces was this precocious politicization of Peruvian Protestantism.

Guatemala: Pentecostal and charismatic influences

The Guatemalan case is also characterized by guerrilla warfare, an extremely fragile democracy and a large indigenous population. But the Protestant field is very different. Guatemala is 30 per cent. Protestant, with an estimated 80 per cent of Pentecostals/ Charismatics. Unlike Brazil, the historical churches are small, but there was a sizeable upper and upper middle class inflow after the Vatican II reforms, mostly to new charismatic churches. In addition, there is a completely different correlation of forces. The weakness of governments, the destruction of war, the proximity of the U.S.A. and the smaller absolute scale of the problems means that Protestants, mostly middle and upper class charismatics,[2] have become key figures in social work and education, areas which the state has virtually handed over to them.

Guatemala's two Protestant presidents, Rios Montt and Serrano were both politicians before conversion to charismatic churches in the 1970s. 'Born-again religion has percolated upward into social strata habitually engaged in politics'.[3] Although Protestantism is still under-represented in the elite, it is strong among 'modern' businesses using imported technology. 'What brought the evangelical movement into politics was less pastoral activism [the Brazilian case] or North American influence [or solicitation of secular politicians, as in Peru] than the movement's extension upward in the class scale', says Stoll. Serrano's election does not appear to have been due especially to the Protestant

---

[2] Known in Central America as neo-Pentecostals. In Brazil, this expression is resewed for new mass Pentecostal phenomena such as the Universal Church.

[3] D. Stoll, in an unpublished paper presented to the Fundamentalism Project, 1991.

vote; it reflects Protestant penetration of the elite and the degree of social respectability it has acquired. Serrano is a lay leader of El Shaddai, an elite charismatic church. At the time of his campaign, the church was engaged in a project of national exorcism known as 'Jesus is Lord of Guatemala'. Promoted by Serrano, the project sought to free the country from a 3,000 year old curse related to pre-Christian religion.

Brazil: New social spaces

Before looking at the third key case of Brazil, it is worth mentioning that in Colombia, a country also tom apart by the drug traffic, guerrilla warfare and an extremely high level of violence, and where the Catholic Church has always enjoyed massive institutional power, the previously small and often persecuted Protestant Church is now enjoying significant growth. The elections for a Constituent Assembly in 1990 were the catalyst for political involvement, co-ordinated by the Evangelical Confederation, for the conquest of evangelical civil rights. Since then, with the effective end of the old two-party system, the many new parties formed around special interest segments have included several evangelical ones, little more than vehicles for the political ambitions of leaders of charismatic mega-churches in Bogota.

On the other hand, in Chile, which has the largest percentage of Protestants in South America and the oldest mass Protestantism, unfavourable electoral systems, considerable institutional power of the Catholic Church and a fairly rigid society which creates a social ceiling beyond which evangelical penetration is virtually non-existent, have led to an almost total Protestant absence from electoral politics. There are currently no Protestants in the Chilean congress. There have only been about three in all of Chile's history, compared to over a hundred in our final key case, Brazil.

In Brazil the transformation of Protestant churches into a mass religion has caused an academic reinterpretation of the phenomenon, going beyond the ideologically restricted analyses of previous decades. Now, Pentecostalism's supposed social 'alienation' is seen precisely as the source of effective changes because it builds communities of discontinuity and transformation, confronts *machismo* more effectively than feminism does, represents the emergence of a new egalitarian society, signals the birth of a truly civil society (*aspasia camargo*), convincingly tackles questions of money, sickness and moral and family crisis (*femandes*) and (through giving identity and values) constitutes the main alternative to the drug culture in the shanty-towns.

However, besides numerical growth Protestantism has penetrated new social spaces, either through targeted proselytizing (to sportsmen, artists, businessmen, prisoners, etc.) or through the corporate muscle which the large popular sects have begun to wield in the media and in politics. Although historical Protestants (Lutherans, Presbyterians, Methodists and Baptists) have been elected to Congress since the 1930s:[4] their presence was always small (never more than about twelve at one time) and discreet. Some, though not all, had a basically Protestant electorate, but none of them had official endorsement from any denomination. They were dispersed among many different parties and had no strong ideological concentration, ranging from the non-Marxist left to the defence of the 1964-1985 military regime. Pentecostals were almost totally absent from Congress[5] But the 1986 election of a Constituent Assembly following the military's withdrawal from power changed the public face of Protestantism.

Pentecostals in the Political Arena

Since 1986, there has been not only a marked increase in the number of Protestant congressmen (up to as many as thirty-four at times), but also a change in the ecclesiastical and social composition of the Protestant political class and in the predominant political style. Pentecostals are now up to two-thirds of the total. The great majority of these are official candidates of their denominations, above all of the Assemblies of God, the Four-Square and Universal Church of the Kingdom of God. (It should be noted that some large Pentecostal groups, such as the Christian Congregation and God Is Love, have remained aloof from electoral politics.) The Assemblies of God have been the most important and in 1985, their General Convention decided to elect one member from each state to the Constituent Assembly. Eighteen state conventions chose official candidates (occasionally a Pentecostal from another denomination), fourteen of whom were elected.

The social origin of Pentecostal congressmen is, on the whole, lower than that of their historical counterparts; in physical type and style of discourse, they typify the clientele of their churches. But they are not average members; rather, they exemplify the desired results of conversion, either in religious leadership or financial success. The tendency of the pre-1986 period for Protestant congressmen to be, if anything, slightly to the left of the average is reversed. The new Protestant political class practices a party nomadism, many switching to smaller parties usually considered havens for time-servers and for those marginalized by the larger parties.

Official Pentecostal candidates are usually one of the following: prominent itinerant evangelists, singers or media presenters of evangelical programmes; sons and sons-in law of head pastors; and Pentecostal businessmen who make agreements with their ecclesiastical leadership.

---

[4] For a detailed history (in Portuguese) of Brazilian Protestant politics up to 1993, see Freston 1993; for a summary in English, see Freston, 1994.

[5] The only significant exception was the election of a federal deputy and a state deputy from Sao Paulo in the 1960s by the Brazil for Christ Church, an initiative which foreshadowed the corporate project of several Pentecostal denominations after 1986.

The basic causes of Pentecostal politicization have to do with the religious field itself.[6] The main beneficiaries of corporate politics have been the church leaders themselves. Unlike the historical churches, with their tradition, middle-class clientele and professional and bureaucratic standards, the Pentecostal field is comparatively young, fast growing, popular and *sectarian.* In addition, Pentecostal pastors often suffer from status contradiction: they are leaders in the church but marginalized by society. Going into politics, or sending in a relative or protégé, can reduce tensions and help professionalize the Pentecostal field. The public connection helps internal structuring, strengthening certain positions and organizations. Politics also help access to the media (half of the Protestant congressmen since 1986 have had links with the media). Politics and the media reinforce each other in structuring the Protestant world in Brazil.

In 1986, the Assemblies of God leaders explained their unprecedented political involvement by talk of a 'threat to freedom of religion' and a 'threat to the family'. 'Religious freedom' should be understood, no longer as the battle for basic Protestant civil rights (as is still the case in a few Latin American countries), but as a code-word for something broader: a statement of intent to join battle with Catholicism for space in civil religion. Having almost an equal number of practising members, Pentecostalism now demands equal status in public life. The 'threat of the family' represented, as elsewhere, an act of cultural defence (cf. Bruce, 1988:7,16), a reaction to changes in the social milieu which threatened to undermine the group's capacity to maintain its culture. In short, the dominant strain of Pentecostal politicization seeks to strengthen internal leaderships, protect the frontiers of sectarian reproduction, and tap resources for religious expansion and dispute spaces in civil religion. It is also, of course, assisted by aspects of the political system (federalist structure, relatively open mass media, weak parties and a proportional electoral system) and the economic crisis (placing strain on traditional urban political clientelism).

Corruption and Vote-selling

The Protestant caucus in the Constituent Assembly became the object of great controversy when its majority faction was denounced by the national press in 1988 for vote-selling and corruption.[7] According to the *Journal do Brasil,* 'many *evangelicos* are making a profitable trade out of preparing a new constitution, by negotiating their votes in exchange for advantages for their churches, and often for themselves. The list of rewards includes a television channel, at least half a dozen radio stations, important posts in government,

[6] For a longer discussion of the reasons why many Pentecostal leaders decided to present their own candidates, see Freston 1994:547-551.

[7] For more details on the Protestant involvement in the Constituent Assembly, see Freston 1994:551-556.

benefits of many types and, above all, a lot of money.'[8] During the corruption scandal in the Congress in 1993, evangelicals were similarly involved. Investigations disclosed a network of corruption involving evangelical congressmen, denominational leaders, evangelical social work organizations and pan-Protestant associations. The 1988 denunciation became the equivalent of the (virtually simultaneous) tele-evangelists' scandal in the U.S.A. Symptomatically, the latter occurred in the private sphere; in Brazil, with its weaker private sector, it followed the tradition of channeling public funds.

Time-serving, vote-selling, and at times, straightforward corruption have thus characterized the new phase of Protestant politics since 1986 and are closely related to the corporate Pentecostal model of official candidates. Corporate politics give access to both concrete and symbolic resources which help to structure this vast popular religious field whose rapid expansion is always producing new leaders anxious to strengthen their positions. Protestant congressional behaviour has also been characterized by an emphasis on questions related to the family (abortion, homosexuality, divorce and censorship) and the media, against democratization of the government-controlled concessionary system which has so favoured Protestant access in recent years. On other issues, Pentecostal congressmen could not initially be classified as especially right-wing. The tendency has, however, increased over time. Of the 30 Protestants elected in 1994 (19 Pentecostals and 11 historicals), 20 are in right-of-centre parties, 7 in the main centrist party and only 3 in left-of-centre parties. Electoral surveys have shown that, while the Protestant electorate is far from uniform, there is a tendency (even after taking social and demographic factors into account) to be more unfavourable to left-wing candidates than the general average. The Protestant electorate may have swung the close 1989 presidential election in favour of the right-wing populist F. Collor. In 1992, the evangelical caucus in Congress was relatively unfavourable to Collor's impeachment for corruption.

The Influence of the Left-wing and Corporatism

However, Brazil is unique in Latin America in having an active and growing evangelical left-wing, largely situated in the historical churches but also expanding among Pentecostals. Two figures exemplify this segment. Benedita da Silva, former shanty dweller, member of the Assemblies of God and of the Workers' Party, is the first ever black women senator. Around 20 per cent. of her 2 million votes in Rio de Janeiro in 1994 seem to have come from Protestants. Although she entered politics through another route, her evangelical electorate has increased at each election.

Although Benedita is at present the only representative of the evangelical left in congress, there has been an increase in the number of candidates in left-

[8] *Journal do Brasil,* 1988:84

wing parties, including the former Communist Party. In 1995, a Baptist state deputy became the Finance Secretary for the Workers' Party administration in the Federal District. He is typical of the new evangelical left which has founded the Evangelical Progressive Movement, distinct from the old Protestant left of the 1960s and 1970s which was linked to ecumenical organizations and non-conservative theologies.

In 1994, an evangelical candidate almost became a governor of Sao Paulo. Francisco Rossi represents a new phenomenon in Brazil: a career politician who converts to Protestantism and continues his career in a new evangelical style. A leading politician since the early 1970s Rossi only joined a Protestant church (an independent charismatic community) in 1993, getting baptized at the beginning of the election campaign. As a politician who has become a Protestant, Rossi is closer to the Guatemalan tradition referred to earlier.

The case appealed greatly to Protestant triumphalism, the much loved idea that they have a manifest destiny and divine right to govern Brazil. The president of the CNPB called on all Protestants to campaign for Rossi.[9] 'As spiritual beings, born again, we are the "cream of society". The church is on a higher level to normal people ... because the church has the answers which the politicians are looking for ... the answer to all the problems which trouble our government ... With the firm and effective action of the church in politics, there will be a glorious future.' [10]

In the legislative elections in Sao Paulo, this triumphalism was expressed by the charismatic Baptist Lamartine Posella. A young tele-evangelist from a business family, he had the support of a prophecy given by perhaps the leading Brazilian tele-evangelist, Valnice Milhomens. As Lamartine said: 'if we evangelicals are one day going to literally dominate on earth, why can't we start taking power now, as a foretaste?' Lamartine got 55,000 votes and only failed to get elected because of the party he was in.

Although triumphalism and corporatism are sometimes mixed, the latter is still the stronger, above all due to the Universal Church of the Kingdom of God. The latter church (founded in 1977 in a poor suburb of Rio, and today present in forty countries, besides owning one of the largest TV networks in Brazil) has been a key factor (as protagonist or antagonist) in recent attempts to unify the Protestant community behind a representative organization. Attempts to create such organizations in Brazil have always been linked to politics, and never more so than now, when the right to speak to government and society in the name of an enormous and expanding community would give immense political clout. The current intense struggle for hegemony in the evangelical world is eloquent of the power of national politics to structure this rapidly expanding and largely lower-class social movement.

---

[9] *Journal do Brasil,* 1994:1-5

[10] *Semeador,* 1994:3

We should not be deceived by the noise made by some evangelical groups in Brazilian politics. Noisiness is a sign that they are still relative outsiders. But their firepower is on the increase. One proof of this is the capacity to influence what other political actors do. Afro-Brazilian religions talk of electing corporate candidates, just like the Pentecostals. The left now starts to search for evangelical candidates who can add votes to their party list, and there are also cases of what look like self-interested conversions at election time by left-wing politicians, a custom previously restricted to other points of the ideological spectrum. Pentecostal practices start to influence the historical churches, some of which become (albeit slightly) politically 'Pentecostalized'. At the same time, to compete with historical Protestants in having an attractive public role, Pentecostals are investing more in the sort of social action which their theology has usually portrayed as irrelevant..

The Sociological Literature: Some caveats and comments

The existing sociological literature offers few clues for interpreting Brazilian evangelical politics. The American religious right, although it may have a certain demonstration effect, functions in a religious and political context which is totally different from Latin America. Despite similarities such as the concern with questions of sexuality and the family and the link with the mass media, the differences (of methods and demands, of background and of prospects) are far more decisive. In Brazil, the key figures are denominational heads and not leaders of agencies like the Christian Coalition which mobilize Protestant opinion, elaborate agendas and monitor the activity even of non-Protestant congressmen. Nor is there in Brazil the nostalgia for a lost past. Brazilian leaders are in a different position in the Protestant field; Protestantism has a different position in the religious world and a different relationship to civil religion and national identity.

The literature on fundamentalism worldwide, although useful, must be deployed with caution, since the political and religious situations treated under this label are very diverse. Nor does the literature on Christian sectarianism give us many parameters. In Catholic Europe, all Protestant groups remain small. In Protestant Europe, the established churches inhibited the growth of sects, or else secularization and unfavourable electoral systems politically marginalized all religions. In the United States, Protestant sects became denominations (and were sociologically transformed) within a generation or two (Niebuhr, 1929); a process helped by the lack of an official church, by rapid economic expansion, by an egalitarian ideology in which sects could grow quickly in size and respectability, and by the constant arrival of new immigrants who pushed the older ones up the social scale (Wilson, 1970, 234). Brazilian sects, however, grow rapidly but do not win social and cultural respectability; there is still a semi-official church; and there is no immigration or economic expansion. It is in this context that the sects have launched themselves into politics.

Even in Latin America the Brazilian case is so far unique. In Peru, where the Protestant field is smaller and less Pentecostal, the sudden entry into politics in 1990 owed a lot to a secular initiative (the Fujimori campaign) and affected above all the historical churches. In Guatemala, the most Protestant country in Latin America, both Protestant presidents (Rios Montt and Serrano) were already politicians before their conversion to high-class charismatic churches. Protestantism entered politics through its penetration of the ruling class. In Brazil, on the other hand, the political vanguard are leaders of popular sects which have grown so much and so fast that they can begin to use the state for their own ends. The Pentecostal eruption into politics from 1986 onwards followed a corporate model: the great majority of Pentecostal parliamentarians are official candidates of their churches, above all the Assemblies of God, the Four-Square Church and the Universal Church of the Kingdom of God. This may be the first case in history in which Christian conversionist sects have achieved such a relationship with the state.

In view of Brazil's historically unique case of relationship between national politics and conversionist Christian sects, is Pentecostal corporatist politics a danger for democracy? There is no simple answer.

There are several factors which suggest that Protestant, and especially Pentecostal, religion may be helpful for democracy, or at least neutral in its effects. Unlike Islamic fundamentalism, it is a product of the voluntarist tradition and thus essentially divided. However much it grows, it cannot form a Protestant neo-Christendom. It is good for democracy that the religion that grows fastest in Brazil and has shown the most political ambition is institutionally divided and functions in a pluralist format.

For some authors, the internal practices of Pentecostalism have an intrinsic democratic worth, since they value individual dignity and train people in leadership skills. Although their leaders are often authoritarian, sects can become bulwarks against the massification produced by the culture industry (as in the opposition in the members of the Universal Church to the most powerful mass medium in Brazil, TV Globo). And Latin American sectarianism may follow the precedent described by Weber,[11] who pointed out that American democracy was precisely not a shapeless heap of individuals but a hive of strictly exclusive but voluntary associations, the result of a process of secularization from the prototype of the sect.

Besides, corporatist politics tends to incite internal ideological competition. Even in the official journal of the Assemblies of God there are signs of the growth of another concept of politics: that of the free citizen who, seeing himself an instrument of the Kingdom of God, joins a party without involving his church. Many Pentecostals do not obey the electoral injunctions of their

[11] See Gorski, 2003:833-839

pastors and do not feel guilty about it. Pentecostalism after all, is a branch of Christianity and subject to its universalist ethical impulse. In the broader Protestant field, initiatives such as the founding of the Brazilian Evangelical Association and the Evangelical Progressive Movement point in the same direction. There is no reason to believe, as some laicist newspapers in Brazil appear to, that any religious presence in politics is *per se* a threat to democracy. The aforementioned survey on religions and electoral behaviour (Prandi and Pierucci, 1994) did not find significant differences between Pentecostal opinions and those of the general population on the democratic regime and its institutions.

There is also no evidence for the claim that Protestant growth in Latin America is necessarily linked to times of political repression. In Brazil, growth has been as strong or stronger in democratic periods (1945- 1964; 1985 to date); in Argentina, Protestant growth took off with re-democratization in 1983. Nor is there evidence that relatively open left-wing governments harm growth: Chilean Pentecostalism continued to grow quickly during the Allende years, and *evangelicos* went from 5 per cent. to 15 per cent. during the Sandinista period in Nicaragua.

Nevertheless, the relationship of Pentecostalism to democracy has another side to it. The same Brazilian survey of 1994 discovered that Pentecostals are much less concerned than the general population about freedom of organization and expression (except of course about religious freedom, which is its corporatist reduction). And although Pentecostal politicians are divided among various parties, their actions and opinions do not generally strengthen the party political system as much. So far, Pentecostal politics has not given support to the idea of a correspondence between doctrine and politics, according to which Protestantism would be necessarily favourable to a universalist and ethical politics, unlike Umbanda with its celestial patronage network. In fact, we cannot just 'read out' the implication for democracy from a religious doctrine.

The Brazilian context is one of sectarian growth in a democratic regime. Triumphalist and corporatist tendencies do carry dangers for democracy. Sectarianism has difficulty elaborating a universalist perspective on politics because it has always been excluded or self-excluded from such concerns. There is no project for society in Brazilian Pentecostalism. Corporatism emphasizes winning a place in civil religion, moral questions, anti-communism and a pragmatic support of the existing government with a view to maximizing returns. The time-serving and vote selling reflect the sectarian concept of mission. To guarantee the best operating conditions for the church, agreements are acceptable. This is not naïveté in the face of temporal power, but a pragmatism authorized by the sectarian view of the world. The benefits received (whether a new roof for the local church in exchange for the congregation's votes for a certain candidate, or a radio station in exchange for a parliamentarian's crucial vote in congress) are not seen as treason to the gospel message, but as a sort of tax which 'worldly' power pays to the truth. This is not constantinianism (the officialization of the church by the temporal power); it is the appropriation of the state by the sect.

'Only the elect of God should occupy the key posts in the nation', says a leader of the Assemblies of God.[12] It is hard for the sect to imagine any other political role for itself. It has always seen itself as morally superior; so, in relation to temporal power, it cannot really accept that it is one player among many others. It must either be indifferent or be in charge.

In the specific context of Brazil, so different from the established denominationalism of the United States in which church-state separation is part of the founding myth and puts constraints on all political actors, it is hard to be as optimistic as Martin (1990). In Brazil, the 'logic' of voluntarist religion may lose its force in the new hybrid pattern which is developing, in which the monolithic church has not completely disappeared. The already destabilizing strength of the Universal Church of the Kingdom of God may be a foretaste of what could happen in the uncharted waters that Brazilian Protestant politics are now entering.

African Evangelical Politics: First impressions of the literature

Obvious religious and political differences between the two continents must be borne in mind. In Latin America Pentecostalism is now much more important than historical Protestantism. Evangelicalism is virtually synonymous with Protestantism in Latin America, something which does not happen to the same extent in Africa. The background of the whole religious field is, of course, very different. In Latin America the economic crisis is not quite so severe, civil society is not quite so weak, and some countries have had a far greater historical experience of multi-party democracy.

I am not sufficiently familiar with the authors to do a sociology of the sociology of African evangelicalism. In Brazil, a phase in which ecumenical Protestant scholars predominated has been replaced by non-religiously committed scholars and (lately) by scholars linked to evangelical churches themselves. The resultant multiplicity of perspectives has enriched the debate, as has the recognition of the need to diversify sources beyond those more easily supplied by the mainline churches. The head of the Evangelical Fellowship of Zambia told me he considered some interpretations offered to have been ways for the National Christian Councils and the AACC to 'get the evangelicals out of their hair' and stop the mainline churches losing their privileged access to governments.

Broadly, of course, one can discern a range of positions from what we call in Latin America 'invasion of the sects' or conspiracy theory, to a position which maintains the dichotomies of that theory while rejecting the invasion as an explanation, to positions in which one or both sides of the dichotomy are

---

12 *Mensageiro da Paz,* 1986:5

nuanced in greater or lesser degree-the mainline churches are not so different, and maybe the evangelicals are not so conservative.

Africa and Latin America: Mainline v. evangelical churches in democracy

In Brazil, the principal mainline church, the Catholic, enjoyed crucial sociological advantages which made it more viable to take a strong line in opposition to the military regime. It is significant that the only Protestant church to condemn the regime was the Lutheran: being the church of the German immigrants, its multi-class nature (and international connections) gave it both the ability to perceive the social situation and the possibility of protest – a combination unique in Brazilian Protestantism and which approximates it sociologically to the Catholic Church. A church (in the sociology of religion sense) is more protected in the adoption of politically risky postures. In addition, it will be more protected from the 'local subversion' factor. These advantages of the mainline over other churches, stemming from social position and sociological type rather than theological factors, are recognized in some of the literature on Africa.

At the same time, it is clear that the actual performance of the mainline churches does not always reflect these advantages, though the implications of this are not always drawn out by the authors. The Catholic Church is more heavily missionary – and foreign-funded, and this is crucial for its socio-political influence (Gifford, 1994). Yet it and other mainline denominations have usually needed a hefty prod in the form of a threat to their institutional interests before opposing regimes. It is not, therefore, only fundamentalists who seem to need a 'trigger issue' (Haynes, 1996). And the mainline churches have clearly supported far more years of authoritarian rule in independent Africa than the evangelical ones. It was the mainline churches of Liberia which supported a century of True Whig rule, which asked the United States to intervene militarily in 1990, which could not speak out against the regime in Monrovia because many members lived at the mercy of Charles Taylor, and whose generally fatalistic approach paved the way for catastrophe. Once the evangelical churches have been appropriately nuanced, as in some of the more recent accounts, one wonders whether, when all other things are equal, there is much to choose at the institutional level between them and their mainline brethren. And they may be, as some in Africa and Latin America have pointed out, better in their overall effect on democratic consolidation, even if the mainliners in both continents have been far more important for democratic inauguration.

But at this level one enters the realm of speculating about potentialities, a favourite pastime of authors on both continents: new political language, new public space, the demystification of power, new values and abilities which can be brought to bear on public life. African and Latin American churches could, in Tocquevillian and Weberian fashion, become the sectarian prototypes of a democracy based on a hive of voluntary associations. The argument is logical – unlike so much that actually happens in the sociology of religion! The value of such arguments is limited when divorced from empirical demonstration of actual trends, but they have the salutary effect of making us wary of equally non-empirical projections to the contrary.

Africa and Latin America: Some correspondences

Amongst the many comparisons and contrasts which a Latin American notes in the African literature are, firstly, the similar growing strength of prosperity doctrine in the two continents' evangelicalism, but which assuredly has a more solid cultural base in Africa. Traditional religion and post-independence political culture would seem to be an ample explanation for its spread in Africa, even if American books and preachers have helped to systematize it and give it a more Christian and universalistic colouring. The actual ideological implications of prosperity doctrine remain, in my opinion, enigmatic in both continents after all, the Brazilian left's proposals of strengthening the domestic market and encouraging small-scale enterprise could be at least as pleasing as neo-liberalism to churches like the Universal Church of the Kingdom of God which encourage members to become self-employed as a necessary complement to giving sacrificially to the church in order to receive many times over from God.

The evangelical left in Brazil would seem to be somewhat paralleled in cases such as the Concerned Evangelicals in South Africa and the outspoken evangelical Anglican bishops of Kenya. Not surprisingly, there are in fact Third World networks linking them, usually overlooked in analyses of evangelical politics. The case of the CPK evangelicals queries the pitch for some generalizations, and throws us back onto non-theological factors such as ecclesiastical insertion and social position.

In a different vein, the Latin American material throws doubt on the idea that a trigger issue is needed for political activism. When conditions are favourable, issues, it would seem, can be found in abundance by mass Pentecostal churches. As to some of the newer, more middle class charismatic communities, their theology of spiritual warfare takes political activism in its stride.

This brings us to the case of Nigeria. Anyone familiar with Latin America can hardly wait for re-democratization to come and the Pentecostal political ebullience to flower in all its ambiguity. Resembling Guatemala in its high-profile politicized middle class charismatic churches, and yet reminiscent of Brazil in its conscious corporatist planning for action in the aborted return to democracy, its use of the language of religious conflict (with Islam taking the place of Catholicism) and its plethora of candidates. Yet clearly (and undoubtedly for many reasons), there has yet been no real corporatist electoral politics *à la brazil* by mass evangelical churches in Africa. Whether there will be is a topic for further research.

Suggestions for further Research into African Evangelical Politics

Some suggestions come directly out of the literature. That one must distinguish between the actions and pronouncements of church leaders and the actual political behaviour of ordinary members, and that more needs to be known about the latter. That we must look beyond the formal declarations to the other contributions to democratic development that evangelicals might be making. That Pentecostalism and fundamentalism must be clearly distinguished conceptually. That the autonomy of Third World evangelicalism, or at least the autonomous appropriation of its messages, must be assumed unless proven otherwise, and not vice versa. That differences between Pentecostal churches (theological, class, organizational) should be studied more carefully. It is only by taking the churches seriously as dynamically evolving institutions that we shall be able to throw light on some aspects of their political behaviour.

Other proposals stem from the comparison with Latin America. Some fascinating comparative studies suggest themselves: the relationship to society of the Assembly of God in Brazil and Zimbabwe (where they make up similar proportions of the population and dominate the Protestant field); a comparison of the Brazilian Universal Church of the Kingdom or God with a new independent church in Nigeria. More generally, the Latin American cases highlight the question of why evangelicals enter politics in certain ways under certain circumstances, the dynamic involving factors internal and external to the religious field, and the probable importance of internal ecclesiastical organizations as well as the role of politics and the media in structuring the evangelical field.

The Brazilian case illustrates vividly a tendency discernible in the evolution of Ruth Marshall's writings on Nigeria. Lately, she seems less sanguine about Pentecostal political potential, as the reality of political action by the leaders makes her more conscious of the ambiguous way in which different levels interact. It may not be too bold to suggest that the Brazilian case could be a useful guide to what may happen in some African states if other non-religious conditions are favourable. As she says, 'growth beyond the local into the politics of influence means entering a civil society moulded by the high politics of patronage. To have representation as a group within the 'political nation' means to enter the high politics of the state. Prebendalism is the form of this engagement in a civilian regime. Whatever the power of the moral vision of civic virtue, the uses to which it is put in the high politics of the state rob it of its radical potential, a process of narrowing and flattening: of identity', what I have called corporatism. She speaks of a totalitarian potential behind a politicization which permits the identity of the 'saved' to become the basis of political power. At the same time, the inner logic of Pentecostalism is radical enough to outlive this short-circuiting and the new political language can be turned back by the discontented within the community into a critique of their churches' own politics, something discernible in sectors of the AG in Brazil.

More generally, there would seem to be a need, in both continents, for more detailed country-level studies. The virtually simultaneous growth of evangelical religion straddles the two continents, but political involvement has been far from uniform in either. We need now not to remain at very general abstract levels of explanation, but to undertake studies which delve into national political fields, the structure of national media and of national religious fields, giving body to, and showing the limits of, global explanations. Evangelical religion means different things to different people at different times, and holds different positions in society and in the religious field of each country. If, for example, the withdrawal of the state is crucial in Africa, leaving institutional churches almost as the effective government in some areas, with Pentecostalism as the unofficial opposition (Ranger, 1994), then we need to look carefully at the dynamics of the religious field in mediating political positions. And if Gifford's study of Liberia, one of the few in-depth country studies available, is critiqued by Haynes precisely in terms of the uniqueness of the Liberian case, this points once more to the need to multiply such studies. If the 'long run' argument adduced by some authors on Latin America is perhaps the key debate today on Third World evangelical politics, it assuredly cannot be answered in the abstract, but only by national studies which cut close to the bone. Between anthropological micro-studies, and continent-wide generalizations, we need country-level macro-institutional studies to understand how evangelical politics are actually developing, enabling us to move beyond conspiracy theories on the one hand, and on the other general theories about the potential of evangelical religion based on historical analogy or on supposed essential characteristics of charismatic Christianity. Nigeria is clearly a prime case for such a study, but perhaps too much coloured by its peculiar religious configuration. Zimbabwe and Zambia might be more typical cases for the contexts in which evangelicalism is flourishing.

There would still not seem to be a really satisfying account of the obviously crucial Zambian case. How exactly did mainline churches, evangelical churches and trade unionism interact? It is affirmed that Chiluba's pre-election declaration that he was born again won him votes, but is there any actual evidence for that? In Latin America, when running for a majority office (rather than a proportional congressional seat), it is not usually considered advantageous to align oneself too closely with a minority religious identity. In addition, since Chiluba is originally from a mainline denomination, one must ask (as in the case of Guatemala's two charismatic presidents) how much charismatic socialization he has really had and what his politics actually mean in relation to the political rise of the born-again community. It is affirmed that fundamentalist leaders got involved because they considered that IMF resources should be disproportionately weighted towards those who would make best use of them, i.e. themselves. But have they in fact benefited? Has there been an effective strategy to obtain these resources? And how did they 'sell' the need to vote for Chiluba to their members? What exactly is the relationship between Chiluba and the church leaders (who regard themselves as having taken up distance from the government), and how do ordinary evangelicals see him? The case of President Serrano in Guatemala counsels caution in jumping to hasty conclusions.

Towards an Evangelical Political Philosophy and Agenda for Christians in the United States[1]

Ronald J. Sider

Ronald J. Sider is Professor of Theology, Holistic Ministry and Public Policy at Palmer Theological Seminary in Wynnewood, Pennsylvania

Evangelicals today probably have more political influence in the U.S than at any time in this century. But we are not certain what to do with it. Unless we find out, we will squander an historic opportunity to nudge this society towards moral renewal and justice for all. To be sure, there are many evangelical voices loudly promoting political agendas But the voices are often confused, contradictory and superficial. Evangelicals lack anything remotely similar to Catholicism's papal encyclicals and Episcopal pronouncements on social and political issues that have provided Roman Catholics with a careful, integrated foundational framework for approaching each concrete political decision. (This deficiency, as Mark Noll points out, is one important aspect of the 'scandal of the evangelical mind.') On the other hand, when evangelicals have acted politically, we have usually jumped into the political fray without doing our theoretical, theological homework. That our confused, superficial activity has had little lasting impact should not surprise us. If that is to change, we urgently need to develop a careful systematic political philosophy to guide and sustain our activism. That, of course, is a task requiring years, indeed decades, of communal work. Here, I want briefly to illustrate some problems that arise because we lack an evangelical political philosophy and outline how I try to move from a biblical normative framework and careful societal analysis to a political philosophy and its concrete application in forming a current agenda.

Present Confusion

It is not hard to illustrate the way the absence of a foundational political philosophy leads evangelical political activists to rush off madly in all directions. Take the area of moral decay. Virtually all Christians, and certainly all evangelicals, agree both that serious moral decay threatens this society and also that religious communities are the only place to look for that radical

[1] Sider, 1997:1-10

spiritual conversion that transforms persons and are the primary moral teachers of the virtues that decent societies require. Some evangelicals think the solution is a constitutional amendment to restore prayer in the schools. Others want constitutional, or at least legislative, action to guarantee equal benefits to adherents of all religious views. And other evangelicals think both of the previous proposals would violate the First Amendment and destroy both church and state. Or consider evangelical pronouncements on the role of government. Sometimes, when attacking government programmes they dislike, evangelical voices adopt libertarian arguments that would preclude almost all government activity to promote economic justice ('Helping the poor is a task for individuals and churches, not the government'). Then when the issues change to abortion, family, euthanasia, and pornography, the same people loudly demand vigorous government action. There might be a good case to be made for private programmes in the first case and legislation in the second. But if one uses arguments in one area that run counter to one's agenda in another, one appears confused and superficial. The absence of a consistent ethic of life leads to absurd inconsistency. Some evangelical political voices make the sanctity of human life (up to birth and just before death) the overriding issue and neglect the way poverty and smoking destroy millions. Other evangelicals point out that racism, poverty and environmental decay all kill and yet seem little concerned with millions of abortions each year. Some of our superficiality and confusion result from the fact that we have seldom taken the time to work out carefully the specific policy implications of biblical faith. Too often we just assume that traditional American values or the Republican (or, less often, the Democratic) Party's platform are right. Christian Coalition director Ralph Reed, for example, says that when he became a committed Christian and started attending an evangelical church, 'my religious beliefs never changed my views on the [political] issues to any great degree because my political philosophy was already well developed.[2] Without testing political agendas on the basis of biblical norms, Christians often uncritically endorse left-wing or (more often) right-wing ideological agendas. I need not go on illustrating this basic point. An evangelical political impact today is weakened because our voices are confused, contradictory, and superficial. We contradict each other. Our agendas are shaped more by secular ideologies than divine revelation. We have no systematic foundational framework for careful dialogue about our specific policy differences or even for successful repudiation of extremists. And, oh, how the secular media love to publicize the worst examples, such as intolerant attacks on the civil rights of gay Americans or the murder of doctors who perform abortions. Evangelicals urgently need a political philosophy. It would not solve all our political problems. But it would help.

---

[2] Reed, 1996:23

Methodology

Jesus is Lord

The centre-piece of all genuinely Christian politics is the Lordship of Jesus Christ. Christians believe that the Galilean champion of the poor and marginalized is the creator of the galaxies, the sovereign of the universe. Therefore, all who believe in him seek to submit every realm of life – whether family, economics or politics - unconditionally to Christ the Lord. Christians, therefore, reject the uncritical embrace of any and every secular ideology – whether right, left, 'green,' libertarian, or communitarian. The Christian's starting point must be the Word of God which is revealed partially in creation, more fully in the Bible, and most completely in Jesus Christ, the eternal Word become flesh. Founding political engagement on ideologies of the left or the right rather than Christ is fundamentally un-Christian.

Four Components

Starting with the Lordship of Christ, however, does not instantly provide detailed political guidance on specific policy issues. Citing specific biblical texts does not instantly solve complex political questions. Serious Christian political engagement must recognize the complexity and ambiguity of political decisions. Every political judgment rests finally on a normative framework on the one hand and careful study of society and the world on the other. It is helpful to distinguish four different, interrelated components of – every political decision: 1) a normative framework; 2) a broad study of society and the world; 3) a political philosophy; and 4) detailed social analysis on specific issues.

Normative framework: If one's political activity is to be genuinely Christian, then the guiding norms for one's politics must come from the core of one's faith. Since biblical faith teaches that some sense of the true and good is embedded in the human conscience, common wisdom (call it natural law if you like) can offer some guidance. Some Christians, especially Roman Catholics, believe that it is still possible to derive major input for one's normative framework from general revelation. My own inclination is to think that since the Fall has deeply clouded the understanding of God's law written on all hearts, general revelation by itself cannot be the primary source of the Christian's normative framework for political engagement. For clarity, therefore, I turn to the revealed truth of the Scriptures. Discovering relevant biblical norms for specific political issues is not, however, a matter of simple proof-texting. The Bible is full of commands, stories, and proverbs - in short, a wide variety of materials written over many centuries. To develop a fully biblical perspective on political issues, we need a biblical view of the world and persons. We also must understand biblical teaching related to many concrete issues (for example, the family or the poor). To develop a biblical framework, we must in principle examine all relevant biblical passages, understand each text according to proper principles of exegesis, and then formulate a comprehensive summary of all relevant canonical material. That requires an understanding both of the basic biblical story and comprehensive summaries (one might call these biblical paradigms or a comprehensive summary) on things such as the poor, the family, work, justice, the dignity of persons, etc.[3]

Broad study of society and the world: By itself, however, the biblical framework is insufficient. Nothing in the Bible talks explicitly about the pros and cons of a market economy or multi-national corporations or the impact of five billion people on the natural environment around them. In addition to a normative framework, we need a broad, comprehensive study of 'our world. That study takes many forms. It includes reflection on the historical development of society, the economy, political systems, etc. (As finite, historical beings, we come to see some things more clearly as history unfolds.) It also includes, in principle, detailed, comprehensive socio-economic, political analysis of everything relevant to any particular political question. This careful study becomes central at two stages of analysis. One's analysis of the history of economics, politics, etc. helps to shape one's political philosophy (see B.3.). For example, as the Marxist experiment worked itself out in the course of the twentieth century, it became more and more clear not only that Marxist philosophy contradicted the biblical view of persons but also that in practice Marxism led to economic inefficiency and political totalitarianism. Similarly, it is becoming increasingly clear that substantial injustice accompanies the functioning of today's market economy. Detailed social analysis of everything relevant to a particular politician or piece of legislation is also crucial (see B.4.).

Political philosophy: In addition to a biblical framework and a broad study of society and the world, Christians engaged in politics also need a political philosophy. It is simply impossible, every time one wants to make a political decision, to spend days (actually years) reviewing the mountains of relevant biblical material and complex studies of society. We need a framework, a road map, a handy guide - in short, a political philosophy. But we dare not adopt our political philosophy uncritically from some non-Christian source. It must emerge from our normative biblical framework and painstaking, extensive socio-economic, political analysis.

Detailed social analysis on specific issues: Even after a Christian has a political philosophy shaped by both a normative biblical framework and a careful study of society and the world, one still needs to do painstaking, detailed social analysis on everything relevant to a particular legislative proposal or a specific election. Two people could, in principle, have identical normative frameworks, identical historical analyses of modem society and identical political philosophies and still disagree on whether or not, for example, to raise the minimum wage. Why? Because they rely on different

---

[3] See e.g. Sider, 1989b:156ff.

economic analyses of the actual effect of raising the minimum wage. The only way to make progress on settling such a disagreement is to go back together and do further detailed economic analysis. Careful detailed social analysis of all the available information relevant to any specific political judgment is the fourth essential ingredient of any responsible Christian political engagement.

Other Introductory Points

Complexity and political necessity: The method just described is complex – in fact, far more complex than I have been able to suggest here. Every one of the four steps intersects with all the others. Our reading of history shapes the questions we put to the Bible as we seek to develop a normative framework. That framework in turn shapes everything else. In real life, we cannot wait to make political decisions until we have completed all the study that is desirable. We must make decisions based on our best current understanding and then remain open to further insight and information.

Co-operation and humility: The kind of study required for faithful Christian political engagement is far too complex for any one individual. We need communal activity, teams of scholars and activists, and organizations and networks working together to develop a common vision and agenda. For successful Christian political engagement, then, we need groups of Christians who can integrate a normative biblical framework, a study of society and the world, a political philosophy (derived from the former two ingredients) and a detailed social analysis as they all approach every major issue of contemporary political life. That means working out concrete public policy proposals on everything from welfare reform to family policy to peacemaking in Bosnia. Knowing the complexity of such political judgments and the possibility of mistakes at every step, we must always hold our specific political conclusions with great humility and tentativeness. But we should dare to advocate boldly for specific policies because we have sought to ground our specific conclusions in a biblical framework and responsible social analysis even as we invite friend and foe alike to help us improve our analysis of both the Scriptures and society at every point.

Resolving disagreements: It would help immensely to reduce political disagreements among Christians if we would be more precise about where we disagree. It is unhelpful to confuse a disagreement over the proper interpretation of Matthew 25 with lack of compassion for the poor or disagreement over the relative merits of capitalism and socialism. To the extent that we can be precise about exactly where we disagree, we can make more progress in overcoming our differences.[4]

Common language: In a pluralistic society one additional crucial step is essential. Many citizens have no interest at all in political proposals advocated on the basis of a biblical framework. Therefore, we must develop a common

[4] See Sider, 1987:11-16

language grounded in the common good of all citizens when we take our specific proposals into the public realm. We must try to develop reasons for our policies that are intelligible and convincing to all people, not just Christians.

The starting point: the Christian community: It is absolutely crucial, however, that Christians first articulate and develop their political agenda and concrete proposals within the Christian community on the basis of biblical norms. If we do not, we will end up adopting secular norms and values and their corresponding political ideologies. The result will be a compromised, often fundamentally un-Christian, political engagement. That is exactly what has happened to many Christians in politics. Too many Christians have uncritically adopted left-wing or right-wing politics. The result has been a sub-Christian religious right that correctly championed the family and the sanctity of human life, but neglected economic justice for the poor, uncritically endorsed American nationalism, ignored environmental concern for God's creation, and neglected to struggle against racism. Equally sub-Christian has been a religious left that rightly defended justice, peace and the integrity of creation but largely forgot about the importance of the family and sexual integrity, uncritically endorsed Marxism, the sexual revolution, and almost everything championed under the banner of gay rights, but overlooked the fact that freedom is as important as justice, and failed to defend the most vulnerable of all, the unborn and the very old. This paper is written first of all for the Christian community. Therefore, it first outlines a normative biblical framework, then sketches a political philosophy, and finally outlines a concrete political agenda for U.S. politics in the last four years of this century. Little attention is given to developing the common language for advocating these policies in the larger pluralistic society - although that is also an essential task.

Normative Biblical Framework

The Biblical Story

The biblical story provides an essential framework for Christian political thought. The entire created order is good and precious because it comes from the hand of a loving God. Persons created in the image of God are called to a servant-like stewardship of the rest of the Creator's handiwork. Tragically, humanity rebelled against God and the result is selfish persons, twisted social relationships and institutions and even a groaning, disordered creation. Unwilling to forsake fallen humanity, however, the Creator began a long historical process of salvation to restore a right relationship between God, persons, and the creation around them. At the centre of that redeeming grace is Jesus Christ, Nazarene carpenter and eternal Word, who is a model for perfect humanity, atones for our sins, and rises from the dead to break the power of evil. History is moving toward the risen Lord's return when all things will be restored to wholeness.[5] This biblical story provides a foundation for thinking about the nature, dignity, and destiny of persons, the status of the non-human world, the importance of the historical process, and the ultimate meaning of all things. From this biblical story as well as all the other relevant biblical material, we can develop comprehensive biblical summaries or paradigms of specific topics that are especially relevant to politics. The following are some of the most important.[6]

Biblical Paradigms

The Special Dignity and Sanctity of Human Beings: Every person – and only human beings – are made in the image of God, called to stewardship of the non-human creation, made to find fulfilment only when rightly related to God, neighbour, the earth, and self, summoned to respond in freedom to God's invitation of salvation, and invited to live forever in the presence of God. We must act on the belief that from the moment of conception, we are dealing with human life. No extended biblical passage explicitly teaches that; none denies it. A number of texts use words for the unborn that are normally applied to those who have been born. For nineteen centuries, the Christian church has been overwhelmingly opposed to abortion. Modern science now demonstrates with astounding detail that from the moment of conception, a genetically distinct human being with a continuous biological development exists. If one is uncertain whether this developing foetus is a human being, one must adopt this as a working assumption. To do otherwise would be like shooting blindly into a darkened theatre with the justification that we cannot know whether we will hit empty seats or murder innocent persons. The directly intended taking of innocent human life - whether in abortion or euthanasia - is wrong.

Freedom of Belief: Throughout biblical history, God gives persons enormous freedom to respond in obedience or rebellion, unbelief or faith to God. Jesus' parable of the wheat and tares shows that God chooses to allow this freedom to persons until the final judgment. Therefore, religious freedom is an essential element of a good society.

The family: Strong, stable families (persons related by blood, marriage, or adoption) are essential for a good society. Keeping marriage vows, accepting God's design that sexual intercourse be reserved for a man and a woman united in a life-long marriage covenant, and valuing singles in the extended family are all important aspects of strengthening the family.

Justice: The two key Hebrew words for justice *(mishphat* and *sedaqah)* are used both to call for just courts and just economic arrangements. Fair courts require honest witnesses and an impartial justice which is not biased towards

---

[5] This is not to argue for universalism (i.e. the salvation every person).

[6] In principle, one would need to examine every relevant biblical passage using appropriate exegetic tools, understand the trajectory of biblical revelation on the issue, and then formulate a comprehensive canonical paradigm in each specific area.

the rich or the poor. Fair economic arrangements require – as the Old Testament treatment of the land (the basic capital in an agricultural society) shows - an arrangement where all families and persons have access to the productive resources needed to earn a decent living and be dignified participating members of society. Sometimes, of course, wrong personal choices rightly result in the loss of these productive resources for a time, but God does not want that to continue forever. Frequently, too, according to the Bible, powerful oppressive people seize these resources from the poorest. Justice requires restoration of equitable arrangements where all have the opportunity to work and thus obtain a generous portion of the necessities of life. In addition, those who are unable to work and provide for themselves must be cared for by their family and the larger community.

A Special Concern for the Poor: Hundreds of biblical texts declare God's special concern for the poor and demand that God's people imitate God's concern. One crucial measure of how obedient people judge societies and policies is by what they do for the poorest, weakest and most marginalized. This special concern to strengthen the poorest is not a bias towards the poor but rather a concern for equal justice for everyone.

Work: Work is essential to the dignity of human beings who are called to be co-shapers of history with God. Every able person has the responsibility to work and people have the obligation to structure society so that every person can work in a way that respects human dignity and earns a decent living.

Peacemaking: Christians look forward to the time when a 'nation shall not lift up sword against nation neither shall they learn war anymore.' Until the Lord returns, unfortunately, persons persistently resort to wars and rumours of wars. Many Christians believe they should, as the lesser of two evils, engage in just wars for the sake of preserving some order and peace. Other Christians believe that killing is always contrary to the teaching of Christ and that he calls us to overcome our enemies with suffering love rather than the sword. But all agree that Jesus' words 'Blessed are the peacemakers' are urgent in our time.

Individuality and Community: Biblical faith holds together both the inestimable value of each person and each person's freedom to shape their own life and also the fact that persons are made for a community and only achieve wholeness in right relationship with others in the family and the larger society.

Rulers: God ordains rulers both to restrain evil and promote good. In biblical thought, the justice which God calls the king to do (Psalm 72: 1-4, 12-14) includes nurturing both fair courts and economic systems that strengthen the poor. God stands far above every political ruler. No politician or government has ultimate authority. The story of Naboth's vineyard demonstrates the rights of individual families over against the king. When the king defied God's law, the prophet challenged and condemned them. Everyone and everything, including rulers and government, have only a limited authority which is subordinate to the divine Sovereign.

Political philosophy

The Bible does not prescribe any particular political philosophy. Political philosophies emerge as people in community over a period of time integrate a normative framework and careful study and reflection on historical experience. As long as we understand our political philosophy as a useful guide (to be improved by further normative reflection and social analysis) rather than an unchanging dogma, it can be a helpful tool for navigating complex political decisions. The following components of a political philosophy are, I hope, consistent with biblical revelation and rigorous social analysis.

Democratization and Decentralization of Power: There is both a positive and a negative reason for decentralizing all forms of power. Each person is called to exercise a creation mandate and become a co-worker with God in shaping history. If a small elite makes most decisions, the majority cannot exercise their God-given mandate. Negatively, as Lord Acton pointed out, power tends to corrupt and absolute power tends to corrupt absolutely. Sinful people in a fallen world will almost always use unchecked centralized power to benefit themselves unfairly and oppress others. Therefore, to avoid totalitarianism and injustice, power must be decentralized. The principle of subsidiarity in Catholic social teaching rightly stresses that other things being equal, activity should be undertaken by a lower level of government or by a smaller societal institution rather than a higher. At the same time, it must be clearly recognized that some things can only be done (or at least done well) in a more centralized way. Careful analysis is needed in each situation.

Democracy: A concern for human rights, individual freedom, and the decentralization of power all lead to a democratic political order. When freedom of speech, secret ballots and universal suffrage exist, people - at least in theory - have the political power to shape society for the benefit of the majority. Separating legislative, administrative and judicial functions and balancing national, state and local governmental realms also decentralize power.

Civil Society: A large group of institutions intermediate between the individual and government decentralize power and provide smaller contexts for human communities to flourish. These include the family, the church, the media, the schools, the economy, and a host of smaller voluntary associations. These intermediate centres of power provide a check on governmental power and thus are a significant foundation of freedom.

Private Ownership and a Market Economy: The history of the twentieth century has shown clearly that when the state owns and controls most of the economy, economic and political power is so centralized that totalitarianism is almost guaranteed. Genuinely decentralized private ownership, on the other hand, nurtures free individuals and serves as a counterbalance to political power. Determining prices and production via supply and demand has also proven to be far more efficient than central planning. Huge privately-owned corporations, of course, can also become centres of enormous economic power. When the same corporations own the media and provide most of the funding for election campaigns, economic and political power is again dangerously centralized. A concern for justice and freedom demands a continuing vigilance against all forms of centralized economic power and a constant effort to strengthen smaller centres of economic life including family-owned farms and businesses, co-operatives, and widespread home ownership.

Religious Freedom and Church-State Relations: The First Amendment's prohibition against the government's establishing any official religion or preventing its free exercise is a crucial aspect of a society that truly respects human dignity and individual freedom. Religious freedom is a gift from God, not the state. A government can only acknowledge and defend it. Avoiding established religion, however, does not mean that religious expression is banished to the private sphere. Everyone, including religious people, should be free to develop and state the implications of their deepest convictions for public policy. Faith-based institutions have a long and venerable history of engagement in education, health care, and social welfare. When a government adopts programmes to enable the voluntary sector to serve the public good in these areas, there should be no discrimination in eligibility on account of religion, nor should there be exclusionary criteria that force these providers to engage in self- censorship or to otherwise abandon their religious character.

Human Rights: The right to life and freedom are inalienable because they come from God, not a government. A government should recognize and protect freedom of religion, speech, and political activity.

Family: A government rightly recognizes and favours the family (those related by blood, marriage and adoption) and especially the nuclear family (wife, husband and children) with its larger circle of extended family (grandparents etc.) as an essential element in a stable society. The family, not a government, has the primary responsibility for raising children. Religious institutions can do far more than government to strengthen the family, but government should do what it can. That includes discouraging (although not preventing) divorce and sexual promiscuity and recognizing that children are best served when they live with both of their parents. It also includes not broadening the definition of marriage to include gay partners and not defining family as any two or more people co-habiting. A government rightly offers tax and other benefits that favour marriage rather than co-habitation or divorce.

Care for Creation and a Sustainable Planet: Responsible care for creation flows from a biblical worldview. We face a long-term environmental crisis. Utilitarian attitudes must be balanced by a recognition of the intrinsic worth of all God's creation and the human responsibility to act as God's faithful stewards. Human beings have far more worth than plants or animals. But very seldom, if ever, do we have to choose between taking a human life and destroying an endangered species. Usually it is a choice between growing affluence and obliterating the handiwork of the Creator. We must aim to develop sustainable economic practices that reduce the stress on natural systems and make it possible for us to pass on a lovely, sustainable planet to our descendants. The needs of the poor and most vulnerable must be central in all environmental decisions; the rich must pay the major cost of reducing environmental damage. We must encourage alternative sources of energy that decrease our reliance on non-renewable resources. We must balance the needs of workers and the environment.

The Role of Government: A government should both restrain evil and promote the common good. Nurturing an economic order where everyone, especially the poorest, has the resources to earn a decent living is a central concern of good government. A government is responsible for providing the legal and social framework in which the other institutions in society can flourish. A government should carefully strengthen rather than replace society's intermediate institutions when they experience trouble. What should be legislated and what not? Why should there be laws against something like racial discrimination in the sale of housing and not against an act of adultery? The following considerations are relevant: 1) Individuals should normally be free to harm themselves (e.g. get drunk regularly at home) but not be free to harm others (drive while drunk); 2) laws must be enforceable in a way that does not undermine other important values (e.g. even if it were good in spite of the first principle, to have a criminal penalty for adultery, it would be impossible to enforce such a law without the kind of police state that would destroy freedom); 3) laws have a teaching function – to some extent people think (wrongly) that what is legal is moral.

Work and Workers: Since work is essential to human dignity, every able-bodied person should have the opportunity to work at a job that pays a living wage that can support a family. An unemployment rate that denies the dignity of work to people other than those properly in transition from one job to another is immoral and socially destructive. Conversely, people who can work have an obligation to do so in order to earn their living. Welfare policies should assist those who cannot care for themselves but dare not discourage work and responsibility. Workers have a right to safe working conditions, a living wage and reasonable job security. The legal right of workers to organize unions counterbalances corporate economic power, encourages justice, and nurtures dignity and self-respect.

The Priority of the Poor: Poverty has many causes. Those who are poor because they are unable to provide for themselves should be given a decent living by their family where possible and the government where necessary. Those who are poor because of personal irresponsibility should suffer appropriate consequences. Those, however, who are poor - whether through an accident of birth, or the neglect or oppression of others - because they lack the education and the capital to be productive, self-sufficient members of society should be empowered by both private institutions and government. Justice at least demands that every person has an equal opportunity to acquire the basic capital (whether land, money or education) that will enable that person to earn a decent living and be a dignified participating member of society. Strengthening the poor by providing such an opportunity should be a central concern of a government. Every significant governmental decision should be judged by its impact on the poorest.

A Consistent Ethic of Life: The first and most basic human right is the inviolable right to life of every human being. The first and most basic responsibility of civil law is to ensure that this right is recognized and protected. Abortion involves the direct, intentional and violent taking of human life. No law which legitimizes the direct killing of innocent human beings through abortion can be just. Therefore, we must work for the legal protection of the unborn, and oppose all public funding of abortions. At the same time, we must develop a wide range of alternatives to abortion - both to reduce the evil of abortion and also in recognition that two people are directly involved, not just one. A caring society will surround women with unwanted pregnancies with love and concrete support including financial assistance and better adoption alternatives. Euthanasia - the direct killing of the aged and infirm either with or without their consent - is wrong. That does not mean that it is immoral to refuse or withhold extraordinary medical treatment when death is imminent or inevitable. But we dare not blur the distinction between on the one hand *allowing* a person to die and on the other *killing* a person. Concern for a consistent ethic of life does not end with abortion and euthanasia. Life does not begin at conception and end at birth. Tens of millions of people die unnecessarily each year of starvation and malnutrition. Tobacco kills millions of people prematurely each year. Capital punishment kills human beings. We should seek to protect the sanctity of human life wherever it is threatened and violated. That is not to deny a significant moral difference between abortion and death from lung cancer caused by smoking. The direct, intentional taking of innocent human life in abortion, euthanasia, and genocide is morally graver than the indirect, unintentional taking of human life in starvation or death from smoking. But all are wrong and all reflect disregard for the inestimable value of human life. Respect for human life is a seamless garment. A consistent ethic of life opposes and seeks to reduce not only abortion and euthanasia but also capital punishment, starvation and cigarette-induced cancer.

Peacemaking: Those who threaten society, from within or without, must be restrained. Historically, that has usually been done through lethal force as a last resort. Historically, too, it is true both that vast numbers of people have been killed and also that a variety of non-violent methods of conflict resolution have successfully replaced lethal force. The courts, for example, replaced duelling. In the twentieth century, Gandhi, King and a host of others successfully used non-violent techniques to end oppression and seek justice. Christians today disagree over the extent to which non-violent models of conflict resolution can successfully replace most or all uses of lethal force. But all agree that the search for non-violent alternatives must be greatly strengthened. Wherever possible, non-violence must replace lethal force.

An Evangelical Political Agenda

Every attempt to spell out a concrete political agenda that in any way makes claim to being grounded in biblical norms must be with humility and caution. Nobody and no group of people know enough to suggest they speak for God. God does have an opinion on every specific political decision we face. But our only access to God's will for politics is through the painstaking, imperfect process of carefully examining both the relevant Christian norms and relevant social analysis. Both are complex. We can make almost an infinite variety of mistakes in both tasks. Therefore, we never dare claim to have the biblical or the Christian position. At the same time, Christians dare not abandon the attempt to ground our political work in biblical norms. Some normative judgments will shape our politics. If they are not Christian, they will come from some other – inappropriate – source. Therefore, we must dare to propose concrete political proposals and show how we have attempted to allow both a normative biblical framework and an accurate social analysis to shape our conclusions. We rightly advocate such proposals with humble confidence even as we invite others to help us modify our positions by showing us how we can more faithfully ground them in biblical norms and careful study.

Towards a Just Economy

In a just economy, all persons able to work have the opportunity (within the limits of particular historical circumstances) to work and earn a living wage that enables the worker and the worker's family to enjoy a decent life. Therefore, full employment is a necessity for justice. In a dynamic economy, of course, there will be temporary, transitional unemployment as technologies change and production moves to locations with a comparative advantage. All citizens should share the burden of those temporarily displaced through generous unemployment insurance, effective job re-training, and help for further education. Unions are essential to balance the power of employers, especially larger corporations. Therefore, public policy should vigorously encourage strong, honest, democratically run unions, and have laws that guarantee collective bargaining, and prohibit firing and replacing striking workers. At this point in the U.S.A's history when unions are especially weak, justice demands that they be strengthened. Knowing the temptations to abuse power for selfish ends, a government should enforce clear, effective standards on health and safety at work in a way that does not unnecessarily reduce productivity. At the present time in the U.S.A., a decline in earnings on the part of the poorest and stagnation at best on the part of a large section of the lower middle class is accompanied by a rapid increase in income and wealth among the richest 20 per cent. When a growing gap between the poorest and the richest results in a declining standard of living for those at the bottom, it is unjust and must be reversed both for the sake of justice and in order to avoid societal conflict that might endanger democracy. Especially threatening is the fact that a variety of factors including changes in the global economy have produced a situation where large numbers of people work part or full-time at jobs that simply do not pay a living wage. To the extent that some low-skill jobs are no longer needed, a government should offer assistance for further education and training. To the extent that these jobs are still essential for society (for example, clerks, fast-food store workers etc.), people ready to work full time must be ensured a living wage. Two possible mechanisms are: raising the minimum wage or increasing the Earned Income Tax Credit so that all workers who work forty hours a week receive a living wage (via wages plus a refundable EITC). Unless a better way can be found, I support greatly expanding the EITC so that single persons over eighteen who work full time are guaranteed approximately $17,000; there should also be an economic incentive for marriage. It is urgent that economists, politicians, business leaders and others undertake a careful study to see what new mix of policies (taxes, education, etc.) can enable the poorest one-third of our citizens who are ready to work full time to earn a decent income. A society that can and does not offer that opportunity is immoral.

Balanced Budget

The budget deficit of recent decades is bad economics. It is also robbing our children and grandchildren. It must end - in seven years, if not sooner. Ending the deficit is more urgent than tax cuts. But it is immoral to ask the poor to bear a large share of the cost. Those most able to afford cut-backs should lose the most in reduced benefits and increased taxes. Cutting effective programmes for the poorest (e.g. Pell grants, EITC, WIC) is wrong. Instead, we should drastically reduce the $85 billion per year in corporate welfare (grants and tax benefits) that the conservative Cato Institute estimates the U.S. government provides. The military budget can be further reduced. Social security and Medicare are extremely important programmes that have dramatically reduced the number of elderly folk who are poor. But there is no reason why seniors with good incomes should not pay taxes on social security income or cover a little more of the monthly cost of Medicare.

Tax Policy

Sweeping changes in tax policy, including the flat tax, are on the table today. Tax policy should be fair, clear, and promote basic societal values (as stated by an underlying political philosophy). That includes strengthening the poorest, nurturing the family, encouraging a wide variety of vital, thriving institutions in civil society, and protecting the environment. The basic principle of the current income tax (higher tax brackets for those with greater resources) reflects biblical values. The capital gains tax should not be lowered unless there is demonstrable evidence that lowering this tax would benefit the poorest one-third of our people. The flat tax abandons the important virtue of the income tax which demands more of those more able to pay. By eliminating all charitable deductions, it would also drastically undermine all the private non-profit-making institutions which have historically been a vital force for freedom and renewal in our society.

Church and State

The 'non-establishment' and 'free exercise' clauses of the First Amendment to the Constitution are essential to our freedom. Constant vigilance to preserve them is essential. Unfortunately, in recent decades an exaggerated understanding – amounting almost to an absolute wall of separation - has gained strength in popular thought, policy decisions and even some legal decisions. That too must be resisted. The proposed amendment by Rep. Istook is misguided and should be opposed. The equal benefits amendment (Hyde, Hatch) is less clear. Its basic desire - not to discriminate against anyone on account of religious expression or belief when government provides public benefits to citizens – is entirely valid. But it is far from clear that a constitutional amendment is the best approach. Only very occasionally and only in matters of great moment should we amend our most basic foundational document. Recent Supreme Court cases have moved in the direction of this proposed amendment. Probably a legislative remedy would be preferable.

Family

It is time for political rhetoric and public policies unequivocally to seek to support the family. That means discouraging sexual promiscuity, divorce, and co-habitation without marriage. It means affirming the choice of remaining single without promoting radical nonsense that claims we should expand the word 'family' to mean any set of people who choose to live together. It means assisting single parents, but in a way that affirms and helps them move towards the norm of the two-parent family. Public policy should favour marriage over co-habitation in tax law and welfare policy. No-fault divorce law should be revised to slow down and make divorce more difficult, especially when children are involved. Much stiffer penalties should be levied on fathers who fail to pay child support. Sex education in the schools should urge abstinence until marriage. Public schools are not the right places to distribute condoms, much less demonstrate their use. A tax policy should also support children. I support an expanded tax credit for each child in lower-income families (up to approximately $30,000 per year).

Homosexuality

Public policy must both defend the civil rights of all citizens including gays and lesbians and clearly affirm heterosexuality as the societal norm. Every citizen, including practicing gays and lesbians should have the right to jobs, housing, etc. and discrimination against homosexuals should be prosecuted under general civil rights laws. Physical attacks on gay citizens should be prosecuted vigorously. Gay-bashing is a sin. So is scapegoating gays and lesbians by suggesting they are the primary cause of the decline of the family. At the same time, public policy should reject all efforts to re-define marriage and extend the special privileges of married couples to gay partners. I question whether special civil rights legislation for gays is necessary if general civil rights laws are firmly and fairly enforced.

Education

Education is an essential means of affirming the dignity of each person. It is also the primary source of capital in an information society. The state has the responsibility, to the extent that historical circumstances permit, to work vigorously toward the equality of education opportunities for all citizens. That does not mean the state must run all or even most of the schools. It does mean that government should, through public funds, guarantee that every child has the financial resources for quality education. Good education is inevitably grounded in ethical and religious foundations. Each child's family, not state structures, should have the basic right to choose the values that undergird their child's education. Elementary and secondary education in the U.S. is abominably unequal. Drastic reform is needed. There is no clear, obvious path to quality education for all. In this context, therefore, a government should encourage maximum experimentation in the next five to ten years to see what ideas work best. That includes a wide variety of experiments in the public schools, new charter schools, increasing parental involvement and choice, and a serious test of educational vouchers in a dozen different types of settings. A fair test of educational vouchers would involve selecting a dozen representative cities and communities and then offering a voucher worth approximately the amount of money currently spent on public education in that area divided by the number of eligible children. There would have to be an extra amount for handicapped children. I would add an extra $100-$1500 for each voucher for children from poor families with incomes below $15,00-$25,000. There are potential dangers and benefits in educational vouchers. Some claim they would divide society, increase racism, and harm the poorest. Others believe the opposite and think they would allow religious faith to return to its rightful role in education without discriminating against anyone since all faiths can operate schools, provide needed competition for the present educational establishment, and return effective control of education to the family. We certainly do not know enough to move immediately to vouchers for a large part of elementary and secondary education. But vigorous testing (and careful analysis of the results) of educational vouchers is surely warranted immediately.

Abortion and Euthanasia

Full legal protection of the unborn will not happen quickly. An incremental, long-term approach that works at all levels – cultural, legislative and judicial – is essential. I oppose all public funding of abortion. I support legislation to ban 'partial birth abortions' and late-term abortions after the 25th week of pregnancy. We must vigorously promote more alternatives to abortion – e.g. we should provide better support for women with unwanted pregnancies and make adoption more affordable and easier. The well-organized campaign for legalized euthanasia must be resisted vigorously. All attempts to legalize 'physician-assisted suicide' should be opposed.

Health Care

It is fundamentally immoral for a wealthy society like the U.S. to tolerate a situation where tens of millions of citizens lack health insurance. I propose no particular mechanism. But I insist that this issue dare not be postponed for another generation. If nothing else, a bi-partisan commission appointed by the President and the Congress must be appointed in 1997 to prepare a feasible proposal within one year.

Welfare Policy

The present system is a disaster. It must be fundamentally reformed. The guiding principles must include: strengthen marriage and the family and foster sexual integrity; encourage the responsibility to work and provide for one's family; discourage long-term dependency; guarantee (yes, as an entitlement) adequate benefits including health care for those unable to provide for themselves. No programme to reform welfare will succeed unless that policy is grounded on two interrelated facts. Firstly, long-term welfare dependency results from a complex mix of both wrong personal choices (about drugs, sex, alcohol, marriage, laziness) and structural problems (the flight of well-paying, low-skill jobs to other countries; the effects of racism on educational quality, the black family etc.). Secondly, persons are not just economic machines that respond to monetary incentives. They are also spiritual beings gifted with freedom. Therefore, long-term change is impossible without spiritual renewal of persons – and that can only happen if public policy recognizes the need for some new kind of partnership between government and other institutions in civil society, especially the religious community. No public officials currently know the magic solution for long-term welfare reform. We need widespread experimentation. State and local governments, private non-profit-making and private profit-making ventures should all be given new expanded space to explore promising alternatives. In particular, I urge a major exploration of different mechanisms that would allow far more needed services (AFDC, drug rehabilitation, support for low-income housing, etc.) to be provided through local non-profit-making organizations. Especially important is the stipulation (rightly adopted in the Charitable Choice provisions in the Welfare Bill of

1996) that government should not demand that religious non-profit-making organizations abandon their distinctly religious character and programme when they are freely chosen as a delivery system for public services. Government funds (even when they come via vouchers) should not be used for worship or other sectarian religious activity. But religious non-profit-making organizations should be free to raise private money to fund their specifically religious activities and be free to integrate their total programme as they deem best. We must continue to search for the best mechanisms to nurture this partnership between government and religious non-profit-making organizations without violating the First Amendment. Tax credits is one possibility. Vouchers to individuals who are eligible for government services is another. Holders of vouchers can then take them to either a government provider or a non-profit-making agency (religious or otherwise). I urge federal and state governments to promote several major tests where a portion of the welfare case-load is granted vouchers which they may choose to take to a religious non-profit-making organization that both offers all the usual welfare services, but also raises private funds to support a programme of nurturing spiritual transformation among its clients. Careful evaluation after five years could then show whether this kind of agency is more successful than current government-run departments of public welfare in reducing long-term welfare dependency.[7] Affirming more state and local control does not mean abandoning the federal government's obligation to guarantee basic benefits. Nor does favouring far more emphasis on non-profit-making organizations (religious and others) as preferred delivery systems mean abandoning the responsibility of government to be the guarantor of last resort of basic benefits to the poorest.

International Affairs

The U.S. is the only global super power today. Neither isolationist policies nor unilateral global policing are warranted. If a great imbalance of power is usually abused, then increasing the balance of power in the global community of nations is desirable. Strengthening the UN is one way to do that. Certainly, I would not want the UN to become a global centre of unchecked centralized power. But that is far from the major problem today. The UN's agencies should be improved (i.e. become more efficient) and strengthened to deal with the vast numbers of refugees, regional conflicts, and global environmental problems. The U.S. should pay the money owed to the UN. Promoting human rights and democratic governments should be a higher priority in US foreign policy than increasing US exports. The US should exercise far more vigorous leadership in a wide variety of peacemaking ventures. The international trade in conventional arms should be drastically reduced. Anti-personnel land mines should be outlawed by a universal treaty. More attention should be given to ending nuclear proliferation and further reducing the stocks of nuclear weapons held

[7] For a more Rolland and Sider, 1996:454-79

by all nuclear powers. Military aid should be reduced. Foreign economic aid should move upward until it reaches at least 0.7 per cent of GDP, but its focus and delivery should be drastically changed. Far less should go in bilateral deals with governments. Far more should go via private non-governmental organizations (NGOs) that are more efficient and do a better job of helping the poorest. The amount devoted to micro-loans should be increased. In 1995, the Intergovernmental Panel on Climate Control concluded that global warming had begun. New efforts to avoid the disastrous consequences of major global warming must be undertaken promptly. We should immediately implement a large carbon tax (with substantial tax reductions elsewhere) to reduce the use of fossil fuels. Chlorofluorocarbons should be banned to protect the ozone layer. Global environmental concerns should become increasingly important in U.S. diplomacy.

Environmental Justice

Public policy must continue to protect endangered species, prevent environmental deterioration, and avoid discriminatory practices that disproportionately locate environmental hazards near communities who are coloured or who are poor. Not every environmental law has been wise. The current political concern to evaluate the wisdom of past legislation is legitimate. Carefully evaluating the cost of environmental regulation is essential. But we dare not abandon a careful, sustained, long-term protection of our environment. Particular vigilance is essential today to make sure that earlier environmental gains are not lost. Legislation and other public policies to protect endangered species here and around the world are essential.

Racial Reconciliation

America's long history of slavery and racial division is one of our nation's most grievous sins. Persistent personal and institutional racism permeates every facet of American society. Racial reconciliation must be one of the highest priorities for Christians in America. While much of the work of racial reconciliation will have to be done in the institutions that constitute civil society - especially, the church - there remains a role for government. The civil rights movement did much to correct racial injustice in American law, but our society continues to suffer the consequences of past sins, and to perpetuate those sins through ongoing, persistent racism. Allegedly colour-blind policies which ignore both historic and present realities, and which attempt for reconciliation without restitution, can in effect serve only to perpetuate existing racism. Yet government policies of affirmative action have been, at best, imperfect mechanisms. While current affirmative action policies may be clumsy and not completely just, eliminating them without replacement would be a grave injustice. Because of persistent racism, coloured people are disproportionately represented among the poor and economically disadvantaged in the United States. Thus, an aggressive, class-based approach to affirmative action might be a just and effective means of redressing the economic effects of racism. Although the civil rights movement helped to end racial segregation as official policy, much of our country remains segregated, particularly in our urban centres. At this time we must vigorously work on two fronts: first to build and strengthen strong black institutions; second to remove the remaining barriers to full participation in society by 'coloured people'. Public policy should ensure that government-funded programmes do become more vigorous and should be fully funded. Even if all the preceding assertions and proposals are correct (and I am sure they are not) and even if they were all successfully implemented, the result would be only a modest improvement. We must rest satisfied with limited expectations from even the best political engagement. Politics will not bring in the Kingdom. Political action is no substitute for evangelism and church planting. Even the best public policy and wise governmental bureaucracy cannot transform persons the way personal faith can do. But the fact that the goal of politics is limited does not make it unimportant. A more biblically rooted and more thoughtfully grounded evangelical political engagement could make a modest, but also a substantial contribution to American public life in the next century.

TOWARDS A LATIN AMERICAN PENTECOSTAL POLITICAL PRAXIS[1]

Douglas Petersen

Dr. Douglas Petersen is Margaret S. Smith Distinguished Professor of World Missions and Intercultural Studies at Vanguard University, U.S.A.

Introduction

Pentecostals throughout Latin America have already begun to demonstrate their potential for mobilizing large numbers of people, ostensibly in their efforts to extend the evangelical faith. It should be noted that in these societies, where discrimination, neglect and indifference are too often characteristic, Pentecostalism has typically gathered strength precisely among the most disadvantaged or dissatisfied sectors such as the peasantry, the urban poor, women, Indians and ethnic minorities, young adults and the independent middle groups. Thus, Pentecostalism, quite unlike some of its stereotypical portrayals as passive, otherworldly and traditional, is deeply involved in its own kind of here-and-now social struggle. Its programme of personal regeneration at the grass-roots, significant both in its degree and volume of effectiveness, has far-reaching implications for social transformation.[2]

Pentecostal Non-involvement in Politics

Since their beginnings in Latin America, Pentecostals have considered politics to be, at best futile and, at worst, a dirty business.[3] The *reglamento local* of *las asambleas de dios* required every member to sign a *pacto de miembro* (membership agreement) that precluded members from participating in political

---

[1] Petersen, 1997:30-33

[2] For a description of alternative examples of Pentecostal social action in several Latin American countries, see Petersen, 1996.

[3] I present an explanation of Pentecostals' rationale for non-involvement and subsequent distrust in the political process, in Petersen, 1996:157-159.

parties[4] Moreover, Pentecostals seldom have been involved in political action because they have had little hope that a revolutionary change of government necessarily would bring change to the social structure.[5] Their pragmatism limits them to certain arenas of action where they have been tepid at best and generally have avoided outright conflict. Everett Wilson succinctly summarizes the traditional relationship between Pentecostal social action and political involvement:

> They [Pentecostals] themselves are primary victims of social oppression, dehumanizing economic policies, and corrupt politics. Their rejection of political initiatives for revolution is based on their perception of options, not indifference. Their policies may be expected to reflect their marginal social status, their rejection of short-term solutions, and their cynicism of political messiahs and temporal ideologies.[6]

With the exception of very few cases the radicalism of the Pentecostal position of non-involvement in political action is still the norm. Though Pentecostal social concern traditionally has avoided most types of political involvement, in the last five or six years one can witness so many 'departures from the norm' as to force the question as to why these departures are happening and how Pentecostals will understand and respond to this new fact?[7] Involvement in politics can no longer be avoided. If Pentecostals intend to live out their faith as a reality in today's world, they cannot avoid coming to grips with what Miguez Bonino articulately calls his '"thing" that shapes individual and collective life, that both confers meaning on and denies meaning to human plans and actions, that encompasses and invades all areas of human existence, and that offers and dispenses both life and death to thousands of millions – political struggle!'[8]

The time has come when Pentecostals' critical reflection upon the 'theoretical implications' of the intermeshing of social action with politics is indispensable. The price of simple pragmatism is too high. Pentecostals cannot ignore the assertion issued in Miguez Bonino's statement 'that theory is necessary, in the first place, because it is unavoidable; whether acknowledged or not, it is present.' Bonino contends that political reflection 'is necessary in

---

[4] *Reglamento Local,* 1992:32. The Reglamento published in 1932, presented the major doctrines of the church and also prescribed the conduct and responsibilities of the membership and the congregational leadership. Wilson 1983:186-98.

[5] See Aguilar *et al.*, 1993:134-135

[6] Wilson, 1987:87

[7] Pentecostal leaders have been active in politics in virtually every Central American country as well as in the South American countries including Colombia, Peru, Chile, Argentina and Brazil. This raises profound theological questions for analysis; see Padilla, 1992:2-7 and Freston, 1994:226-242.

[8] Bonino, 1983:8

order that we can make explicit to ourselves the presuppositions and assumptions of our action as well as expose and critically examine forms of action suggested to us.'[9] This last sentence holds a challenge to Pentecostals to move beyond their unwillingness to deal with political issues and constructively devise acceptable social and political structures to cope with the problems and give viability to the hopes of our situation. Further reflection certainly must address the social and political dimension and implications of Pentecostal activity.

As a starting point for this essay, I would offer three basic facts of social action that would enable the church to come to terms with this all-pervasive factor of politicization. First, and in my opinion most fruitfully, Pentecostals should create their own alternative institutions that can function as instruments of human justice. Second, any active and direct participation should begin with community-based and grass-roots political structures. Third, contrary to popular wisdom and seldom as effective as the first two, Pentecostals will have to involve themselves directly with national political powers and creative political reforms.

Pentecostalism and Institution-Building

Pentecostalism has been criticized consistently for its lack of 'political involvement' beyond its own context and within civil society.[10] To balance this critique, Pentecostals could argue legitimately that they are creating their own alternative institutions that function as instruments of human justice. Through the process of institution building, it is possible that constructive alternative instruments of social justice actually may enable the church to 'break the spell cast over the modem mind that uncritically equates social action axiomatically with political action.' [11] Social action and political action have become almost interchangeable terms in some circles of Christian social ethics.

As an alternative institutional organization committed over the long-term to be effective as a transforming agent in the social system, Pentecostals have the capacity potentially to create and attract a following that governmental entities cannot ignore.

Latin America Child Care, a ministry of compassion directed primarily toward the poor children in the slum areas in the cities of Latin America, can be used as a case study to demonstrate how institution-building has been utilized effectively by a Pentecostal organization to bring about structural change. LACC demonstrates the structural validity of the widespread conviction of sociologists and political analysts that the positive condition of children care, education, ethical formation – is essential for any kind of structural change that

---

[9] Bonino, 1983:9

[10] Rocha, 1991:202-203; Diamond, 1989); Huntington, 1984:2-11

[11] Dempster, 1991:37

will include democratic participation and produce a stable future. LACC represents the creation of an expanding infrastructure within Latin America designed to alter the existing social structure.

LACC is committed to providing education as one way that effectively breaks the chain of poverty in the generational reality of Latin America. Education with a Christian base from kindergarten to the university level is needed in each country. Teaching children that they have value and dignity is basic. Equipping them with the academic skills necessary to have a real impact on society is a long-term goal. Right thinking and right doing, faith and action, combine to present a whole gospel in culturally relevant terms. While it is recognized that spiritual transformation in the form of a personal encounter with Jesus Christ is absolutely necessary, faith is not separated from social action designed to change the structural conditions of Latin America through institutionalizing new educational opportunities.

In 19 countries of Latin America the results of this pastoral action have been most rewarding. In 1996 there are 75,000 children enrolled in 300 different schools. Education ranges from pre-kindergarten to a government accredited university. Over 2,000 teachers committed to the claims of the kingdom of God have been in action. LACC not only builds a new infrastructure but effects changes in resisting the *status quo* by being instrumental in bringing basic amenities such as electricity, water wells or running water that impact on the entire slum community. Latin American Child Care, a historical project, is already making a difference.

LACC is a prime example that Pentecostals are creating institutional structures capable of performing various educational, community development, social service and political functions. LACC is an authentic expression of an alternative institutional social action programme and as such has an opportunity to effect political change. As an alternative institutional organization committed over the long-term to be effective as a transforming agent in the social system, LACC, along with other Pentecostals, is creating institutional alternatives that provide fertile avenues attracting a following that governmental entities recognize.

At the same time, it must be acknowledged, Pentecostals have experienced difficulty in transferring this 'substitute society' into the larger forum of secular society. Rowan Ireland presents a critique that should be taken seriously by Pentecostals who desire to affect social change in the larger arena of society. It is Ireland's contention that Pentecostals, in spite of their obvious numbers, have a tendency to be hermetic, even when they form alternative structures. He questions the overall validity of such alternative societies if, 'their experiments in new ways of naming and addressing the problems of life at the grass-roots stay locked within the group.' This isolation will result, argues Ireland, 'because they [Pentecostals] lack the horizontal linkage to poor neighbours of other faiths and vertical linkage to individuals and organizations with more direct access to the means of cultural production'.[12] When Pentecostal groups, no matter the magnitude of their size, are content to form their own enclaves rather than opt for extended community involvement, they will forfeit the opportunity to participate in radical change or structural transformation.

Pentecostals and Involvement in Community Associations

An important question would be the manner in which Pentecostals break the norm of non-involvement in politics. It would seem unwise for Pentecostals to move from a stance of non-involvement to direct participation in political parties or worse still, to the creation of Christian political parties. When people arrive at political positions or enter political parties without the necessary experience they often become discouraged or get caught up in 'bad politics.' It is Miguez Bonino's contention from his experience that the best way for Protestants in general, and Evangelical Pentecostals in particular, who have rejected political participation, to take part in public life, is by participating in 'social movements' at the local level-neighbourhood associations, groups concerned with specific issues, associations related to public schools, consumers' associations and many other forms of civilian participation and social movements of the same type at provincial and national levels.[13] In the first place, the goals and purposes of such associations and groups are limited and better defined and Pentecostals may share these goals and purposes confidently. In the second place, relationships are more personal, face to face, similar to what Pentecostals are used to in their communities. Third, there is less 'money' involved and, therefore, competition is not usually so strong and a power struggle is less vicious. In this sense, Pentecostals can receive 'training' while they also contribute significantly to public life. When they clearly develop a lucid political vocation, they can enter party life in a more significant way. At the same time, modern constitutions in many Latin American countries are beginning to include different forms of active participation for these social movements and similar-concern groups.

Pentecostals and Overt Political Involvement

A third step, and a much more dangerous one for Pentecostals, involves coming to terms with the all-pervasive factor of national politicization. In Pentecostal theologian Murray Dempster's judgment, Pentecostals must 'desacralize the political power of human governments.'[14] The ultimate authority for the basis for justice in human rights is a 'God-given obligation.' The church needs to be willing to declare to the state 'that the compliance of the Christian community

[12] Ireland, 1991:222
[13] Bonino, 1994
[14] Dempster,1991:35

to any political authority is conditioned on the government's commitment to promote human dignity and social justice through its laws.'[15] Christopher Rowland and Mark Comer, similarly express the same sentiment that when the state institutes and practices laws that are directly contrary to God's laws of justice, then Paul's injunction in Romans 13:l that 'everyone must submit himself to the governing authorities' should not be understood as an absolute doctrine about the state. Rather one should turn to passages like Revelation 13 that describe an apostate state that functions as 'a servant of Satan.' Rowland and Comer forcefully aver that the state which functions in constant violation of God's laws of justice 'can never demand unqualified allegiance from those committed to the Kingdom of God whose goodness and values usually differ quite drastically from those of the powerful of the world.'[16]

A most beneficial approach to Pentecostal involvement is what Stephen Mott terms 'creative reform through politics'. The explanation is drawn as follows:

> Creative reforms are ... those changes which modify power relationships, set forth a new order of priorities, and provides new models of life and culture. They are changes which limit the power of those currently holding disproportionate power, which makes the weak more aware of their human rights, and which grant the poor and members of the working class (both in capitalism and in state socialism) more control over their lives.[17]

Pentecostals' involvement in such a political forum is valid when a government's role is decisive in structuring laws that result in greater justice on behalf of those who have no voice. The church does not involve itself, therefore, for self-serving reasons, but rather to promote and encourage official actions that are in the best interests of the powerless and the marginalized.[18] Murray Dempster, in recognition of the vast implications for the church to be involved in 'creative reform' calls for 'pragmatic flexibility and careful deliberation' when the church evaluates all of the variables involved in this exercise.[19] Many scholars agree that Pentecostals in the future may well be positioned to provide leadership that will further advance their fundamental position of changing lives in order, then, to change society:[20]

---

[15] See Dempster,1991:35 For a comprehensive treatment of 'strategic noncooperation' with governmental structures by the church community see Mott, 1982:142- 166.

[16] Rowland and Corner, 1990:88-89. For a thorough description of the political role of the believer and church community to submit to governments that are diabolically inspired see Rowland, 1993:133-141.

[17] Mott, 1982:203

[18] Mott, 1982:36

[19] Mott, 1982:37

[20] See Burdick, 1992 and) and 1993). Also see Ireland, 1991

It is true that Evangelical-Pentecostals could not consider Jesus, in any formal sense, to be a social reformer.[21] However, because Jesus was not involved in direct political activity cannot be construed that he did not or could not affect political change. If one asks how this political change happens, the answer is aptly phrased by Rowland and Comer:

> It was the power of the charismatic leader who attracts a following, the kind of leader who is at the edge of conventional life and whose political thrust consists in the position of marginality which makes an alternative political culture, however embryonic its form, a possibility.[22]

A word of caution – Pentecostals can easily miss the essential theological and ethical reflection and move from analysis to action similar to the process employed by secular political ethicists.[23] However, when Pentecostals follow the example of an integral ministry, as exemplified by Jesus, and are directly involved in activity filled with an evangelistic spirit then there is nothing that precludes them from playing an active part in bringing about change in the socio-political reality of the region.

Any hopes of Pentecostals taking active and effective involvement in political creative reform must move beyond theory and basic community practice to active visible involvement. However, unless Pentecostals, in their initial stages of political involvement, begin at the grass-roots and work out from there, the gargantuan leap from grass-roots' Pentecostal 'substitute societies' to effective national political involvement is at best, nearly impossible, and at worse, disastrous.

Summary of Pentecostals and Political Involvement

I have argued in this essay and elsewhere that perhaps the most appropriate place for Pentecostals to begin addressing social structures is in the creation of alterative institutions.[24] But still Miguez Bonino's injunction that politics will not go away requires Pentecostals to address directly the political sphere whether they care to or not. Probably the most suitable method at this juncture and at least at these initial stages, would be in community involvement that could provide political experience on a much smaller and more familiar scale. As Pentecostals begin to assume an active role in political life, in the wide sense of the word, it will be necessary for Pentecostal theologians and ethicists to develop a more precise theological analysis of specific issues related to political life and participation in order to offer guidelines for direct and overt

[21] Rowland and Corner, 1990:90
[22] Rowland and Corner, 1990:90
[23] See Schubeck, 1993:212-222.
[24] See Petersen, 196:197-246

action for the people who take these options. The Pentecostal leader must present in the congregation a study of an Evangelical Pentecostal social ethics, so that the people who take an active role may be supported by the sympathy, the understanding, and the prayer of the believing community and will not feel isolated or rejected.[25]

In spite of Pentecostals' critical weakness in these and other areas, corporately they present an authentic expression of an alternative institutional social action programme and as such have opportunity to affect political change. When Pentecostals model an integral society as exemplified by Jesus, though directly involved in activity filled with evangelistic fervour and compassion, they are not precluded from playing an active part in bringing change in the socio-political reality of the region. Pentecostals can offer not only a kind of spiritual refuge, but also authentic social action alternatives. A clear expression of serious and committed Pentecostal views is essential in order for them to articulate an initial agenda for a further discussion of social and political concern.

---

[25] Petersen, 1991:44-58. Also see Dempster, 1989:1-7; Dempster, 1993:51-64; and Dempster, 1987:129-153. See also Villafane 1992

PART THREE

CHRISTIAN FAMILY IN CONTEXT

Family, Covenant and Kingdom of God: Biblical Reflections[1]

Christopher J.H. Wright

Dr. Christopher J.H. Wright is International Director of Langham Partnership, U.K.

Introduction

Biblical material on the family presents a series of ambiguities. It closely mirrors the ambiguity of human life itself. The human family shares the ambiguity inherent in every human being: made in the image of God and yet at the same time fallen and sinful.

On the one hand, composed of persons made in God's image, the family reflects something of God's own self. The Bible affirms a high view of the family as God's creational context for human lives. On the other hand, composed of sinful persons, the family can magnify the horrors of human oppression and wickedness, and become an idolatrous substitute for the true worship of God. The Bible also depicts dysfunctional families. The family is recognized as a potential source of the temptation to idolatry, and a potential rival for that ultimate loyalty which is due to God alone through Christ. We ought to avoid a naïve or simplistic view of 'the Family', and assume that anywhere and everywhere the Bible will affirm that it is A Good Thing. God created it, like everything else in his creation, to be 'very good'. But it has the power, like all things human, to be distorted into something very evil. Christians sometimes use the term as a 'warm-glow' word. But there is also community among thieves and evil-doers. We need to be discerning. We will survey some major parts of the biblical canon and to explore both sides of this ambiguity.

Genesis 1–11

The material related to the family in the creation narratives and primal history of Genesis 1-11 is well known.

---

[1] Wright, 2002a: 11-19

Family as a Central Feature of the Created Order

'So God created the human being in his own image, in the image of God he created him; male and female he created them. God blessed them and said to them, "Be fruitful and increase in number; fill the earth and subdue it..." God saw all that he had made, and it was very good' (Gen. 1:27-31). This text, along with the parallel text in Genesis 2 giving special attention to the creation of woman, articulates several of the essential familial aspects of humanity: 1. Our sexual differentiation and complementarity is God's idea and reflects something that is true of the Creator: that God exists in relationship. That which our created sexuality enables – loving familial relationship – is true within the Creator: God exists in personal and familial relationship. 2. Marriage as the foundation of family life is articulated in Genesis 2:20-24, monogamy and marital faithfulness implied. 3. Although the procreation of children is not mentioned here, that purpose of marriage has already been expressed in the command to 'be fruitful and increase in number' in Genesis 1:28, and is implied in Gen. 2:24 – a man establishes an independent family unit in which he and his wife will become father and mother in their turn. 4. The whole arrangement is placed under the blessing of God and his approval as 'very good' (Ps. 127-128).

Family as a Context of Fallen Rebellion

The entrance of sin into human life moves quickly from the realm of the relationship between husband and wife, to that between siblings, to the whole of human society. God warned Adam and Eve that if they ate the forbidden fruit they would die. They did eat, but they did not die – at least not physically or immediately. The first actual death in Scripture came by human hands, the murdering hands of an angry and jealous brother. This sharply locates the explosion of human violence within the very first human family. God's question to Cain, 'Where is your brother?' and God's refusal to accept Cain's attempt to evade responsibility (Gen. 4:9), both point to a fundamental human duty, which may be universalized to all our 'brothers' in the wider human family, but certainly applies first to kinship duties. Cain went to live 'east of Eden', away from the presence of God. He began two building projects: building a family and building a city (Gen. 4:17). Probably to underline the significance of this double human effort to find a place of security in the absence of God, it records that he gave the same name, Enoch, to his son and his city.[2] The ongoing family of Cain manifests a dual capacity for great cultural achievement (in agriculture, music and crafts – Gen. 4:19-22), with simultaneous moral decline (bigamy and boastful violence – Gen. 4:23-24). It is within the family that Lamech of the line of Cain boosts his macho image to his two wives by boasting of outdoing his ancestor in excessive revenge, as if to

[2] See helpful comments in Walter, 1979:190. See also, Ellul, 1970

imply that his very manhood depended on such prowess. When God acts to save humanity and the earth from total obliteration by the flood, it is through a family. When Noah was born, his father Lamech of the line of Seth named him thus in the hope that he would 'comfort us in the labour and painful toil of our hands caused by the ground the Lord has cursed' (Gen. 5:29). Noah himself, described in terms that portray him virtually as a second Adam before the fall ('righteous, blameless, walked with God' – Gen. 6:9), is saved through a covenant with himself and his family (6:18). When he and his family come out of the ark, the new beginning for creation is heralded in the language of Genesis 1 – blessing, fruitfulness and family multiplication (Gen. 8:15-9:17). Tragically this 'second Adam' experiences a second fall, which again involves the fruit of the earth and again affects his family, injecting discord among his sons (Gen. 9:20-27).[3] The human family is again the focus of both salvation and blessing on the one hand, and sin and suffering on the other.

Genesis 12–50

The so-called patriarchal narratives (often now referred to by the more gender-inclusive term ancestral narratives, since so many of the stories relate to the women in these families, not just the patriarchs) exhibit the same positive and negative duality.

Ancestral Families of Israel: Models of redemption

1. The call of Abram heralds a fresh start. The text highlights yet again those keynotes of divine involvement, blessing and fruitfulness through the family. God's covenant promise to Abram (Gen. 12:1-3, often repeated) not only depends for its fulfilment on the gift of a family to Abram and Sarai themselves, but also has in view the ultimate blessing of 'all families (or clans, *mispehot*) of the earth' (Gen. 12:3). Although the Abrahamic covenant more often speaks of 'all nations (*goyim*) of the earth' (e.g. Gen. 18:18, 22:18), its original form, 'all families', reminds us that God's redemptive intention includes that most primal context of all human existence – the family. 2. When, however, the child of covenant promise is eventually born and grows up, God makes a demand which seems to put the whole project in jeopardy – the mysterious 'testing' of Genesis 22 and the 'binding of Isaac'. Abraham had, of course, sought to speed the divine promise during the anxious days of Sarah's continuing childlessness through taking Hagar and fathering Ishmael. Perhaps a major purpose in this event was to impress on Abraham and Israel that although God's mission of blessing humanity would proceed through a human family, the redemptive source and dynamic lay with God, not in human procreative or

---

[3] On this comparison of Noah with Adam, and the way in which Genesis 8-11 mirrors Genesis 1-7 in a repetition of the creation-decreation sequence, see Wenham, 2000 and Tomasino, 1992:128- 130.

parental capacity. Could Abraham believe that God would carry on with his promise, even if the child of promise was given back to him in sacrifice? The divine word at the end of the chapter links Abraham's faithful obedience with God's renewed promise to bless all nations on earth (Gen. 22:15-18).[4] 3. The narratives of the ancestral families were clearly written to teach certain desirable values and ideals. Gordon Wenham points out the emphasis on family reconciliation in the Jacob and Joseph cycles and the contrast this provides with the stories of Cain and Lamech in the primal history. There are also stories of inter-ethnic conflict resolution.[5] Wenham points out the rhetorical advocacy of such virtues as piety, courage, generosity, integrity in speech and action, filial duty, and brotherly love in the stories of the ancestral families.[6]

Ancestral Families of Israel: 'Anti-models' of divine patience and triumph over evil

One of the prayers of blessing in the Marriage Service of the Book of Common Prayer always made me uncomfortable as it invokes the God of Abraham, God of Isaac, God of Jacob and asks for blessing on the newly-weds as on Abraham and Sarah. I used to wonder if the couple in front of me knew the full range of stories about that couple, not to mention the marital relationships of their son and grandson. The catalogue of deception, lies, half-truths, abuse of other women, favouritism, jealousy, competition, failure and grief, is appalling. And that's only the marriages. Add in all the sibling rivalry, parental favouritism, murderous jealousy, simmering hatred and lingering fear, and you could fill a comprehensive casebook on dysfunctional families. Genesis does not conceal the horrendous wickedness and misery that stalked these proto-Israelite families. While the strength and durability of these families is apparent, as is the relationship that various key individuals have with God, Genesis 12-50 reflects family life in its Genesis 3-4 aspect as much as in its Genesis 1-2 aspect. And yet God carried on his mission of redemptive blessing. Genesis shows that God's determination to bless 'all families of the earth' will ultimately be in spite of human failure and inadequacy, not because of human prowess or success. Maybe the prayer in the wedding service is appropriate

4 It is possible, however, that the effect of this costly obedience was to cause a rift between Abraham on the one hand and Isaac and Sarah on the other. Genesis 22:19 tells us that Abraham and his servants went and stayed in Beersheba, with no mention of where Isaac went. Sarah, however, died at Kiriath Arba and Abraham 'went to mourn for Sarah' (Gen. 23:2), implying he may not have been with her at the time. Isaac, meanwhile was living at Beer Lahai Roi (Gen. 24:62, 25:11). If these geographical notes do indicate a family split, it would not be the last time that obedience to God's commands produced tension within families.

5 Wenham, 2000: 39

6 Tomasino, 1992:87-102

after all. If God is willing to be known as the God of Abraham, Isaac and Jacob, he can doubtless cope with the rest of us.

The Torah and Israelite society

Israel's kinship structure is not an abiding model to be replicated elsewhere (though it does have many similarities with traditional societies in the majority world today). But when we read laws or narratives relating to the family in Israel we must understand its social structure in its own context. Israel's kinship structure had three tiers, each of which is reflected in the way Israelite names were recorded:

The father's house: (*bet-'ab*). This was the smallest unit, but still a fairly large group of people. It consisted of all those living within the household of a single living male ancestor, who was known as the 'head of a father's house'. It would thus include his wife or wives, his sons and their wives and their sons and wives and unmarried daughters. It would also have included any servants or resident aliens living as part of the household.

The clan: (*mispahah*). This was a group of related households, named after one of the grandsons of Jacob. A clan often seems to have had a territorial identity as well, and sometimes village names and clan names were identical. The clan functioned as a protective association of families, with a variety of economic, social, judicial and military duties.

The tribe: (*sebet/matteh*). The tribe was the largest kinship grouping, named after the sons of Jacob (with Joseph sub-divided into Ephraim and Manasseh), and the tribes' major significance was in territorial land-holding. Of these, the first two were of far greater social and economic significance in the everyday life of average Israelites.[7]

Family as Focal Point of Covenant Faithfulness and Social Stability

The sign of the covenant between Yahweh and Israel was circumcision, an act carried out within the family. Appropriately, therefore, the family was also the prime place for the teaching of the faith, history, laws and traditions of Israel, and circumcision itself became a metaphor for covenant obedience – 'circumcise your hearts' (Deut. 10:16).

Israel had suffering in the latter stages of their bondage in Egypt through genocidal intrusion into their families. Egypt's state-sponsored campaign to reduce the population by the extermination of male births was part of an oppression that eventually led to Yahweh's intervention. In a form of poetic justice, the climax of Yahweh's plagues upon Egypt was the death of Egypt's firstborn. And in the context of that event two rituals were instituted in Israel which focus on the family for the experience and celebration of redemption. 1) The Passover: The social inclusiveness (with careful limitations) of this annual family ritual is based on the composition of normal Israelite households (Ex.

[7] For details, see Wright 1992b:761-769

12:43-49). 2) The Consecration of the Firstborn (Ex. 13:1- 16): That which Yahweh had delivered from death belonged to him. But in claiming the firstborn son in every family, Yahweh effectively claimed the whole succeeding generation. This symbolized the continuity of the covenant relationship through the generations.

In the Exodus context, the Decalogue forms the charter of freedoms and responsibilities for a redeemed people. The protection of the family is an essential aspect of its 'second table', including the preservation of parental authority (5th commandment), of sexual integrity (7th commandment), and of economic viability (8th and 10th commandment). Each of these central principles is then reinforced by other groups of laws and institutions.

Parental authority is buttressed by the penalties on cursing or striking a parent (Ex. 21:15, 17, cf. Deut. 27.15), and by the law which makes incorrigible profligacy on the part of a son an offence which parents may bring before the civil courts (Deut. 21:18-21). Parental authority is balanced, however, with responsibility – particularly the responsibility not to show favouritism or deprive a firstborn son within a polygamous family of his rights (Deut. 21:15-17).

Sexual integrity is buttressed by the prohibitions on marriage between certain degrees of kinship (Lev.18:6-18, 20:11-14, 19-21). These provided clear boundaries on sexual relations between the nuclear families living within the larger 'father's house'. Social and economic viability is buttressed by mechanisms to prevent families falling into serious economic decline, or to rescue them for a fresh start if they had done so. These include the following: the original division of land (Joshua 13 ff.); the law of inalienability (Lev. 25:23); the law of redemption and the year of Jubilee (Lev. 25:24-55). All these mechanisms preserved families as participating members in the economic and social community, and so preserved their place within the covenant community as well. In ancient Israel, kinship and land together played a major role in belonging within the covenant community. Loss or lack of either family or land or both created vulnerability.[8]

Since the Israelite family was the focus of covenant membership, it had significant functions in the judicial realm. It was also the prime vehicle for the teaching of the historical traditions and the requirements of the law (Deut. 6). Therefore, Israelite households were as socially inclusive as possible. The worship of Yahweh at the recurring annual festivals, or the triennial tithe, or at the grand reading of the law in the seventh year, drew together family members, the landless (Levites and aliens), the family-less (widows and orphans) and the lowliest of slaves (Deut. 14:27- 29; 16:11, 14; 29:10-12). The social and ethical duties of an Israelite family embraced the needy in the wider community. The Book of Ruth illustrates a number of these positive aspects of

[8] See Wright, 1990

the family in Israel, while also portraying some of the factors which could make people vulnerable.

Waldemar Janzen argues that what he calls 'the familial paradigm' was the dominant motif in the ethical consciousness of Israel. He lists the major components of the familial paradigm as the gift, the continuance and enhancement of life, the possession of land, as the prerequisite of familial viability, and the ethical imperative of hospitality – especially to those beyond the kinship boundaries.[9]

Family as context for covenant unfaithfulness and social collapse

The OT also describes serious conflict within key families, or acts of rebellion involving whole families, that disturbed the relationship between God and Israel. Examples worthy of note include: Aaron and Miriam opposing Moses (Num. 12); the rebellion of Korah, Dathan and Abiram and their families (Num 16); Achan's breaking of the rules of *herem* at Jericho (Josh. 7); the tragic divisions and violence that engulfed David's family in his later reign.

The strength of family loyalty could rival the primary covenant loyalty owed to Yahweh alone. Family ties could be a source of temptation to the worship of other gods – thus breaking the bond of Israel's covenantal monotheism. Marriage to non-Israelites was not prohibited on grounds of ethnic purity – Moses married a Cushite wife, and there is no condemnation of Elimelech's sons for marrying Moabite women, but rather clear approval of Boaz for marrying Ruth in kinsman duty in spite of her foreignness. Marriage with Canaanite women was prohibited on the grounds of the threat posed to Israel's covenant faith. Intermarriage would inevitably lead to the intrusion of other gods into family piety (Deut. 7:1-4). This was the undoing of Solomon (1 Kgs. 11:1-6), and the cause of the reforms of Nehemiah and Ezra (Ezra 9-10; Neh. 10:30, 13:23-27).

With immense realism and perception, Deuteronomy 13 anticipates that the temptation to go after other gods may come from within the bosom of one's closest family: 'your very own brother, or your son or daughter, or the wife you love, or your closest friend' (vs. 6-11). Even so, it is to be resisted with a steely firmness that puts loyalty to Yahweh alone above even such familial ties. This was a choice that Jesus himself faced, in the sense that when his family pressed him to return to his family responsibilities they were inadvertently drawing him away from obedience to the will of his Father. Jesus highlighted the stark nature of that choice when he re-defined his family in terms of those who put the will of his Father above all else (Matt. 12:46-50).

Perhaps the most ambiguous of all family-based institutions in the OT was the royal dynastic principle. The first time it emerges it is greeted with apparent shock and resistance. Gideon seems to reject dynastic monarchy as

[9] Janzen, 1994:26-54

incompatible with the theocratic rule of Yahweh (Jg. 8:22- 23). Yet the Hebrew narrator tells us that Gideon, for all his protests, behaved like a king – accepting a handsome reward in gold and taking many wives (contra Deut. 17:17). It was a son of Gideon who made the first attempt at monarchy, which included the ruthless murder of seventy other sons of Gideon – a less than promising start for the whole idea, which is accordingly shelved until the next book.

When the monarchy eventually did get established after Saul's disastrous 'reign', the dynastic principle is affirmed by Yahweh in his covenant promise to David (2 Sam. 7). This dynastic covenant becomes the foundation for Davidic rule in Jerusalem, and also for a messianic theology and eschatology which Christians are happy to endorse in the person of 'great David's greater Son'. Yet just as the patriarchal families were simultaneously models of faith and obedience, but also of horrific abuse and wickedness, so also the royal households of the two kingdoms of Judah and Israel display every horror known to any family: patricide, matricide, fratricide, suicide, adultery, murder, incest, conspiracy, intrigue, betrayal and vengeance – and some of these done in the name of the loyalty of one part of a family to another and reciprocal hatreds and feuds.

The Prophets

Championing the Family under Attack

The positive view of the family in the prophets is implied rather than expressed. They attacked current practices which destroyed families: socio-economic forces and judicial corruption that led to dispossession, poverty, debt and apparent loss of covenant inclusion. These dislocated and destroyed families, and threw ordinary people into material poverty and distress, but also into a kind of socio-religious limbo in relation to the covenant. Did they really belong any more? Were they not to be counted among 'the wicked' and 'cut off'? No, said Amos. The poor and dispossessed are 'the righteous', while those who prospered on the back of such oppression were 'the wicked'.[10]

Eschatological Vision – a 'Familied' Future

In several of the prophetic visions of the future messianic age, visions which usually include not only the restoration of God's people, their wholehearted obedience to God and enjoyment of his blessing, but also the renewal of creation and its abundance, the place of the family is prominent. The new creation described in Isaiah 65:17-25 will be a place in which families are safe from infant mortality or early death and the fruit of family labour will not be frustratingly swept away.

---

[10] See discussion in Wright, 1990:109

The Wisdom Tradition

Some scholars consider that the fundamental roots of OT wisdom literature lie in the familial soil of ancient Israel's tribal society. It is basically clan wisdom and lore. Although the social origins of this material are probably more complex than that, it is true that family relationships constitute one of the major concerns of the wise men and women of Israel.

Family as a Focus of Strong Moral Support

In Proverbs especially, family relationships are of paramount importance for those who desire to act wisely and live well. After the prologue, the opening advice reflects the fifth commandment about honouring parents (Prov. 1:8-9), and this is amplified again and again throughout the book. Similarly, reflecting the seventh commandment, the integrity of marriage is upheld vigorously against adultery (Prov. 2:16-19, 5:1-23, 7:1-27). In the case of adultery, the main warning is the disaster that adultery will bring upon one's own family not just from the social disgrace, but also from the loss of standing in the covenant community that would be the consequence of the loss of the family's substance (Prov. 5:9-14). In contrast, the book's climax is its praise of wisdom with a portrait, not of a model wise man, but of a model wise woman – the 'wife of noble character' in Proverbs 31:10-31. The description reflects not just on the woman herself, but is a window on some features of the ideal Israelite home and family: not only a place of blessing and security for husband and children, but also of hospitality and generosity for the needy.

But what if Family Fails

The OT wisdom literature also incorporates a kind of deconstruction of some of the strong and positive affirmations of the book of Proverbs, and of the idyllic portrayal of sexual love in marriage in the Song of Solomon.

1. Ecclesiastes explores the theory that wealth creation is a good thing because you can pass it on to your son and heir. But what if that heir is a fool who squanders it? And is it fair that he should get for free from your life of toil what he has not personally worked for? (Eccles. 2:18-23). To be a workaholic, with nobody to pass it on to, seems no better (Eccles. 4:7-8). Even if you believe it is good to accrue wealth to pass on, 'some misfortune' can rob you of it so that you depart as naked as you arrived and your heirs get nothing (Eccles. 5:13-15). The joys of marriage are all very well, and a gift of God, but do they really count for much in view of the death that awaits us all? (Eccles. 9:7-10). It seems that the author's experience of the other sex had not even had that mitigation (Eccles. 7:28).

2. Job raises even sharper questions in the midst of the experience of massive bereavement – the loss of his children, his wealth and his health. With pathetic nostalgia he recalls the status he had once had in the community (Job 29 – note vs. 5-6). This description matches the picture of the respected

husband in Proverbs 31:23 and the social security that comes from having a quiver-full of sons (Ps. 127:3-5). But what if you lose the whole lot – sons and substance? The social reality is painted graphically by Job in chapter 30 – disgrace, contempt, marginalizing. Would such loss expose Job's piety as a mere pretence which would not be sustained once he lost his goods? Or would Job prove that his faith in God was truly located in God, not merely in the abundant family and fortune God had entrusted to him? Even through the darkness of God's hiddenness and silence, Job maintained his integrity under the pressure of the accusations of his friends and his own agonized protests, preserved his faith in God and was finally commended.

Job forces us to ask hard questions about the blessings of family, health, and abundance. If they become our security in themselves, then they rapidly become idolatrous and we are vulnerable in times of loss. Perhaps this very thought lies behind Psalm 127 – the same Psalm which celebrates children as a heritage and a reward from Yahweh. 'Unless the Lord build the house, its builders labour in vain' – a sentence which in Hebrew as in English has a double entendre: literal house-building, and the building of a family. For all your genealogy and ancestry, where does your true identity come from? For all your family heritage in persons and property, where does your real security come from?

The Gospels

In the NT we find the same dual treatment of the family, rendered even more sharply defined by the claims of Christ, the demands of the kingdom of God and the eschatological era which has now begun in Christ and in which we meantime live. A very helpful survey of the different perspectives on the family to be found in each of the gospels has been published elsewhere,[11] so only a brief survey is needed here.

Jesus' Affirmation of Family

Positive appreciation of the family includes the following: 1. The narratives of Jesus' own birth and childhood in Matthew and Luke, particularly the latter who emphasizes the role of Mary, mother of Jesus, both in his gospel narrative and at the beginning of Acts (1:14). Luke preserves the ambivalent narrative of Jesus as a boy in the temple, an action in which he seems to put his heavenly Father's house or business above his parents' anxiety, but immediately follows it with the observation that as he grew up in Nazareth, Jesus was obedient to his earthly parents (Lk. 2:49-51). 2. Jesus' presence at the wedding in Cana, and his remarkable gift to the couple in their embarrassment (Jn. 2). 3. His strong affirmation of marriage in his teaching on divorce (Mk. 10:2-12; Matt. 5:31-32; 19:1-9). 4. His affirmation of the fifth commandment's duty to parents in

[11] Barton, 1992:226-229

rebuke to those who had sought to evade it under a cloak of piety (the Corban issue, Mk. 7:9-13; Matt. 15:3-6). 5. Many of the healing miracles of Jesus were compassionate responses to the family members of those who implored him on their behalf e.g. especially children, Simon's mother-in-law. And even on the cross his compassion for his mother overrides his own agony for a moment (Jn. 19:26-27)

Jesus' Relativizing of the Family

On the other hand, the gospels show that following Jesus meant a radical reassessment of family ties and could inject serious disruption into the sphere of family and household. Mark shows Jesus calling his first disciples who promptly left their family businesses, including their father, and followed him – an act often portrayed as an admirably radical commitment which we should be willing to emulate, but which would have been scandalous in the social perception at the time. The breaking in of the kingdom of God in his own person meant, for Jesus, subordinating his own family to the imperative of proclaiming the kingdom. Likewise all who follow him must put the kingdom of God above all else, including even family duties where necessary. Indications of this priority include the following:

1. His words to his mother and brothers, distancing himself from their demands and identifying his true family as those who do the will of God (Mk. 3:31-35).
2. His reply to the would-be disciple who wanted first to go and bury his father: 'let the dead bury their dead' (Lk. 29:59-60).
3. Jesus required that, in comparison with love for Jesus, the disciple's love for his parents and family must be regarded as hatred – a characteristic form of Hebrew hyperbole or comparative negation (Matt. 10:37; Lk. 14:25- 26).
4. Such radical detachment from family commitments and securities for the sake of Christ and the kingdom of God, however, would find compensation in a whole new experience of 'family' – the family of God in Christ. (Matt. 19:29).

Acts and Epistles

It was the experience of the early church that the new 'family' in Christ, in its spiritual fellowship and its social and material expression, could replace the loss of natural family securities resulting from a profession of loyalty to Christ. Yet the early Christian movement did not set itself against the normal forms of family life in society, but sought to sustain and redeem them under the Lordship of Christ. Thus again, we have a dual dimension to the way the family is viewed in the early Christian church.

Church as Family

The NT church made prominent use of the family metaphor for the church itself, drawing on both the Graeco-Roman social institution of the *oikos*, and the OT Jewish background of the *bet-'ab*, as described above.[12] In relation to the latter, the church family provided a number of functions comparable to those provided for individual Israelites by the household and kinship network: a place of identity, security and inclusion; a structure of authority; and a context for worship, teaching and nurture. Other familial metaphors include the language of adoption to describe our new relationship with God, and the awareness that all Christians are now brothers and sisters in Christ.

In addition to this metaphorical understanding of the Christian community, there was also the empirical fact that actual households provided natural contexts for evangelism (e.g. the conversion stories of Lydia and the Philippian jailer), baptism (1 Cor. 1:16), and church meetings (Rom. 16:3-4,10-11). This is the social as well as spiritual context for Paul's teaching on appropriate sexual ethics within families (1 Cor. 5), and the demands of Christian behaviour within households – spouses, parents, children, and slaves (Eph. 5:22-6.9; Cor. 3:18-4.1).

Family as a Place of Pain and Divided Loyalties

Jesus' warning that loyalty to himself would create divisions came true very quickly. The gospel injects a conflict of loyalties into any situation where people have existing commitments to one another which are disturbed by someone's new commitment to Christ. 'Christian belonging was not necessarily conducive to strong family ties and a happy family life.'[13]

The clearest indication of this is in the area of marriage, where one partner becomes a Christian and the other remains unconverted. The matter is addressed both by Paul (1 Cor. 7), and Peter (1 Pet. 3:1-6). However the eschatological new age brings new priorities, affecting all human concerns including the family. Paul offers a radical relativizing of everything that we normally attach such weight to: marriage, family bereavements and joys, purchased possessions and business deals. All such things have their rightful place in God's created order. But all of them, including the family bonds which God himself instituted, must be held lightly in comparison with the urgency of the times. 'For this world in its present form is passing away' (1 Cor. 7:29-31).

---

[12] See further in Wright, 1992b: 768-769

[13] Barton, 1992:226

Redeeming the South Asian Family: Mission as Extending the Household of God[1]

Charles Hoole

Dr. Charles Hoole was Principal of Baldaeus Theological College at Trincomalee, Sri Lanka

Joint-Family in Transition

Major changes in the pattern of family life in the Indian sub-continent can be traced back to the advent of British colonial rule. Structurally there was a change from the joint to the nuclear family; culturally, the change usually included westernization. The most affected groups were the urban middle classes and the industrial proletariat. Geographically, the process was unevenly distributed and is confined almost wholly to urban areas or provinces which have been subject to intensive industrial development. Such changes to some extent are, of course, inevitable. The joint-family system is efficient to the degree that well-defined duties are learnt by the emulation of elders living in close proximity. The younger gènerations gradually fill these positions in the corporate function of the family unit without anxiety, resentment or revolt. But once the chain of occupational uniformity is broken and a young man learns a new job through training outside the home and caste, stress is felt and the system loses both its *raison d'etre* and its efficiency. Where individuals from a joint-family background have had the chance of higher education and increased mobility, these have given the initial psychological impetus: a sense of individuality with a desire for greater independence. In turn this greater degree of individual liberty fosters the desire for a higher standard of living. But these changes in the pattern of family life should not be exaggerated. All too often social historians accustomed to western models confidently forecast the inevitable destruction of the extended-kinship system (joint-family and caste) by economic change. Social predictions of this kind are however based on superficial observations. In South Asia the nuclear families living in urban areas often maintain close kinship ties with the original joint-family, usually

---

[1] Hoole, 2002:37-41

located at some distance from the city in the ancestral village.[2] Recent evidence shows that despite modernization the traditional family structures remain deeply entrenched in South Asian life. In the changing cultural landscape of today, the western nuclear family system exists alongside the traditional extended family, including the joint-family system. So far there is no indication that the latter will gradually disappear. In this respect it is remarkable that the kinship network among South Asians settled in a western metropolis such as London, New York, Los Angeles, Toronto and Sydney remains intact, notwithstanding the inevitable strain in kinship ties.

Joint-family in tradition

In South Asia, as in much of Asia, the family and kinship ties have an importance far beyond that to which the West is accustomed. This is a fact of great relevance to many aspects of social life in the sub-continent. It partially masks unemployment, profoundly affects personal attitudes towards authority and individual initiative. These are only some of the by-products of family life in South Asia. In the Indian sub-continent the individual is thought of always in a family setting. Contacts are maintained with kin far beyond the immediate family, and some obligation is owed even to distant kin. The kinship group[3] often has a closeness almost as great as that of the average western family, while the family units within it have a closeness inconceivable in the West. The ideal family consists not just of a man and his wife and children, but rather of a larger patriarchal 'joint-family' in which sons bring their wives to a paternal home and rear their children within it. Sometimes, the joint-family also includes married grandsons and their wives and children. Whatever their size, the family groups used to live together under a single roof, sharing a common hearth. They held in common all the family property and often worked together at a common undertaking whether agriculture, a craft, or business. By the efforts of those who were able and energetic, the old and infirm members of the family were supported. The group respected the authority of the elders in general, but of the oldest male in particular, who was traditionally authoritarian. It was he who made many of the decisions regarding the lives of family members. The eldest woman in the household if wise and strong, often gained considerable authority over time, and, in any event, could control the women. Within this system, a marriage is regarded not so much as a union between two

---

[2] Singer, 1972. The extended family's tremendous capacity to adapt to the changing milieu can be readily evidenced in the life of 100,000 Jaffna Tamil expatriates settled in Greater Toronto. Individual apartment blocks are dominated by extended families, and some prominent villages have been transplanted into neighbourhood apartments. Consequently, traditional village identities, rivalries, turf warfare, have continued in a western setting.

[3] *Contakkarara* is a key concept in Tamil social life.

individuals as the establishment of a relationship between two families. It is arranged after long negotiations between the parents of the prospective bride and groom, during which horoscopes would be exchanged and agreement upon financial terms concluded. A recent innovation has been to permit the prospective couple to have a brief glimpse of each other and allow them to veto the match.

Women in the family

The position of women deserves special comment because it is one of the key factors that continue to buttress the traditional family. Until the arrival of the modern Protestant mission the legal and social position of women appeared extremely low. Polygamy, child marriage, *sati*,[4] female infanticide, the low status of widows and *purdah* seclusion were customary. The *purdah*, although introduced to India by the Muslim conquerors, became widely accepted because it coincided to a great extent with the increasing tendency of the Hindu family and caste system to seclude their women. In fact the custom of *purdah* seclusion has been adopted by many local Brethren and Pentecostal type of churches.[5] The status of women in South Asia is related to Hindu belief. The Laws of Manu which became the canon law of Hinduism, declares that 'a woman must never be independent': In childhood a female must be subject to her father, in youth to her husband, when her lord is dead to her sons. Women, who like the goddess are feared, must like the goddess be kept under male control. Through male control and her own chastity, the Hindu woman controls her dangerous sacred powers[6] and is able to use them for the benefit of the family. There is strong evidence that the attribution of sacred powers to women derives from the beliefs and practices of the indigenous peoples of India and images of sacred femininity are prevalent in the earliest Tamil literature.[7] The attribution of sacred powers to the Indian woman must be baffling to the western observer because, of all the women in the world, Indian women appear to many westerners to be among the most powerless. Furthermore, the scriptural view that an Indian woman must regard her husband as a god and regard herself as a servant, *sudra*, seem to contradict the concept of *sakti*, implying that women have power, that they are *sakti*-filled. However, this

---

[4] The custom of *sati* was practiced only in North India.

[5] Pastor Muralee, one of its spokesmen in Sri Lanka passionately argues that this Hindu-Muslim custom is also biblical.

[6] *Anangu sakti*, in the classical Tamil tradition.

[7] Hart, 1973:233- 250. Beneficent or terrible powers are available from the self-denying action of chastity. This is the central theme of the Tamil epic *Cilappatikaram*, in which the chaste heroine wreaks vengeance for her (unchaste) husband. With her *sakti*, she destroys the city of Madurai whose king has allowed injustice to take place by wrongly executing her husband.

contradiction between subordination and power may be explained with reference to the Tamil culture, which expresses this contrast in terms of *akam* (inner) and *puram* (outer). The contrast forms a major division in ancient Tamil poetry.[8] As applied to women the contrast is between inner chastity and outer modesty and shyness. Inner chastity is an immanent, unobservable force related to *sakti*. Based on this distinction, Jaffna Tamil culture views women as inwardly powerful and outwardly enslaved. These ideological representations call attention to a contrast between expected public behaviour (public submission of females) and expected private behaviour (private covert power wielded by women). All this evidence shows that the women of South Asia despite their low social status, do wield considerable influence particularly at home. For it is central to Indian thought that power is acquired through suffering and servitude, i.e., through certain forms of self-denial and sacrifice.[9] Alluding to the great influence of the woman at home, the well known Indian Christian leader and missionary in Sri Lanka, Christian David, is reported to have once said that the conversion of one woman is of more importance than that of six men.[10] Following his advice the nineteenth century missions made great strides in the training of women, and it resulted in strong churches being established.

Plurality of families

The idea of the joint-family can often give the impression that the traditional South Asian family is of one type. But in actual fact the concept of the joint-family has historically embraced a tremendous variety of marriages and families. Plural marriages, such as polygyny, polyandry and polygamy have been widely accepted in Sri Lanka. Divorce was considered very flexible. In the up-country Kandyan kingdom both women and men commonly wed four or five times before they settled into a long term relationship.[11] If they have had children prior to divorce, when they part the Common Law allocates the males to the man, and the females to the woman. The co-existence of such diverse marriage and family practices is of course integral to the caste system. For caste morality recognizes no universal morality equally applicable to all human groups; it is based on the assumption that humanity is composed of groups of different nature (*guna*) and status. There are thus differences in the social-moral codes of different castes. This has led to a multiplicity of behavioural patterns in South Asian society and the acceptance of the concept of relativity in moral

---

8 Ramanujan, 1970

9 Bhakti tradition shows that tears have power to melt another's heart. Women are regarded as inherently more religious than men, because they have naturally this power of feeling (*unarcchi*), which enables them to wield power over others.

10 Hoole, 1995:250

11 Knox, 1981:93-93

standards. Caste morality is, therefore, strongly opposed to the Christian view of marriage and family, for it maintains that different forms of marriage, such as monogamy, polygamy and polyandry can be considered equally legitimate under appropriate social conditions.[12]

Extended family of God

The Bible reveals that God is concerned for the family and, therefore, in his redemptive work the church becomes a close-knit family of God. At the same time the biblical idea of family is close to the South Asian extended family. The modern western notion of family as consisting of father, mother and children is somewhat alien to the Bible. In the NT, family (Gk. *patria*) is mentioned as such only three times, although the related idea of house or household (Gk. *oikos, oikia*) occurs more frequently. Importantly, the church itself is thought of as the household of God (Eph. 2:19) or the household of faith (Gal. 6:10). The meeting places of the Pauline groups, and probably of most other early Christian groups, were private houses. In four places in the Pauline letters specific congregations are designated by the phrase, '*te kat' oikon auton ekklesia*', 'the church that meets at their house' (Rom. 16:5; 1 Cor. 16:19; Philem. 2; Col. 4:15). An intimate connection with existing households is also suggested by 1 Cor. 1:16, where Paul says he baptized 'the household of Stephanas', and later in the same letter (16:15 f.), where he commends the Stephanas household (*oikia*) as the 'first converts in Achaia' who have 'devoted themselves to the service of the saints'. The conversion of a person with all his or her household is mentioned several times in Acts as well.[13] We hear, too, of Christians in the household of Chloe (1 Cor. 1:11), and even in the household of Caesar (Phil. 4:22). All these passages show that the local structure of the early Christian groups was thus linked with what was commonly regarded as the basic unit of the society. The phrase *kat' oikon* does not designate merely the place where the *ekklesia* met, although the commonest English translation is 'the church in their house'. For that, *en oiko* would be the more natural expression (see 1 Cor. 11:34; 14:35). Rather, Paul probably uses *kat' oikon* to distinguish these individual household-based groups from the whole church, which could also assemble on occasion (1 Cor. 14:23; Rom. 16:23; 1 Cor. 11:20). The *kat' oikon ekklesia* is thus the basic cell of the Christian movement, and its nucleus was often an existing household. The household was, as stated earlier, much broader than the family in modern western societies, including not only immediate relatives but also slaves, freedmen, hired workers and sometimes tenants and partners in trade. However, the *kat' oikon ekklesia* was not co-terminous with the household. New converts would certainly have been

---

[12] See Hoole, 1995:39

[13] Acts 16:15 Lydia; 16:31-34, Philippian jailer; 18:8, Crispus). It has its antecedents in the OT, cf. Gen.7:1.

added to existing household communities. Furthermore, not every member of a household always became a Christian even when its head did, as the case of Onesimus shows. The relation of the Christian groups to the household had certain implications for the way we conceive of the Pauline mission. If the existing household was the basic cell of the mission, then it also afforded the motivational base for becoming part of the *ekklesia*. On occasion, a household became Christian more or less *en bloc*. Furthermore, the household base ensured that the church would not become a ghetto, for it directly linked the church to an existing network of relationships, both internal kinship ties and external ties of friendship and occupation. It needs to be appreciated that such an approach to mission risked compromising the gospel because the traditional structure of *oikos* was hierarchical, structured by superior and inferior roles. Pauline Christian groups were on the other hand anti-hierarchical, based on egalitarian beliefs and attitudes (cf. Gal. 3:27-28). In the Pauline mission, therefore, we see a fruitful dialectic between 'structure and anti-structure' that Victor Turner describes, and which appears again and again in the tensions addressed by the Pauline letters (1 Cor. 12:13; 1 Cor. 11:2-16). To exist in creative tension, the *ekklesia* in the house had to maintain a high level of cohesion and group identity, while being made aware that they belonged to a larger movement (1 Cor. 1:2). These features in the Pauline groups are exhibited in the regular use of terms like brother and sister, the emphasis on mutual love, and the prominent role accorded to the Spirit and its gifts (*charismata*), which result in spontaneous actions by members of the community (*communitas*). In the end the Pauline mission based in the household proved to be highly successful. Without the Christian mission the contemporary closely structured, hierarchical society would have probably collapsed, plunging the Greco-Roman empire into much turmoil and uncertainty. However, by taking the existing extended family as the base cell of the mission, the church was effective in redeeming a collapsing world, by transforming the kinship, trade and neighbourly relationships integral to the household.

Redeeming the South Asian family

As everywhere in the world where industrial urbanization occurs, the interdependence and comparatively well-defined duties of traditional South Asian family life, following an immemorial pattern, tends to break down, to be replaced by nervousness, restlessness and a sullen feeling of a world devoid of love. The caste-group oriented individual finds little stimulus to develop consistent personal integrity and sincerity. In compensation, there is a widespread tendency among the disenchanted to project on individual charismatic figures[14] the role of the authoritative and sheltering parent in a

[14] Usually religions and political leaders, movie and sports stars.

relationship of dependence; such an attachment cannot, under normal day-to-day conditions, be other than precarious. If the old kinship structure is to be redeemed, then the gospel must be allowed to impact on the extended family, whereby the individual is able to participate in the new humanity of Christ. Such participation unleashes a process of re-socialization by which individuals are adopted as God's children and thus received into a new family of brothers and sisters. This process involves breaking with the past, the caste and joint-family structures and the integration into the new family. In the language of baptismal ritual, those who have been 'baptized into Christ' or 'into one body' have 'put on Christ' or the 'new human' (Gal. 3:28; 1 Cor. 12:13; Col. 3:11). In the Indian sub-continent, this particular experiment is not altogether new. In the early nineteenth century when the caste and joint-family institutions were all-powerful the Protestant pioneers used the mission compounds to construct the new human family, which functioned as an egalitarian *communitas*, existing parallel to the traditional hierarchical society. In the new community, the missionary patrons were addressed as *amma* (mum) and *Iyah* (dad), while the other members were referred to as *anna* (elder brother), *acca* (elder sister), etc. During this period marriages of members were arranged by the missionaries, and even a customary dowry was given for the bride.[15] But the social context of mission has changed a great deal in the last two centuries. The forbidding wall around the traditional *oikon* has all but collapsed; there is, therefore, a new opportunity to build the *ekklesia* in the *oikon*, which ought to become the basic cell of the Christian movement in the twenty-first century.

[15] American missions gave £4-10s for the purchase of dress and ornaments.

Family and Faith[1]

Ida Glaser and David Zac Niringiye

Dr. Ida Glaser is Senior Teaching and Research Fellow based in Oxford, U.K. and Rt. Rev. Dr. David Zac Niringiye is Assistant Bishop of Kampala, Uganda

Jesus said: 'If anyone comes to me and does not hate his father and mother, his wife and children, his brothers and sister – yes, even his own life – he cannot be my disciple' (Luke 14:26). The false witnesses said: 'This fellow never stops speaking against this holy place and against the law. For we have heard him say that this Jesus of Nazareth will destroy this place and change the customs Moses handed down to us' (Acts 6:13-14).

Jesus, say the religious people, is a threat to community stability. For different reasons, says Jesus, they are right: following him will divide families. Those who oppose the spread of the gospel often do so because it threatens to divide families, disrupt communities and change cultures; and they have discerned rightly. It is true that Christians wish to build up family life; but it is also true that the gospel offers one of the deepest challenges to all community loyalties, because it calls to a community and a loyalty that supersedes all. Because of this, the good creation of the family, the basic building block of community, can also be one of the greatest challenges to Christian discipleship: it can function as an idolatrous alternative to the kingdom of God. This paper explores this tension first by considering its basis, and then by reflecting theologically on various practical challenges to today's church.

The basis for the tension

There is a fundamental link between family and faith. Traditionally, the family is the place of transmission of faith; and faith is the major means of transmission of the family tradition. Depending on the particular faith and culture, continuity of faith can also ensure continuation of property and prosperity, name and honour, and respect for forbears. This means that continuation of faith is the basis of the family and, therefore, of community security. This is widely recognised in our world. Two phrases common in

[1] Glaser & *Niringiye,* 2002:23-33

current western discourse are 'religious tradition' and 'faith community'. Such language acknowledges that religion, tradition, faith and community are inter-linked; but it also suggests that they are co-extensive. This is even the basis of part of the 1981 'Declaration of elimination of all forms of intolerance and discrimination based on religion or belief' of the United Nations Commission on Human Rights, that bastion of concern for individuals. On the one hand, each individual is said to have the right to self-determination in matters of faith: on the other hand, the family has the right to determine its children's induction into faith. The questions then are: What 'community' is the 'faith community'? How does it relate to the family? What happens if the child wishes to reject the faith or tradition of the parents?

Biblical families

The Bible does not have either Greek or Hebrew words that translate exactly the English word 'family'. Rather, it has words that imply household or kin, or sometimes both.[2] We will find it useful to distinguish these two concepts: the *household* might include people who are not kin (e.g. slaves). It is the socio-economic group that lives together, interacts together and provides for the welfare of its members. It is the place of responsibility, protection and nurture; *Kin* (who can be called 'house'!) can include anything from close relations to a whole clan related to a particular (male) ancestor – what we might call an 'ethnic group'. Eventually, all human beings are kin, being descended from Noah and thus from Adam. Kinship provides identity, continuity, and history. It is the place of belonging into which one is born and which cannot, therefore, be changed; although marriage creates new kinship relationships. The Bible affirms the family as a primary characteristic of human beings made in the image of God. But that which has potential for good also has potential for evil, and Genesis indicates the disruption of the family as a major result of the fall.[3] This means that the family can be opposed to God, and God can, therefore, be opposed to the family.

In Genesis 11, God himself disrupts the kin descended from Noah. The reason is that, rather than worshipping God, they are working together to use religion to establish their own name. I would describe this as turning the group into an idol. It is into this situation that God calls, not Abram as an individual, but Abram as the father of a family.[4] He is to reverse the sin of Babel: far from Abram building a faith which will establish his family and its name, God will build a family that will embody his mission and carry his name. The primary purpose of the family-faith link is neither the establishment of the family nor

[2] See C.J.H. Wright's paper above

[3] See C.J.H. Wright's paper.

[4] This is evident even from his name. 'Abram' means 'exalted father', and the new name, 'Abraham', given in Genesis 17:5, means 'father of a multitude'.

the propagation of a faith but the mission of God; and, since God works according to his own creation, his mission is in, through and to human beings, it is expressed through the creation of groupings of families.

This divine mission has, necessarily, a human, socio-economic expression. As in the surrounding nations, the kinship network and the community of faith are generally assumed to be co-extensive. However, as the OT story unfolds, it becomes increasingly clear that kinship with Abraham and membership of the household of Israel does not guarantee participation in Israel's faith. Further, as the story of Ruth indicates, it is possible to cross from one household of faith to another household, of another faith. And, as in the story of Naaman, it is also possible to live in one household while holding to the faith of another. Faith and family are not, in fact, co-extensive, and we begin to wonder whether they should be.

This becomes more evident when we move to the NT, where it is underlined that kinship is no guarantor of faith. Rather, the language of kin is most often used to describe the kingdom of God. God is the Father, and Jesus is the firstborn Son. Believers are God's children, by rebirth and/or adoption, and speak of each other as siblings. It is even possible to call Jesus brother. It seems then that when we enrol in God's kingdom, we enter a new kinship network, which we will call the kingdom family. This is not only a family under God's rule, but a family of which God is a member. God is, we might say, the member – it is not only that he is the source of fatherhood or that he defines what fatherhood is (Eph 3:14-15), but that he is in fact the Father within this family. The language of household as well as of kinship is used to describe Christian relationships (Eph 2:19-22, Heb 3:1-6). Not only do we join a new kinship network as believers: we also have a new place to belong, under new management, and with a new purpose. Being 'born again' gives us a whole new identity, which looks towards its fulfilment in heaven. What then of previous loyalties? Some of the 'family' language of the NT is used to indicate that *ethnic loyalties are transcended by kingdom loyalties*.

In particular, the pictures explored above re-appropriate aspects of Israel to the new, trans-ethnic kingdom. The Messiah inaugurates an inclusive people! One of the tensions here is that the ethnic group – the kinship of Abraham – had its own *traditions*. These were challenged not only by the inclusion of people from different ethnic groups, but also by Jesus' insistence that the needs of individuals be put before a faith tradition. The religious leaders also saw the threat to the people in terms of threat to their own authority. We might say that tradition and authority together guarantee the continuation of the community. Where the kingdom family offers both a higher authority and a choice of tradition, tensions will inevitably arise with the natural community and, therefore, within the extended families of which it is built. This takes us to Jesus' statement quoted at the start of this paper: 'If anyone comes to me and does not hate his father and mother, his wife and children, his brothers and sister – yes, even his own life – he cannot be my disciple' (Luke 14:26). It is not only ethnic loyalties, but also family loyalties in the narrower sense that are transcended by the kingdom family. The question is, 'In what sense are they transcended? What are our continuing responsibilities to kin and household?' While Jesus repeatedly makes it clear that loyalty to him should take precedence over loyalty to the family,[5] he also offers interpretations of the law that intensify the call to family commitment,[6] and his various healings of sons, daughters and servants as well as Peter's mother-in-law affirm the importance of the family.

Similarly, Paul, whilst affirming singleness for the sake of the gospel, also insists on marital faithfulness, filial obedience, family responsibility and household order. A superficial reading might suggest contradiction here. Deeper consideration would suggest that, although the kingdom family must transcend the natural family, it does not negate it. Rather, the kingdom affirms and seeks to restore all that is good in God's creation: the problem is that, as we have seen, the natural family is fallen, and is, therefore, likely to be rejected in the kingdom. Add to this the centrality of the family in creation and its tendency to become an idol, and the family can become the single greatest challenge to the kingdom. Even where the family affirms the kingdom, it can be that this very good gift of God can be given precedence over specific calls to service and the cross. This is why faith in Christ is not only the way to healthy families: it also has the potential to disrupt families (Matt 10:34-36). As the family stories of Genesis show,[7] we can see that families can be disrupted through faith when 1) People break faith with God and therefore break faith with each other; 2) A family member is ejected from the family because he/she has broken the faith; 3) Someone has to leave the household in order to obey the call of God; 4) Someone leaves a household because he/she does not share its vision of faith; 5) People within the family react sinfully to God's particular choice; 6) A marriage is made outside the faith/tradition/ ethnic group.

A Contrasting Model

Family tensions arise in the above cases not only because family members have different faith commitments, but also because different faiths have different views of families. The contrast with one other faith will assist our understanding of Christian views of the family; it will also clarify some of our family/faith tensions in a particular context. Here is the Qur'anic story from which I started my reflections for this paper:

> So the Ark floated with them on the waves (towering) like mountains, and Noah called out to his son, who had separated himself (from the rest): 'O my son!

[5] From Matthew alone, we could cite 4:22, 8:21-2, 10:34-9, 12:46-50, 19:16-30.
[6] E.g. Matt. 5:27-32, 15:1-6, 19:1-9.
[7] See C.J.H. Wright's paper.

> Embark with us, and be not with the unbelievers!' The son replied: 'I will betake myself to some mountain; it will save me from the water.' Noah said: 'This day nothing can save, from the command of Allah, any but those on whom he hath mercy!' And the waves came between them, and the son was among those overwhelmed in the flood. Then the word went forth: 'O earth! Swallow up thy water, and O sky! Withhold (thy rain)!' And the water abated, and the matter was ended. The Ark rested on Mount Judi, and the word went forth: 'Away with those who do wrong!' And Noah called upon his Lord, and said: 'O my Lord! Surely my son is of my family! And thy promise is true, and thou art the Justest of Judges!' He said: 'O Noah! He is not of thy family; for his conduct is unrighteous, so ask not of me that of which thou hast no knowledge! I give thee counsel, lest thou act like the ignorant!' Noah said: 'O my Lord! I do seek refuge with thee, lest I ask for that of which I have no knowledge, and unless thou forgive me and have mercy on me, I should indeed be lost!' (Surah 11:42-47).

Biblical covenants are with families; and God perseveres with these families despite the sin that mars them. Qur'anic covenants are different: they are not unbreakable relationships with whole groups of people, but agreements to follow the guidance of God.[8] The story of Noah's drowned son signals that faith comes before the family: the one who chooses disobedience is not only excluded from the Ark, but also from the family. However, this does not mean that families are less important to Muslims than to Christians. It can mean the opposite. Because the Muslim family is the building block of the Muslim community, its preservation is essential to the security of the community; and because leaving the faith implies leaving the family, it is the more important that people remain Muslim as well as within the family. Strong families are, therefore, not only important to Muslims because of their essential humanity and because of the traditional cultures from which they usually come, but also because of the nature of Islam. There are several contributing factors here:

1. Islam, like Judaism, is something into which one is born: members of Muslim families are Muslims unless they deliberately choose to leave the faith. In fact, Islam teaches that all human beings are born Muslim – with a natural acceptance of God's lordship and laws. Christians believe in original sin rather than original submission to God, and therefore recognise that each family member needs to *choose to appropriate* the faith. Any Christian family lives with the possibility that some members might choose otherwise. For Muslim

---

[8] The difference in ideas of covenant are reflected in Christian and Muslim views of marriage: while Christians think of marriage as an irreversible covenant relationship between two people, Islamic marriage is essentially a contractual agreement. It does not fundamentally change the two people involved – the woman does not usually change her name, and her property is legally separated from that of her husband – and it can be terminated. Muhammad even approved marriage contracts of specified duration, for example, for soldiers who wanted partners while away from home. Such marriages are still approved in Shi'ite law.

families, that some might deliberately choose against Islam is generally unthinkable.

2. The Muslim community – *ummah* – is not a mystical fellowship of believers but a socio-political entity that lives by the laws of God. Turning from Islam is, therefore, a threat to the security of the state. The family feels implicated by the defection of one of its members, which also brings shame on the family.

3. Islamic law covers not only what might be conceived as 'religious' and 'civil' laws, but also many aspects of cultural tradition. This means that the maintenance of tradition and the maintenance of faith effectively coincide. Turning from Islam is, therefore, a threat to the family tradition.

4. Islamic law also covers family relationships, rights and responsibilities, including marriage and divorce, inheritance rights and guardianship of children. Turning from Islam therefore threatens family structure and stability. Underlying all this are different views of the nature of God and of human beings. In Christian thinking, family reflects the very nature of God: in orthodox Islamic thinking, it is blasphemy to suggest that anyone or anything is like God. Of course, Christian families and other families share many of the characteristics of Muslim families mentioned above.

The links between family and faith, community and tradition are common human traits. However, as we have seen, for Christians, such natural expressions of family are secondary to its rooting in the image of God. Genesis 1:26-8 tells us that family is the first consequence of our being made in that image. The Bible continues to describe people and events through relatedness: genealogies are one of the important ways of structuring and relating history. Muslims would agree that we are in families because of creation, but would not see human relatedness as reflecting divine relatedness – either relationship within God or relationship between us and God.[9] These ideas of God being part of our families, and of us being part of his, should make Christian thinking about the family and faith radically different.

Practicalities

We are now ready to explore some of the theological principles raised by particular family-faith tensions. We will look at these in the context of Christian faith and other faiths, but recognise that similar tensions can also arise relative to different traditions within Christianity.

Challenge 1: An unbelieving member of a believing family

Moses' call to the Levites to place loyalty to God above family affection (Ex. 32:26-29), and the law on disrespect to parents in Leviticus 20:9, raise the

[9] There are exceptions here. For example, Sufi poetry uses the language of lover and beloved to describe the believer's longing for God.

question of the unbelieving family member. If faith in Christ supersedes family loyalties, should we then regard those who turn from him as no longer members of our families? Should we see ourselves as responsible for disciplining or even killing them? Our answers will be based on our perceptions of the necessity of relatedness, the basis of family security, and the position of God relative to the family. The biblical Noah is saved from the flood with all his family, including the sinful son who will later receive his father's curse. The Qur'anic story has an unbelieving son drowned in the flood, and his father rebuked for pleading for his salvation. This raises two issues: 1. *The eternal welfare of the individual.* Both the Bible and the Qur'an recognise the eternal consequences of unbelief: membership of a believing family is not sufficient for salvation. If someone chooses to turn from the faith, they will come under judgement. This Qur'anic story might suggest that they are beyond even prayer. 2. *The temporal response of the family.* Both the Bible and the Qur'an also recognise the question of how the family should respond to the unbelieving member. Technically, Islamic law requires the death sentence for apostates – those who turn from Islam and are seen as its enemies. Interpretation and practice varies greatly here, but families often feel responsible to discipline or reject a convert. Christians have reacted, in various ways to family members who turn from Christ. There have been times when death has been the public penalty for those considered heretics, even if they still professed to be Christian. At the other end of the scale, in the twenty-first century West, the right of the individual to determine his or her own identity and belief is inviolable, and most Christians would concur with this ideal. The question is, should Christians take similar positions to Muslims on this? What will be best for the family and the individual? Even, should we encourage people from other faiths to disrupt their families by turning to Christ?

Case 1a: A member of a Christian family becomes a Muslim: Disloyalty to parents is punished so severely in the OT, the Levites had to kill their faithless brethren, and Islam is so uncompromising over apostasy for one reason: the link between faith and community. The faith needs to be kept in order for the community to be kept. In the Islamic case, the legislation is rooted in the need to establish the Islamic state in Medina, where apostasy was treason. In a different way, Jewish thinking developed the idea of keeping the community pure. It was the holiness of the community that reflected the holiness of God, and it was important to preserve this pure community as God's people. In practice, family honour may be even more important than these community considerations: it is shameful for one's child to leave the faith, and, at least in the case of Islam, the honour of the whole Muslim community can be at stake. The question then is, as Christians, do we need to defend the community in the same way? Do we need to ensure family honour or purity of faith or even continuity of the faith community and tradition by expelling the miscreant? I want to suggest that the answer is 'No!', because: There is nothing that can destroy our relatedness; our family security is not our major concern; God, as the Father within our families, is the One who is ultimately responsible for their welfare.

One apparently relevant NT passage is the discussion of 'handing this (apostate) over to Satan' in 1 Cor. 5:1-13, but it implies expulsion from the church rather than from the family – although it is also possible that this was a household church. Further, this is not for turning to another faith, but for overt sexual immorality; and it is not for the sake of the church, but for the sake of the offender. The church's problem is not a threat to community but a scandalous sin: its concern is to be for its witness rather than its security. Perhaps more relevant is the challenge to concerns for community purity in the parables of Luke 15. They are usually taken to be about God's concern for the lost, but they are told in the context of religious people criticising Jesus for welcoming non-religious people – the concern is not primarily who God accepts, but who a believer can welcome. Jesus did not have a house, but he had, in effect, a household – the group of people who travelled with him, so maybe we can think of his 'welcoming sinners and eating with them' (v.2) as affording them the hospitality of his household.

We can then read the prodigal son story as the story of a believing household, from which one son defects. The father does not disown him or seek to harm him – he recognises that he is in effect 'dead' to the family (v.32), but this is by his own choice and actions and not because his father has rejected him. The father does not, as might some religious Jews today, say the funeral rites and disown him. Rather, he waits for him, and is ready to welcome him home. In his view, he is still his son, however prodigal. The story goes on to show that the apparently believing son was no better than the prodigal – perhaps he was worse. Kinship cannot be destroyed even by leaving a household, while remaining within a faith community is no guarantee of salvation. The picture of God as Father is also relevant – it was within the power and the prerogative of this Father to await and welcome the return of the son. If we see God as the head of our households, we can trust in his ability to maintain the family. We can, therefore, be free from the pressure to defend our families and can focus instead on the prodigal's welfare.

Our questions will then be different: Does it make any difference for what reason and to what activities the person leaves the faith? Is it better for him to practice a different religion, or to remain nominally Christian and get into sexual immorality or financial corruption? Or even to remain outwardly 'good' while inwardly not really accepting God's grace in Christ? What should we do to ensure that he has the greatest possible chance of returning home?

Case 1b: A member of a non-Christian family becomes a Christian: People from most avowedly non-Christian families experience opposition when they turn to Christ: those from atheistic families may be mocked and marginalized; those from Jewish families may be considered traitors, and even be expelled from home and have the funeral rites read for them; those from Muslim families may be expelled from the family and, in extreme cases, be killed; those from Hindu families may be seen as breaking family tradition and insulting their parents. This is not only because of spiritual obduracy or enmity to Christ, but also because of the anticipated disruption of household, tradition and community and the loss of family honour.

The NT sees such opposition as normal (e.g. Matt 10:34-6): it is the cost of following Jesus. Yet what is the ongoing responsibility of the (new) believer to his or her unbelieving family? A person can leave a household, but cannot leave the kinship group of which they are part by creation. Since faith in Christ enables us to be what God made us to be, we can expect conversion to lead to increased awareness of family and ethnic identity and responsibilities despite the prior commitment to the kingdom family. Jesus himself left his natural household to lead a travelling household of disciples in order to fulfil his ministry. He clearly stated that his primary family is not his physical kin, but those who follow him (Matt 12:46-50), but he did not disown his family. We recall his provision for his mother from the cross (Jn. 19:25-7).

It seems that his own interpretation of 'hatred' of his natural family was a continued honouring of family responsibilities while giving priority to the kingdom family. The convert is called to affirm his or her natural family as far as possible, while necessarily remaining separate from its idolatrous aspects. A key question here is whether there are ways of enabling converts to remain within their families. In some situations, Christian and other communities not only have different faiths but also different cultures and languages. Thus changing faith is seen as changing community and even ethnic allegiance. If our analysis is correct, the latter is not possible and the former is undesirable. Changes of culture and language are quite unnecessary. In many such situations, people are experimenting with ways of being Christian within a non-Christian community.[10]

Challenge 2: Marriage outside the faith

For traditional families, including OT families, propagation of the 'house' is through descent and, therefore, through marriage. The choice of marriage partner affects not only the transmission of the family ethos but also the retention of land and wealth.[11] In most religious traditions, marriage within the faith also ensures that children will be brought up in the faith. It is interesting that, while Muslims oppose their women marrying non-Muslim men, Jews oppose their men marrying non-Jewish women: amongst Muslims, a bride generally joins her husband's household. The primary bonding is, traditionally, between mother and son, and the wife adjusts to the ethos of the household and the authority of her mother-in-law.[12] Thus the husband retains his Islamic

---

[10] See, e.g., Parshall, 1980

[11] See, e.g., Steinberg 1993

[12] See, e.g., Mernissi, 1985

environment and the children are brought up within Islam. Amongst Jews, for reasons now veiled in history, descent is matriarchal. Since Jewishness is as much an ethnic as a religious identity, it is only through Jewish mothers that the Jewish community can be propagated.[13]

The issue for Christians is different, since one becomes Christian by re-birth rather than by birth. Questions of unequal yokes (2 Cor. 6:14ff), remaining married to unbelievers (1 Cor. 7:12ff) and keeping one's wife pious (1 Tim. 3:11) are about present discipleship rather than family propagation; and refraining from marriage is a commendable option. Further, the very nature of Christian marriage as reflecting Christ and the church assumes that both partners are believers. However, since Christians also form natural communities, they share some of the community concerns of other groups, and these can be clearly seen in the OT. The influence of wives over their husbands is frequently recognised – not least the bad influence of Jezebel, and the good influence of Esther. It is this question of moral and religious influence that is at the heart of the OT concern about mixed marriages, rather than concern about the purity of the race. Because of the link between culture and faith, all this overlaps with the concern for the continuation of tradition in the Jewish context. However, since the NT relativizes culture, mixed ethnic marriages raise practical rather than fundamental theological questions for Christians. The major question is whether the marriage will encourage individuals and families in their walk with Christ. The minor one is what language the partners and their children will speak. We will consider below the specific instance of Muslim-Christian marriages, which illustrate some of the questions for Christians that arise in different cultural contexts.

Case 2a: A Christian girl marries a Muslim: This is not, in general, a problem for the Muslim family. In a western context, the questions for the Christian family may not be much different than those in 2b below. In a traditional context, the strong links between family, household and faith can produce different tensions. This is of particular current concern in parts of East Africa where there are deliberate attempts to encourage Muslim boys to marry Christian girls, and thereby to increase the percentage of Muslims. Typically, the Christian girl is told that she can continue to practice her faith, as Islamic law stipulates. However, she may find this difficult when surrounded by her Muslim family; and the mother-in- law may make it difficult for her to attend church. The girl may eventually become a Muslim. The church may treat this marriage as a breach of Christian discipleship, and, therefore, discipline the girl. The family may also deal with her harshly. Such treatment, of course, makes her conversion to Islam more likely. Our reflections so far suggest that: all Christians should be encouraged to make marriages that give priority to the kingdom, and these will be with fellow believers with whom they can establish

---

[13] Whilst this is Halakhic, some groups now also accept children of Jewish fathers and Gentile mothers.

believing families; if we believe that the cross of Christ is the one way of salvation, we should work towards such girls accepting that salvation and not turning from it; these girls continue to be human beings. They continue to be related to their kin and their kin continue to have responsibility for their welfare; harsh treatment of one girl will not necessarily dissuade another from following the same way.

Case 2b: A Muslim girl marries a Christian: This is not very likely to happen in traditional communities, since Islam does not recognise the marriage of a Muslim girl to a non-Muslim, and usually requires the male guardian's permission for a woman's first marriage. In Europe, however, there are increasing incidences of Muslim girls choosing to marry boys from Christian homes. This may be because they have absorbed much western culture and reacted against some of their traditional marriage patterns, yet retain a lively belief in God. A Christian boy who is not so committed that he would not consider marrying a non-Christian might have quite a similar outlook to such a girl. How should his church and family react? Many of the above considerations apply. In addition, it needs to be recognised that such a couple could not have a Muslim wedding: they can have a civil wedding, but if they want a religious ceremony it will have to be Christian. The sensitive welcome and counsel of a Christian minister can be a great help.[14] Further, the girl will inevitably face opposition from her own family and community, and may even be expelled. Her welcome into the boy's family will, therefore, be essential to their welfare – spiritual as well as temporal.

Challenge 3: Renunciation of family

The Luke 14 passage which stands at the head of this paper finishes with the words 'Any of you who does not give up everything he has cannot be my disciple' (v. 33). Throughout Christian history there have been people who have quite literally given up their families in order to follow Christ. For example, there are traditions of celibacy and monasticism. These traditions continue today, but may take different forms. We have a stream of students coming to study at Selly Oak, for whom the cost is being parted from their families for months or even years. We have others preparing to leave their families in the U.K., and live elsewhere in the world. Some may take their children to places where their lives may be at risk. We can also look back at pioneer missionaries and evangelists who have not been celibate, but have chosen to live apart from their spouses and children; and at Church of England vicars who have allowed their marriages to come under great strain in their attempts to serve God. All these are examples of people taking seriously the priority of faith over family. Experience shows that this can be damaging to families: our analysis would suggest that, while we can trust the Heavenly

14 See the publication on Muslim-Christian marriages in Europe, available from Church House, Westminster.

Father to care for our families because they are also his, we are also called to remain faithful to family responsibilities.[15] We need to test very carefully any apparent divine call to split families.

Challenge 4: Ordering the Christian household

The three challenge situations above point to the church as counter-cultural in its understanding of the family. In the world of the NT, both the Jewish and Roman worlds saw households as the building blocks of society and of faith. It is not surprising that the Christian teaching that put Christ above all appeared to threaten the whole fabric of society then as much as it does in, for example, today's Hindu contexts. The epistles and some of the early Christian writings deal with this problem: they affirm the importance of household order. It is interesting that, in doing so, they also affirm the accepted household order of the time. The prevailing system had households comprising husbands and wives, children and slaves. One might ask why, when it challenges so many aspects of life, the NT appears simply to affirm this patriarchal, slave-based order.

Dunn[16] suggests that this is because Christianity needed to be seen as upholding social order rather than tearing it down, but he points out that, despite retaining the basic patterns, Christians do in fact challenge contemporary thinking in two ways. 1. They always speak first to the less powerful partner – the wife, the children, and the slave. 2. Most importantly, they have a very different basis for their exhortations. The relationships are always to be seen as being 'in the Lord'. For example, wives, children and slaves do not submit or obey because of the power of the *pater familias*, as to a dictator, but because they choose to do so, as to their loving Saviour. The kinship language of the kingdom family informs and directs the contemporary language of household order. This is strikingly seen in the epistle to Philemon: 'I am sending (Onesimus) back to you … no longer as a slave, but better than a slave, as a dear brother. He is very dear to me but even dearer to you, both as a man and as a brother in the Lord' (vv. 12, 16-17). It seems that it is possible to prioritise the kingdom family even in the context of following the household patterns of the surrounding culture. But this very following of cultural patterns will also deeply challenge the cultural order, by changing its basis; and the changed basis will change the nature of family relationships. This is because the Christian family is not defined by divine regulations, but by God being the participating head of the family.

---

[15] This needs not only to be recognised by the individual, but also by churches and mission agencies. I think, for example, of two single women whose mission agencies needed to adjust policy: one was a orphan, with responsibilities towards siblings, and the other a convert from Islam with a divorced mother.

[16] Dunn, 1996:43-64

Challenge 5: The church as family?

While all of these situations pose questions about the Christian's secondary loyalty to family, they also pose challenges to the community of primary loyalty: the church. We not only have responsibilities to our families: we also have needs. Human beings were made to relate, and we have seen that God himself is committed to families. We need to belong, to have identity, to have the succour that a functional family can offer. What is the church's responsibility here?

Case 5a: Converts from non-Christian families:

The Bible expects and encourages movement from non-Christian families into the household of faith, but it is not blind to the issues that this may raise. The OT story of Ruth offers interesting insights into this situation. For those who must, in some sense, leave their family to follow Christ, and for those whose families have not been able to offer succour, there is an expectation that the new, kingdom family will not only demand loyalty but also offer a refuge. The family language of the NT underlines these expectations: sadly, in many cases, this results in disappointment. It is often noted that many who come to Christ from other faiths subsequently fall away.[17] Investigation indicates that these are not turning from Christ, but returning to their home communities and living as hidden disciples. They find that they cannot survive without their family and community, and that the church cannot be a satisfactory substitute. Many turn back to their faith communities in order to find marriage partners for themselves or for their children.

Case 5b: A post-modern mixture:

While traditional communities may expect kin, household and faith communities to coincide, a post-modern western society may show little relationship between the three. In the inner city area in which I lived, household, faith and kin coincided in the Muslim community, but amongst the indigenous people there were many households in which people were not related to each other, many single person households, and many households that contained only part of a divided family. Believing Christians were few, and were scattered amongst these households. There were only a few homes inhabited by related people who followed Christ. Opposition to faith is more likely to be in terms of mockery than of family betrayal. However, the lack of traditional structures brings its own problems. If households are the places where the life of faith is embodied and transmitted, we not only have to ask how we can compensate for fragmented family structures, but also how faith is transmitted where there is little correlation between household and faith.

[17] I hear numbers from 50 to 80%.

The Key Question: Is the church a new/replacement family?

Converts from other faiths expect to find a new family amongst Christians. In the current western context, many people expect the church to replace their dysfunctional kin, and many churches deliberately present themselves as a 'family'. At first sight, this would appear to be biblical and healthy, but it can produce problems. The family picture can result in the minister being seen as a father and the laity as children. Quite apart from the power dynamic that this sets up, it can put the minister under intolerable strain while making the laity function as dependents. It can mean that members see the church primarily as a place where they receive rather than as a community to which they give. Perhaps most seriously, it can mean that the church focuses on itself rather than on others: family responsibilities tend to be inward rather than outward-looking.

I want to suggest that the distinction between kin and household is helpful here. The church – not only local but universal – is certainly the primary kin of believers. It is here that we find our primary identity. In it, God and not the vicar is Father. However, for actual living we all need to belong to *households*. The local church needs to ensure that people belong to groups that function as believing households, but it does not have to function as a household in itself. For example, in the 'post-modern mixture' explored above, I have seen three models that work fairly well: 1) The establishment of consciously Christian households. These might represent kinship groups, but might also be groups of Christians unrelated by kinship but committed to representing Christ in the area; 2) A network of believers, living in different households, scattered through the community. These believers visit each other, meet not only on Sundays but also for prayer and study during the week, support the weak and sick, and use their homes as centres for discussions with non-Christians; 3) A religious community.

The Franciscans have both households in inner city areas and larger households in quiet country places that can offer hospitality to those who need a rest from the city. All this cannot, however, replace natural kinship networks. We also need to work towards helping people to perceive and accept the nuclear and wider families and ethnic groups to which they belong: to live in the identity with which God has created them. This is not only because of their responsibility to their kin: it is also because fragmented communities have histories of sin and pain which need to be forgiven and healed.

In Conclusion

Family matters. It is the building block of community, and faith is inextricably linked to its continuity, structure, ethic, identity and tradition. The United Nations Commission on Human Rights affirms this in guarding the right of parents to bring their children up in their faith; and most peoples see it as reprehensible to turn from the faith of one's birth. Evangelism questions all this: we call people to put Christ before families, and potentially 'bring the sword' rather than peace.

Our cultures ask, 'Is evangelism to people of other faiths ethical?' Particular issues arise over the evangelism of children: this is so acute that some agencies working amongst Jews have stated policies of not working amongst under-18s. If we believe that the kingdom family does transcend natural families, we will insist that evangelism is not only ethical but essential. If Christ died for all, then what is unethical is to withhold the gospel from anyone for any reason. The idols of family, community, culture and tradition must bow before him. However, in that the Bible affirms our creation families, our evangelism and discipleship need to take heed of the question, and to ensure that our methods of evangelism are ethical. We need to be aware of possible family disruption, and in particular to treat people as members of their families. We need also to recognise and teach that, in the end, the kingdom family is for the welfare of our natural families. In entering it, we are 'born again' – we are changed in our very beings, so that our being-in-family is also changed, and we are enabled to minister to our families in love and in truth. God does not want to destroy our families, but to redeem them.

Practically, we are left with some hard questions: Is the church prepared to receive those who lose family ties for Christ's sake? How do we relate to family structures and loyalties in our evangelism? How can we see the gospel redeeming kin and household even as it challenges them? Underlying all this is the challenge of Jesus: Is the kingdom really worth the family disruption that it brings? What will we pay to follow Christ? We have to answer that the kingdom is worth it, and that, as Christ's appointed witnesses, we will pay whatever it costs. It is not only that the convert has to 'hate' his family. Jesus tells us that every one of his followers is implicated: 'Anyone who does not carry his cross and follow me cannot be my disciple' (Lk. 14:27).

Cultural/Religious Factors in our Understanding of Family[1]

Gloria L. Kwashi

Gloria L. Kwashi is chairperson of the Mothers' Union in the diocese of Jos, Nigeria

In this paper I will focus on the African family, using Nigeria as our frame of reference. This will enable us to look at our own family life more carefully and critically. The family is the most important single factor in moulding or shaping a human being. In the family a person is either equipped to reach his or her fulfilment as an individual and as a member of the community, or he/she is crippled and inhibited from attaining the original potential. Culture and religion are two important factors which are indispensable in moulding the family.

Family, Culture and Religion

A family comes into being when a man and woman agree to live together, and have children. A family is also a group of people living for one another and living together with one another (for example: a child who comes to live with you comes to be a member of the family). Family has been defined as 'any group of people related by blood or marriage'; and 'parents and their children, a person's children, a set of relatives. All the descendants of a common ancestor, their line of descendants.' The family is the basic unit in which society is organized. It is a natural and instinctive grouping, bonded together by ties of blood and marriage. If this grouping is broken or torn apart all members of the family suffer pain and loss. Different societies have different expectations, taboos, and assumptions concerning the life of the family, and there are different understandings of how restricted or how broad may be the group which is called 'family'. In no society, however, is the family unit totally ignored or unknown. Culture may be defined as the custom and civilization of a particular people or group; or the way of life of a people; the beliefs, customs, institutions, arts and all the products of human work and thought created by a people or a group at a particular time. Religion, according to some, is the belief in the existence of a superhuman controlling power, especially of God or gods,

[1] Kwashi, 2002:19-23

usually expressed in worship. It is a controlling influence in a person's life. All family members are products of the culture and religion of their parents and undoubtedly these factors will set the base upon which the families of the next generation will be shaped and raised. It may therefore be asked in what particular ways cultural and religious factors shape the life of the family. How do our beliefs and customs and the great influence which is exerted on our lives by God or the gods shape our understanding of the family?

The Impact of Culture

Central to all definitions of culture is that it is a complex whole, the way of life of a people. It is the powerful influence behind the beliefs and practices that govern the daily behaviour and conduct of a people. Culture is dynamic and differs from place to place and from people to people. However, many African countries are home to cultures which are similar to each other, which have not changed, and which may not change significantly. In Africa, and particularly in Nigeria (which is itself made up of many varied traditions), culture shapes our understanding of the family in the many ways. The following list would apply to many but not necessarily to all African cultures:

1. *Leadership of the family*. The man automatically assumes the leadership of the family. Women may even be seen as property which can, therefore, be acquired, changed or given to someone else.

2. *Domestic chores and child rearing:* Cooking and other household chores are the woman's responsibility. The raising of children, particularly in the early months, is also primarily the woman's responsibility. For example, if the father has carried the child for a short while, and the child then cries or gives trouble, it is not uncommon to hear him say to his wife, 'Come and carry your child'.

3. *Education*: Women should not be highly educated because their place is in the kitchen. Female children are, therefore, not given an expensive education, and married women are not considered to need further education. In contrast, the man is given every possible opportunity for education.

4. *Slavery*: The woman is meant to serve the man, to toil and labour without being adequately appreciated. The woman merely slaves to keep the family and the marriage going.

5. *Economic control:* The woman has no rights at all with regard to the family income. The man controls the finances and he alone decides what, when and how family resources should be used. Even when the woman earns an income, the man may take control of this too.

6. *Right to inheritance*. Inheritance or rights to property is the prerogative of the man. At the death of the father and mother, the male child or children may inherit what belonged to both parents, at the expense of the female children. In some cases involving the inheritance of property, even a widow is discriminated against by the family of her deceased husband.

7. *Divorce:* Men may marry and divorce at will. Like a worn out dress, a woman may be thrown aside and a new marriage contracted.

8. *Ownership of children:* The children belong to the man, rather than to both the man and the woman. In the event of separation or divorce the children remain with the father, and the mother may or may not be allowed to visit them. Both the woman and the children are the property of the husband.

9. *Communication:* The wife and the children are not free to speak to the husband and father at will. The man is viewed almost as a demigod, and therefore he may not be approached at random. Sometimes, for very serious issues, the wife and children may have to communicate with the man through some respected members of the extended family. Where direct communication is permitted it is expected to take place in a private place and not in public. Similarly some cultures do not allow free discussion between elderly men, women and children, so that when elders are seated, discussing a matter, the women and children are not allowed to approach.

10. *Child-bearing:* It is often thought to be essential that a married couple must have children, and especially boys. A childless marriage encourages the man to marry again. It is generally assumed that the 'fault' lies with the woman and that she is responsible for the lack of children or for the lack of male children.

The Impact of Religion

Religion in Nigeria and Africa shapes our understanding of the family in various ways, including the following:

1. *Religious roles*. In a few cases men, women and children as seen as equal before God, but most religious traditions give the man complete leadership in all matters of faith and worship. Religious roles are strictly for men; the men are more exposed to the secrets of their religion; only the man can commune with the deity. The man therefore leads in prayer, scripture reading and any ritual performance. Sometimes when the man is absent, the women and children are forced simply to wait for his return. The women and children are assigned only minor, supporting roles, such as providing the food and drink.

2. *Bread-winning*. The man is expected to meet all the needs of the family, including the provision of food, clothing, health and education expenses. If he fails in this, his leadership is threatened. If laziness is the cause, he stands to lose his respect from other family members. Some religious practices are very strict in reserving this role for the man, whereas others allow the woman to participate in providing for the needs of the family.

3. *Freedom of association*. Some religions allow freedom of association between men and women, whether married or unmarried, but others do not allow close contact even between husband and wife except in the bedroom. In public, and even in religious gatherings, husband and wife sit apart from each other; they do not eat together, nor are they free to discuss matters of mutual

interest. It is common to hear men comment that when the men are talking, women, like the children, should keep quiet.

4. *Jobs/courses*. Some religions are liberal and open-minded here, but others are very restrictive. In the latter case, women are not allowed to read engineering courses, to join the armed forces, the police force or any paramilitary organization, or to play football or other vigorous sports. Men may be prohibited from following 'domestic' courses such as catering or nursing. In some cases women are allowed no 'job' other than child-bearing.

5. *Participation in politics*. There is a diversity of opinion as to who may or may not take part in politics. While some religious practices allow all people to be involved, others regard politics as the exclusive preserve of the men.

6. *Divorce, remarriage and polygamy*. Some religions frown at divorce, remarriage and polygamy, but others freely permit these practices. In the latter case a man may marry many wives, and sometimes a woman may be allowed to divorce and remarry.

7. *Movement*. Some religious traditions take the position that women should not leave their homes in the daytime but may visit relations and friends at night with their head covered. Other traditions allow freedom of movement in the daytime, but women and children are expected to be at home in the evening. Men are not restricted in their movement. Indeed where the woman is restricted in her movements, it is essential that the man move out in order to earn the money to keep the family.

8. *Headship of the family*. As with most cultures, most religious practices see the man as the head of the family. This is particularly so when decisions are to be made. He is the permanent representative of his family in every matter outside the family, and particularly in discussions concerning marriage. Sometimes questions posed to other family members will receive no response in his absence. His presence gives the family a feeling of security and well-being.

9. *Gender issues*. Most religions tend to view women as being the weaker sex physically, mentally and spiritually. Women should therefore be treated with caution and care. On the other hand, however, a very considerable amount of physical labour may be expected of the woman, both in and around the home and even on the farm.

10. *Discipline*. Discipline, especially in Africa, is seen as a common responsibility of all within the family. A child is corrected immediately by an older person, without waiting to report the child to the immediate parents.

11. *Social life*. Especially in Africa, social events concern all members of the family and community, whether it is a matter for rejoicing (such as birth, marriage, promotion), or of sorrow (such as sickness, death or disaster). The younger people are expected to treat older people with maximum respect, to carry their loads and to assist them with whatever work they may be doing. Greeting is a most cherished aspect of African culture. To say 'Hi!' and pass on, is not sufficient! The welfare of the whole family is enquired after. The

person who is poor at greeting is generally considered to be either proud or foolish. The African is an informal person. He is not bound by time. He does not need an invitation before attending a function.

Some Observations

Culture and religion are basic ingredients in determining what family life is like. These two factors are closely interwoven, influencing and shaping each other. Cultural and religious beliefs are all based on values and virtues. Our values and virtues shape our understanding of what a family should be. Cultural and religious factors which are open and positive lead to high aspirations which in turn encourage self-esteem and the attainment of individual and corporate development peaks. In contrast, cultural and religious factors that place unnecessary restrictions on family members are bound to threaten, cripple and hinder the attainment of the individual's potential. Cultural and religious traditions tend quickly to become absolutes. They are then very difficult to change. Worse than that, it becomes very difficult to see what may need to be changed: familiarity leads to blindness.

A country such as Nigeria, where Christianity is very young, is, therefore, at both a disadvantage and an advantage. It is at a disadvantage because very many people have never heard the gospel and therefore, have no knowledge or experience as to how Christianity might affect family life. It is at an advantage because Christianity comes with a freshness to highlight and challenge factors in family life which are cultural and 'religious', but pagan (for example: polygamy; the slavery of women; the lack of concern for education or health; oppression and male dictatorship). We would do well to consider very carefully what aspects of our family life are truly in accordance with the gospel of Christ, and what are purely cultural, traditional and 'religious', but at the same time pagan. The influence of one culture or religion over another is sometimes exercised through colonization, trade, subjugation or diplomacy.

This influence is usually gradual but steady. Just as in the Roman Empire the Latin language was used everywhere, and in the British Empire English was the common tongue, so still language today can be a tool whereby one culture can influence another or indeed a culture can influence religion. One obvious case of another culture influencing our own culture through language is seen in the common use of English terms for family relationships. To the best of my knowledge no Nigerian language has a word for aunt, cousin, half-brother or half-sister. Your aunt is simply your mother and your cousin or half-brother is your brother. Again, in Nigeria in the early days of the missionaries it was those who could speak English and went to church who were considered to be Christians (was this true?). Thanks be to God that Jesus Christ has broken the barriers made by distinctions, differences and classifications. In Christ we are one culture, one religion and one big family.

As Christians the ways, beliefs and practices we must adopt and allow to shape our understanding of the family should be none other than those of our Lord Jesus Christ. His influence must transform our lives, our culture and our religious practices. This will then lead to equality, justice and love. Husband and wife, man and women, girls and boys have all been endowed with gifts and their potential must be drawn out, fulfilled and used to the glory and honour of God. All are made in the image of God; all are potential co-heirs with Christ. Non-Christian cultural and religious practices have an evil side. Only in Christ can perfect holiness, purity and righteousness be found. Christianity is the only religion that enjoys the singular privilege of preparing and building individuals and families here on earth for the larger heavenly family of God the Father through his Son Jesus Christ.

The kingdom of God has been pictured in terms of a city, a chosen people, a holy nation. Might we not do well to think of the kingdom of God as the fulfilment of the family? If the family as we know it on earth is seen as the first fruits of the kingdom of God, then the family will have a focus and a vision which will bring inspiration and encouragement. Above all, the family will then be open to that transformation which can come only through Jesus Christ and the power of the Holy Spirit: 'Do not be conformed to this world, but be transformed by the renewal of your mind, that you may prove what is the will of God, what is good and acceptable and perfect' (Romans 12:2).

Conclusion

A family can be a family put together by culture or a family put together by religion. In these modern times individuals have exercised their freedom to belong to or to reject membership of certain families. For example, converts from one religion have left their original families and joined a new family of their new religion. Other individuals have changed nationality and adopted new nationalities and new cultures. For us as evangelical Christians, when we are born again we become heirs of the kingdom of Christ and members not only of the body of Christ but also of the family of the children of God. This brings us to a totally new level of culture and religion.

The implications of this are that to belong to Christ is to agree to be like Christ by depending on his word in daily devotion and study, and also by living by the Holy Spirit. This new family, as Paul puts it in Galatians 3:8, is not only international but consists of the saints triumphant and the saints militant, those known to us and those unknown to us. The culture that makes and shapes this family is based on the Holy Scripture with a common experience of being born again by water and in the Spirit. 'There is neither Jew nor Greek, there is neither slave nor free, there is neither male nor female; for you are all one in Christ Jesus' (Gal. 3:28).

SLAVERY AND FAMILY LIFE IN THE SEYCHELLES[1]

French Chang-Him

Rt. Rev. French Chang-Him is Metropolitan in the Anglican Communion of the Seychelles

How does, a nation that boasts a population of almost 100 per cent. Christians, have about 80 per cent. of its children born out of wedlock? In many households, the father remains on the periphery and leaves the mother to carry the full responsibility of bringing up the children alone. He sees nothing wrong in having other partners and children. Families are weak and matriarchal. The tradition of co-habitation and the weakness of family life in the Seychelles is deeply rooted in slavery and its aftermath, which the majority of the population experienced during the nineteenth century.

Origins of slavery in the Seychelles

The slaves that were brought to Mauritius, and eventually to the Seychelles in the eighteenth century, came mainly from Madagascar and East Africa.[2] From their arrival in Mauritius, the trauma of capture and of marching from one trader's transit camp to another, to the final sea voyage under conditions of untold misery and deprivation, the slaves were left in a state of physical, moral and spiritual destitution. Families had been fragmented and family members, even if they had managed to arrive at their destination by the same slave ship, were finally separated on being allotted to different estate owners.

The Impact on Marriage

The shattering of the kinship group also destroyed most of the social organization that the African possessed in his tribal environment. Kinship was, and is today, the basis of the tribe's economic, religious and political structures. Once the fragmentation of the family group had been effected, the kinship structure was destroyed and with its destruction the other structures disappeared

---

[1] Chang-Him, 2002:48-51

[2] It has been estimated that about 45 % came from Madagascar, 40 % from East Africa, especially Mozambique, 13 % from India, especially Pondicherry, and 2 % from West Africa. Benedict, 1980:138.

as well.[3] One of the most serious losses of tribal traditions through slavery was the tradition surrounding marriage. With the loss of these social traditions, marriage for the slave was no marriage at all and was reduced to that of sex alone. Slaves in Mauritius and the Seychelles were hardly ever allowed to marry.

The relationship between a black slave and a white French slave-owner was regulated by the *code noir*. Although the Code seemed lenient in places, when put into practice, marriage for the slave was almost impossible. There was a further impediment arising out of the current belief that the Negro slave was unable to participate in the spiritual nature of the sacrament of marriage. For the Negro, according to the white French settler, marriage meant sex and was equivalent to the sex act among animals, so slave marriage could not be worthy of the spiritual blessing of Christian marriage. The loss of a tradition of marriage for the slave inevitably led to miscegenation between master and female slave. The rise of a proportionately large population of mixed blood (Creoles) provides evidence of this practice. The female slave provided sexual services for the white master, while the master made certain that his own marriage bed remained undefiled. Slave quarters on the estates were of poor quality. Very few huts had separate compartments for male and female slaves, and promiscuous living was rife. The slaves themselves would seek permanent or semi-permanent partners[4] but these unions were rarely blessed. Masters would discourage such unions, as they made the sale of one partner without the other difficult, and if they had been married according to Christian rites the forced separation of a married couple would have been frowned upon by the clergy.

Thus, slave marriage was extremely rare. The emancipation of slaves in the Seychelles took place in 1835, as happened throughout the British Empire. Gradually, there developed a system which became known as the 'Moitie system' whereby the emancipated slave was allowed to remain in his previous slave quarters and instead of paying rent, he would provide three days' labour for his master free of charge. Whereas this system provided the ex-slave and his master subsistence crops, it made no difference to the conditions under which the ex-slaves lived.

The Arrival of 'Liberated Africans'

Between the 1861 and 1874, about 2,500 African slaves, who were liberated from Arab slaver dhows captured by the Royal Navy along the east coast of Africa, landed at Mahe. These Africans, mainly in their twenties, were allotted to the white estate owners to work in their plantations, where they experienced similar conditions as the former slaves had experienced before emancipation.

[3] See Benedict, 1980:155-156

[4] See Benedict, 1980

But now the former population called themselves Creoles, whereas the new arrivals were called Liberated Africans. They spoke no Creole, but most of them knew Swahili. Most were baptized as soon as they arrived at the plantations of their new masters, but little more was done for them for a number of years. The conditions under which most of the adults lived led to wholesale co-habitation, and many of the younger girls soon lived lives of prostitution and casual sex. Most of these Liberated Africans took little notice of the exhortations of the Catholic priests to give up co-habitation and get married, since there was little evidence of marriage in the surrounding Creole population, whom they were being called upon to emulate. Consequently very few gave up the practice of co-habitation which by now had firmly taken root among them.

The Catholic Campaign against Co-habitation

In 1884 a Roman Catholic mission began a vigorous campaign against co-habitation. It began with two strong pastoral letters from the Roman Catholic bishop, Symphorien Mouard. The island had just recovered from an epidemic of smallpox that had broken out in the second half of 1883 causing an alarming number of deaths. Bishop Mouard arrived back in the Seychelles after a visit to the United Kingdom bringing with him a statue of St. Roch, a saint to whom the sick would address their prayers. As soon as the statue arrived in the Seychelles, the epidemic abated,[5] which was claimed to be a miracle. In this climate of religious fervour, the campaign against co-habitation was launched, the epidemic of smallpox having been declared as evidence of God's wrath against such an immoral state of affairs. Marriage was now seen in a new light. The pastoral letters, in which veiled threats of excommunication were made for those who persisted in co-habitation, had their effect, and the campaign was brought to a conclusion. However, the large number of marriages at this time included the marriages of many who were already co-habiting, but who now decided to marry in order to make legitimate their existing children. From 1861 to 1874, when the last Liberated Africans arrived at Mahe, most of them co-habited. Gradually both Roman Catholic and Anglican missions began to have an effect upon them, and in 1884, of the 233 marriages registered, 88 were of Liberated Africans, of whom almost all were co-habiting before marriage.

The Roman Catholic campaign against co-habitation eventually failed. It began well by raising the marriage rate from an average of 5.4 per thousand in1882 to 9.6 in 1883. But as it has been suggested above, the success campaign masked the true number of those who continued to co-habit. And the marriage of already co-habiting Liberated Africans also contributed to skewing

[5] The medical profession had already pronounced that the epidemic had run its course in February 1884, in a report which had been transmitted to the Secretary of State for the Colonies.

the figures. From 1900 onwards, political prisoners were brought to the Seychelles. The first was King Prempeh of the Ashanti with 58 tribal chiefs and their wives and concubines. The other prisoners were the kings of Uganda also with their wives and concubines. The prisoners greatly influenced the already largely African population of the Seychelles, who may have argued that if an African king could have concubines accepted by the administration, why should they also not have theirs as well?

We know also that the descendants of the ex-slave population, who now called themselves Creoles, looked down upon the Liberated Africans who were recently arrived. The latter, however, wished to emulate the Creole population and because the tradition of co-habitation was strong among them, they would have preferred to co-habit rather than marry. And the Creole partner, too, would have preferred co-habitation to marriage. Thus, once the Roman Catholic marriage campaign had ceased, the preferred pairing between Liberated Africans and Creoles would have been co-habitation.

It would appear then that the Roman Catholic campaign of 1884-1893 never completely broke the tradition of co-habitation that had begun with slavery. Religious teaching accompanied by sanctions against those who co-habited certainly had an effect, but it was not lasting. A repetition of this occurred in the 1990s with the establishment of the Pentecostal Assemblies of God in the Seychelles. New converts, mostly from the existing Christian denominations, were officially considered as members after re-baptism by immersion following the confession of faith as adults and after marriage on the part of co-habiting partners. Thus followed a number of weddings most weekends for a number of months. Marriages now in the new Pentecostal churches, which have branched off into smaller units under different names and leaders, are mostly of couples who had not previously co-habited.

The Effect of Economic Factors on Marriage Rates

It has been suggested that economics is a factor in determining marriage rates. When the economy slumped or went into recession, it is said, people simply could not afford the expense of a wedding, and so began co-habiting without the bother of getting married.[6] During the First World War there was extreme poverty among the labouring classes, and the Inspector of Schools reported in 1916 that many children were coming to school without having had any food, some of them fainting with hunger during classes. There is no doubt that poverty did have an effect upon the number of marriages contracted during the period 1900 to 1935. But thereafter this does not seem to be the case.

[6] Marston, 1994

The Legacy of Slavery and a Pastoral Policy

Why have the men remained on the periphery of life? Under slavery, the women mostly worked in or around the homes of the white settlers. They learned new skills as they carried out their daily tasks, which would include the nurture of children and the management of a house. The men were always outside working on the plantations or fishing. A man's legal slave wife or concubine was first and foremost the possession of his white master. The only time the slave men were at the centre of anything was during the Moutia dance. The children the slave men fathered did not belong to them but to their masters. Their tribal role as husband and father had been forcibly taken away from them. Much healing of the past is needed at all levels of the Seychellois society.

The church has in the past used excommunication as a means of disciplining couples who co-habit. However, we are now doubtful whether co-habiting couples who remain faithful to each other in their relationship should be excommunicated. There is an effort to understand the historical and other reasons why people choose to co-habit instead of accepting the sacrament of marriage. Nationally, there is a widespread and urgent need for role models. Infidelity and promiscuous living is now creating the threat of HIV/AIDS. For the last two years, partly as part of the millennium resolution and partly due to renewed activities on the part of the churches, a significant increase in the number of marriages has been observed. The future of Christian marriage and a strong concept of family life lie in a sound education, starting with young children, marriage preparation and counselling.

BIBLIOGRAPHY

Abhishiktananda, 1984.
Saccidananda: A Christian Approach to Advaitic Experience rev. ed. (Delhi: ISPCK)

Adeney, B.T., 1995.
Strange Virtues – Ethics in a Multicultural World (Leicester: Apollos)

Adeyemo, T., Samuel, V.K. & Sider, R., 1984.
'Introducing Transformation,' *Transformation* 1.1 (January) 1-2

Aguilar, E.E. et al. 1993.
'Protestantism in El Salvador: Conventional wisdom versus survey evidence', *Latin American Research Review* 28.2, 119-1 40

Anderson, A. 1997.
Zion and Pentecost: The Spirituality and Experience of Pentecostal and Zionist/Apostolic Churches in South Africa (Pretoria 2000)

Anderson, A. 2005.
'The origins of Pentecostalism and its Global spread in the Early Twentieth Century' in *Transformation,* 22.3 (July)

Anderson, N., 1984.
Christianity and World Religions – the Challenge of Pluralism (Leicester: Inter-Varsity Press)

Athyal, S. P., 1993.
'Southern Asia', in James M. Phillips and Robert T. Coote (eds.) *Toward the 21st Century in Christian Mission* (Grand Rapids, Mich.: Wm. B. Eerdmans) 57–68

Augustine 1984.
The City of God new ed. (London: Penguin)

Baillie, J., 1945.
What is Christian Civilization? (London: Oxford University Press)

Bakhtin, M. 1968.
Rabelais and his world. (Cambridge, Mass.; London: M.I.T.Press)

Bakhtin, M. 1984.
Problems of Dostoevsky's Poetics. (Manchester: Manchester University Press)

Barclay, W. 1975.
The Gospel of Matthew v.1 (Edinburgh: St Andrew's Press)

Barth, Karl 1936-1977.
Church Dogmatics (Edinburgh: T. & T. Clark)

Barth, K., 1960.
The Humanity of God, (Richmond, Va.: John Knox Press)

Barth, K. 1962.
'Church and Culture', in T. Torrance (ed.) *Theology and Church : Shorter Writings 1920-28* (London: SCM Press)

Barth, K. 1962.
'The Principles of Dogmatics According to Herrmann', in T. Torrance (ed.) *Theology and Church: Shorter Writings 1920-28* (London: SCM Press)

Barth, K. 1972.
The Humanity of God (Richmond, Va.: John Knox Press)
Bartleman, F. 1911.
'The object of the baptism in the Holy Spirit', *The Latter Rain Evangel* 3 (May) 8–9
Bartleman, F. 1970.
Another Wave Rolls In! ed. John G. Myers (Northridge, Calif.: Voice Publications)
Barton, S.C. 1992.
'Family' in J.B.Green and S. McKnight (eds.) *Dictionary of Jesus and the Gospels* (Downers Grove, Ill.: InterVarsity Press) 226-229
Bastide, R. 1970.
'Mémoire collective et sociologie du bricolage,' in *L' Année Sociologique*, 3. Série, v. 21, pp. 65-108
Bauckham, R. 2003.
Bible and Mission: Christian Witness in a Postmodern World (Carlisle; Grand Rapids, Mich. : Paternoster Press; Baker Book House)
Bediako, K. 1995.
Christianity in Africa: The Renewal of a Non-Western Religion (Maryknoll, N.Y.; Edinburgh: Orbis Books; T. &. T. Clark)
Benedict, B. 1980.
'Slavery and Indenture in Mauritius and Seychelles' in J.L. Watson (ed.) *Asian and African System of Slavery* (Oxford: Blackwell)
Bevans, S.B., 2002.
Models of Contextual Theology rev. ed. (Maryknoll, N.Y: Orbis Books)
Bharucha, R. 1993.
The Question of Faith (Delhi: Orient Longman)
Bhattacharjea, A. 1996.
'A summary report of the debate,' in *Indian Express*, 5 July
Birch B.C. and Rasmussen, L.L. 1989.
Bible and Ethics in the Christian Life rev. and expanded ed. (Minneapolis, Minn.: Augsburg Press)
Bloch, M. 1965.
Feudal Society, tr. L. A. Manyon (London: Routledge & Kegan Paul)
Boesak, A. 1983.
'The eye of the needle', *International Review of Mission* 72 (January)
Bonino, J.M. 1983.
Toward Christian Political Ethics (Philadelphia, Pa.: Fortress Press)
Bonino, J.M. 1994.
'Letter to author,' 6 November
Bosch, D.J., 1991.
Transforming Mission – Paradigm Shifts in Theology of Mission (Maryknoll, N.Y.: Orbis Books)
Boyd, R.S. 1975.
An Introduction to Indian Christian Theology (Madras: Christian Literature Society)
Brandon, G. 1993.

Santería from Africa to the New World: the Dead Sell Memories. (Bloomington, Ind.: Indiana University Press)

Braun, H. 1969.
Jesus (Philadelphia, Pa.: Fortress Press 1979)

Bruce, F.F.,. 1954.
'Rome and the Emperor' in *The Book of Acts* (Grand Rapids, Mich.: Wm. B. Eerdmans)

Burdick, J. 1992.
'Rethinking the Study of Social Movements: The Case of Christian Base Communities in Urban Brazil,' in Arturo Escobar and Sonia E. Alvarez (eds.) *The Making of Social Movements in Latin America: Identity, Strategy and Democracy* (Oxford: Westview Press)

Burdick, J. 1993.
'Struggling Against the Devil: Pentecostalism and Social Movements in Urban Brazil,' in Virginia Garrard-Burnett and David Stoll (eds.) *Rethinking Protestantism in Latin America* (Philadelphia, Pa: Temple University Press)

Burrows, W.R. 1993.
Redemption and Dialogue: Reading Redemptoris Missio *and Dialogue and Proclamation* (Maryknoll, N.Y.: Orbis Books)

Busch, E., 1976.
Karl Barth: His Life from Letters and Autobiographical Texts tr. John Bowden (London: SCM Press)

The Call, 1981.
The Call to Conversion (San Francisco: Harper & Row)

Chakkarai, V., 1981.
Jesus the Avatar (Madras, 1932); reproduced in P.T. Thomas (ed.) *Vengal Chakkarai* v. I (Madras: Christian Literature Society)

Campbell, J. 1995.
Songs of Zion: The AMEC in the USA and South Africa (Oxford: Oxford University Press)

Chang-Him, F., 2002.
'Slavery and Family Life in Seychelles,' *Transformation* 19.1 (January) 48-51

Chilton, B. and McDonald, J.I.H. 1987.
Jesus and the Ethics of the Kingdom (Grand Rapids, Mich.: Wm. B. Eerdmans)

Choudhury, N. 1991.
Indian Express, 21 October

Christian, J. 1999.
God of the Empty-Handed: Poverty, Power, and the Kingdom of God (Monrovia, Calif.: MARC)

Comaroff, J. 1985.
Body of Power, Spirit of Resistance (Chicago: Chicago University Press)

Costas, O.E. 1979.
The Integrity of Mission: The Inner Life and Outreach of the Church (San Francisco: Harper & Row)

Crokett W.V. & Sigountos, J.G. (eds.) 1991.
Through No Fault of Their Own? (Grand Rapids, Mich.: Baker Book House)

Cullmann, O. 1950.

Baptism in the New Testamen, tr. Reid, J.K.S. (London: SCM Press)

Cullman, O. 1959.
The Christology of the New Testament (London: SCM Press)

Daneel, M. 1971.
Old and New in Southern Shona Independent Churches (The Hague: Mouton)

Dillon-Malone, C. 1978.
The Korsten Basket-Makers: A Study of the Masowe Apostles, An Indigenous Religious Movement (Manchester: Manchester University Press)

Dayan, J. 2003.
'Querying the Spirit: The Rules of the Haitian lwa' in Allan Greer and Jodi Bilinkopf (eds.) *Colonial Saints: discovering the Holy in the Americas, 1500-1800* (New York; London: Routledge) 31-50

Dayanandan, T. F. (ed.) 1992. *The Christian Bhakti of A.J. Appasamy: A Collection of His Writings* (Madras: Christian Literature Society)

Dempster, M.W. 1987.
'Pentecostal Social Concern and the Biblical Mandate of Social Justice,' *PNUEMA: The Journal of the Society for Pentecostal Studies* 9 (Fall) 129-153

Dempster, M.W. 1989.
'The Church's Moral Witness: A Study of Glossolalia in Luke's Theology of Acts,' *Paraclete: A Journal of Pentecostal Studies* 23 (Winter) 1-7

Dempster, M.W. 1991.
'Evangelism, Social Concern, and the Kingdom of God', in Murray W. Dempster, Byron D. Klaus and Douglas Petersen (eds.) *Called & Empowered: Global Mission in Pentecostal Perspective* (Peabody, Mass.: Hendrickson) 22-43

Dempster, M.W. 1993.
'Christian Social Concern in Pentecostal Perspective: Reformulating Pentecostal eschatology,' *Journal of Pentecostal Theology* 2 (April) 51–64

Dempster, M.W. 1994. (guest ed.) Special Issue: 'Church Mission and Social Concern: The changing global face of classical Pentecostalism' *Transformation* 11.1 (January)

Dempster, M.W., 1999.
'Social Concern in the Context of Jesus Kingdom, Mission and Ministry,' *Transformation* 16.2 (April) 43-53

De Silva, L.A., 1979.
The Problem of Self in Buddhism and Christianity (London: Macmillan)

Devasahayam, V. (ed.) 1997.
Frontiers of Dalit Theology (Madras: ISPCK; Gurukul)

Devasahayam, V. 1998.
'Conflicting roles of the Bible and Culture in shaping Asian theology: a tale of two Indian theologies,' *Transformation* 15.3 (July) 21–27

Diamond, S. 1989.
Spiritual Warfare: The Politics of the Christian Right (London: Pluto Press)

Dodd, C.H. 1971.
The Founder of Christianity (London: Collins)

Dower, N. 1988.
What is Development? A Philosopher's Answer (Glasgow: Centre for Development Studies, University of Glasgow)

Dreze, J. and Sen, A. 1995.
India: Economic Development and Social Opportunity (New Delhi: Oxford University Press)

Driver, T., 1987.
'The Case for Pluralism', in *The Myth of Christian Uniqueness. Towards a Pluralistic* (Maryknoll, N.Y.: Orbis Books)

Dunn, J.D.G. 1996.
'The Household Rules in the New Testament' in S.C. Barton (ed.) *The Family in Theological Perspective* (Edinburgh: T & T Clark) 43-64

Dunn, J.D.G. 1998.
The Christ and the Spirit: Collected Essays v.2 (Edinburgh: T. & T. Clark)

Dupuis, J., 1997.
Toward a Christian Theology of Religious Pluralism (Maryknoll, N.Y.: Orbis Books)

Earhart, H.B. 1984.
Religions of Japan – Many Traditions Within One Sacred Way (New York: Harper Collins)

Ellul, J. 1970.
The Meaning of the City (Grand Rapids, Mich.: Wm. B. Eerdmans)

Escobar, S. 2000.
'Evangelical Missiology: Peering into the Future at the Turn of the Century,' *Global Missiology for the 21st Century: The Iguassu Dialogue* (Grand Rapids, Mich.: Baker Academic) 101-112

Fakultätsalbum, 1927
Fakultätsalbum der Evangelisch-theologischen Fakultät Münster (Münster Faculty Album)

Farmer, R. 1987.
'The kingdom of God in the gospel of Matthew' in Wendell Willis (ed.) *The Kingdom of God in 20th-Century Interpretation* (Peabody, Mass.: Hendrickson)

Farquhar, J.N., 1971.
The Crown of Hinduism (New Delhi: Oriental Reprints)

Fee, G.D. 1991.
'The kingdom of God and the church's global mission,' in Murray W. Dempster, Byron D. Klaus, Douglas Petersen, (eds.) *Called & Empowered: Global Mission in Pentecostal Perspective* (Peabody, Mass.: Hendrickson)

Forrester, D.B. 1980.
Caste and Christianity: Attitudes and Politics of Anglo-Saxon Protestant Missions in India (London: Curzon Press)

France, R.T. 1985.
The Gospel According to Matthew: An Introduction and Commentary (Leicester: Inter-Varsity Press)

France, R.T. 1989.
Matthew: Evangelist and Teacher (Exeter: Paternoster)

Francis, T.D. (ed.) 1992.
The Christian Bhakti of A.J. Appasamy: A Collection of His Writings (Madras: Christian Literature Society)

Freston, P., 1992.

'In search of an evangelical political project for Brazil' in Evangelicals and Politics in Latin America: A Pentecostal 'showvention',' *Transformation* 9.3 (July) 26-32

Freston, P. 1994.

'Brazil: Parachurch Agenciesand Politics' in G. Cook (ed.) *New Face of the Church in Latin America* (Maryknoll, N. Y.: Orbis Books) 226-242

Freston, P. 1997.

'Evangelicalism and Politics: A Comparison between Africa and Latin America,' *Transformation* 14.1 (January) 23-29

Gärtner, B. 1965.

The Temple and the Community (Cambridge: Cambridge University Press)

Gilroy, P. 1993.

The Black Atlantic: Modernity and Double Consciousness (Cambridge, Mass.: Harvard University Press)

Gispert-Sauch, G., 1999.

'Atman,' Vidyajyoti Journal of Theological Reflection 63.1

Gitari, D. 1988.

Let the Bishop Speak (Nairobi: Uzirna Press)

Gitari, D.M., 1991.

'Church and Politics in Kenya,' *Transformation* 8.3 (July) 7-17

Glaser, I. and Niringiye, D.Z. 2002.

'Family and Faith,' *Transformation* 19.1 (January) 23-33

Glasser, A.F. 1983.

'A Pradigm shift? Evangelicals and Interreligious Dialogue,' in Arthur F. Glasser and Donald A. McGavran (eds.) *Contemporary Theologies of Mission*, (Grand Rapids, Mich.: Baker Book House) 205-219

Glazier, S.D. 1983.

Marchin' the Pilgrims Home: Leadership and Decision-making in an Afro-Caribbean Faith. (Westport, CT.: Greenport Press)

Gnanadason, A., 1993.

'Towards a Feminist Eco-Theology for India,' in P. Kumari (ed.) *A Reader in Feminist Theology* (Madras: Gurukul) 95-105

Gnanadason, J. 1994.

A Forgotten History: The Story of the Missionary Movement and theLiberation of People in south Travancore (Madras: Gurukul)

Gorski, P.S. 2003.

Review of Weber, M. *The Protestant Ethic and the Spirit of Capitalism, and: The Protestant Ethic and the Spirit of Capitalism and Other Writings* in *Social Forces* 82.2 (December) 833-839

Goudzwaard, B. and de Lange, H. 1995.

Beyond Poverly and Affluence (Geneva: WCC)

Grams, R.G., 2001.

Review of *Walking with the Poor*, in *Transformation* 18.1 (January) 62-64

Grams, R.G. 2004.

'Narrative Dynamics in Isaiah's and Matthew's Mission Theology.' *Transformation* 21.4 (October): 238-255

Grams, R.G. 2005.

Rival Versions of Theological Enquiry (Prague: International Baptist Theological Seminary)

Grams, R.G. 2006.
'Paul Among the Mission Theologians' *Missionalia* 34.3

Grams, R.G., 2007.
'Transformation Mission Theology: It's History, Theology and Hermeneutics,' *Transformation* 24.3/4 (July/October) 193-212

Gray, S.W. 1989
'The least of my brothers, Matthew 25:31–46. A history of interpretation', *SBL Dissertation Series* 114 (Atlanta, GA.: Scholars Press)

Gunton, C. 2000.
'Salvation', in J. Webster (ed.) *The Cambridge Companion to Karl Barth* (Cambridge: Cambridge University Press)

Green, M., 1970.
Evangelism in the Early Church (London: Hodder and Stoughton)

Green, M., 1990.
Evangelism through the Local Church (London: Hodder and Stoughton)

Guga, T.H.I. 1965.
'Research into the History of the Usambara-Digo Church' (Makerere University Archive)

Habgood, J. 1995.
'Presidential Address to the General Synod,' 10 July

Halbwachs, M. 1992.
On collective Memory. [*Les cadres sociaux de la mémoire*]. (Chicago: University of Chicago Press)

Hart, G. 1973.
'Women and the Sacred in Ancient Tamilnadu', *Journal of Asian Studies*, 32, 233-250

Hauerwas, S. 1981.
A Community of Character: Toward a Constructive Christian Social Ethic (Notre Dame, Indiana: University of Notre Dame Press)

Haye, S. De la, 1971.
Tread Upon the Lion: The Story of Tommie Titcombe (Agincourt, Ont.: Sudan Interior Mission)

Henry, C.F.H. 1964.
Aspects of Christian Social Ethics (Grand Rapids, Mich.: Wm. B. Eerdmans)

Heron, A.I.C. 1983.
The Holy Spirit: The Holy Spirit in the Bible, in the History of Christian Thought, and in Recent Theology (London: Marshall, Morgan & Scott)

Heschel, A. J. 1972.
The Insecurity of Freedom (New York: Schoken Books)

Hick, J. and Knitter, P.F. (eds.) 1987.
The Myth of Christian Uniqueness – Towards a Pluralistic Theology of Religions (Maryknoll, N.Y.: Orbis Books)

Hiebert, P.G., 1987.
'Critical Contextualization', *International Bulletin of Missionary Research* 11.3, 104–111.

Hiebert, P.G., 1994.

'The Flaw of the Excluded Middle', in *Anthropological Reflections on Missiological Issues* (Grand Rapids, Mich.: Baker Book House) 189–201

Hiebert, P.G., 1994.
Anthropological Reflections on Missiological Issues (Grand Rapids, Mich.: Baker Book House)

Hogan, J. P. 1989.
'Because Jesus Did', *Mountain Movers* 31 (June) 10–11

Hollenweger, W.J. 1997.
Pentecostalism: Origins and Developments Worldwide (Peabody, Mass.: Hendrickson)

Hollenweger, W. 1999.
'The Black Roots of Pentecostalism', in A. Anderson and W. Hollenweger (eds.) *Pentecostalism After a Century* (Sheffield: Sheffield Academic Press)

Hoole, C.R.A. 1995.
Modern Sannyasins: Protestant Missionary Contribution to Ceylon Tamil Culture (Bern: Peter Lang)

Hoole, C.R.A. 2002.
'Redeeming the South Asian Family: Mission as extending the household of God,' *Transformation* 19.1 (January) 37-41

Hooper, J.S.M. 1938.
The Bible in India (London : Oxford University Press)

Houk, J.T. 1995.
Spirits, blood, and drums: the Orisha religion in Trinidad (Philadelphia, Pa.: Temple University Press)

Hrangkhuma, F. (ed.), 1998.
Christianity in India: Search for Liberation and Identity (Delhi; Pune: ISPCK; CMS)

Hunsinger, G. 2000.
'Karl Barth's Christology', in Webster, J. (ed.) *The Cambridge Companion to Karl Barth* (Cambridge: Cambridge University Press)

Huntington, D. 1984.
'The Prophet Motive,' in NACLA Reporton the Americas 18 (January-February) 2-11

Huntington, S., 1993.
'The Clash of Civilizations?' *Foreign Affairs* 72/3 (Summer) 22–49

Huntington, S., 1996.
The Clash of Civilizations and the Remaking of World Order (New York: Simon & Schuster)

Hurtado, L. 2003.
Lord Jesus Christ: Devotion to Jesus in Earliest Christianity (Grand Rapids, Mich.: Wm. B. Eerdmans)

Hwa Yung, 1997.
'The Resurgence of Asian Religions and Cultures: A Christian Response' in *Taking the Whole Gospel to Asia Today: The Fouth Asian Leadership* (New Delhi: Asia Lausanne Committee) 61–80

Hwa Yung, 1997.
Mangoes or Bananas? The Quest for an Authentic Asian Christian Theology (Oxford: Regnum)

Hwa Yung, 1998.
'Christian Ethical Thinking in the Asian Context', in *Christian Reflections within an Emerging Industrialized Society*, Thu En Yu, *et. al.* (Kota Kinabalu, Malaysia: Seminari Teologi Sabah) 153–180.

Ireland, R. 1991.
Kingdoms Come: Religion and Politics in Brazil (Pittsburgh, Pa.: University Press)

Irudayaraj, X. (ed.) 1990.
Emerging Dalit Theology (Madras: Jesuit Theological Secretariate and Tamilnadu Theological Seminary)

Jacob, P.S., 1979.
The Experiential Response of N.V. Tilak (Madras: Christian Literature Society)

Janzen, W. 1994.
Old Testament Ethics: A Paradigmatic Approach (Louisville, Ky.: Westminster John Knox Press)

Jeffery, P.M. 1938.
Dr. Ida: India. The Life Story of Ida S. Scudder (New York: Fleming H. Revell)

Jeremias, J. 1963
The Sermon on the Mount (Philadelphia, Pa.: Fortress Press)

Jeremias, J. 1966.
Rediscovering the Parables tr. S. H. Hooks and Frank Clarke (New York: Charles Scribner's Sons)

Job, G.V. et al. 1938. (Chenchiah, V. Chakkarai, Devasahayam, D.M., Jesudason, S., Asirvatham, E. & Sudarisanam, A.N.)
Rethinking Christianity in India (Madras: A.N. Sudarisanam)

John Paul II, 1990.
Redemptoris Missio. On the Permanent Validity of the Church's Missionary Mandate. Encyclical letter, December 7 (Washington, D.C.: Office of Publishing and Promotions Services, United States Catholic Conference)

John, T.K. (ed.) 1991.
Bread and Breath: Essays in Honour of Samuel Rayan S.J. (Anand, Gujarat: Gujarat Sahitya Prakash)

Journal do Brasil, 1988 & 1994
7 August 84 and 11 September 1-5

Kaiser, W.C. 1983.
Toward Old Testament Ethics (Grand Rapids Mich.: Zondervan)

Kelsey, D., 1975.
The Uses of Scripture in Recent Theology (London: SCM Press)

Kim, K., 2002.
Mission Pneumatology, with Special Reference to the Indian Theologies of the Holy Spirit of Stanley Samartha, Vandana and Samuel Rayan. PhD thesis, University of Birmingham, U.K.

Kim, K., 2003.
Mission in the Spirit: The Holy Spirit in Indian Christian Theologies (Delhi: ISPCK)

Kim, K., 2006.

'Indian Contribution to Contemporary Pneumatology,' *Transformation* 23.1 (January) 30-36

Kinnamon, M. (ed.), 1991.
Signs of the Spirit. Report of the Seventh Assembly of the WCC, Canberra (Geneva: WCC)

Kirk, J.A. 1999.
What is Mission? Theological Explorations (London: Dartman, Longman, and Todd)

Knitter, P. F., 1985.
No Other Name? (London: SCM Press)

Knox, R. 1981.
An Historical Relation of the Island of Ceylon (London: Richard Chiswell)

Koshy, N. 1995.
Religion and Politics: The Debate at the End of the Century (Geneva: WCC)

Kothari, R. 1994.
ISA Journal, December

Kraft, C.H. 1979.
Christianity in Culture (Maryknoll, N.Y.: Orbis Books)

Kraft, C.H. 1989.
Christianity with Power (Ann Arbor, Mich.: Servant Books)

Kuzmic, P. 1998.
'Kingdom of God,' in S.M. Burgess, G.B. McGee, P.H. Alexander (eds.) *Dictionary of Pentecostal and Charismatic Movements* (Grand Rapids, Mich.: Zondervan) 525–6

Kwashi, G., 2002.
'How Cultural and Religious Factors Shape our Understanding of Family,' *Transformation* 19.1 (January) 19-23

Ladd, G.E. 1951.
The Presence of the Future (New York: Harper & Row)

Ladd, G.E. 1964.
Jesus and the Kingdom: The Eschatology of Biblical Realism (Waco, Tex.: Word Books)

Ladd, G.E. 1974.
The Presence of the Future (Grand Rapids, Mich.: Wm. B. Eerdmans)

Latourette, K. S., 1929.
A History of Christian Missions in China (New York: Macmillan)

Leopold, A.M. and Jeppe S..J. (eds.) 2004.
Synretism in Religion: A Reader. (London: Equinox)

Lévi-Strauss, C. 1966.
The Savage Mind [La pensée sauvage] (London: Weidenfeld and Nicolson)

Lévi-Strauss, C. 1988.
The Jealous Potter (Chicago: Chicago University Press)

Lillie, W. 1961.
Studies in New Testament Ethics (Edinburgh and London: Oliver and Boyd)

Lindbeck, G. 1984.
The Nature of Doctrine: Religion and Theology in a Postliberal Age (Louisville, Ky.: Westminster John Knox Press)

Lohia, R. 1950.

Fragments of a World Mind (Bombay: Parivartan Prakashan)

Lovelace, R.F. 1979.
Dynamics of Spiritual Life: An Evaneglical Theology of Renewal (Leicester: Inter-Varsity Press)

Lu, M. 1992.
Confucianism – its Relevance to Modern Society (Singapore: Federal Publications)

Macchia, F.D. 1989.
Spirituality and Social Liberation: The Message of the Blumhardts in the Light of Wuerttemberg Pietism, with Implications for Pentecostal Theology (D. Theol. Dissertation: University of Basel)

Macpherson, C.B. 1962.
The Political Theory of Possessive Individualism (Oxford: Clarendon Press)

Macquarrie, J. 1967.
Principles of Christian Theology (London: SCM Press)

Marston, N. 1994.
Report by Report on a study of marriage and family life in Seychelles, SNA F/2. 880

Maston, T.B. 1967.
Biblical Ethics (Waco, Tex.: Word Books)

Massey, J. 1994.
Roots: A Concise History of the Dalits (Delhi: ISPCK)

Maxwell, D. 1999.
'Historicising Christian Independency: The Southern African Pentecostal Movement 1980-1950', *Journal of African History*, 40

Maxwell, D. 2006.
Gifts of the Spirit (Oxford: Oxford University Press)

McArthur, H.K. 1960.
Understanding the Sermon on the Mount (New York: Harper & Row)

Mbiti, J. S. 1971.
New Testament Eschatology in an African Background (Oxford: Oxford University Press)

McClung, L.G.Jr., 1988. (also cited as *DPCM*)
'Missiology', in S. M. Burgess and G. B. McGee (eds.) *Dictionary of Pentecostal and Charismatic Movements* (Grand Rapids, Mich.: Zondervan)

Mernissi, F.1985.
Beyond the Veil: Male-female Dynamics in Muslim society (London: Al Saqi Books)

Mensageiro da Paz, 1986
(September) 15

Mojzes, P. and Swidler, L. eds. 1990.
Christian Mission and Interreligious Dialogue (Lampeter: Edwin Mellen Press)

Moltmann, J., 1992.
The Spirit of Life: A Universal Affirmation tr. Margaret Koh (London: SCM Press)

Moltmann, J. 2000.

'The Mission of the Spirit-The Gospel of Life,' in T. Yates (ed.) *Mission: An Invitation to God's Future* (Calver, Hope Valley: Cliff College)

Monk, R.C. et al., 1987.
Exploring Religious Meaning (New York: Prentice-Hall)

Montoya B.. 2000.
'Karneval in Kolumbien: *Mismedad* und *Otredad* in Aufführungen und Inszenierungen,' in B. Montoya, B.E. Schmidt (eds.) *Teufel und Heilige auf der Bühne: Religiosität und Freude bei Inszenierungen mestizischer Feste in Südamerika* (Marburg: Curupira) pp. 11-79.

Mott, S.C. 1982.
Biblical Ethics and Social Change (New York: Oxford University Press)

Moule, C.F.D., 1967-68.
'Fulfilment-Words in the New Testament', *New Testament Studies,* 14 , 300-1
'Sidetracked!', 1989. *Mountain Movers* 31 (March)

Myers, B. 1999.
Walking With the Poor: Principles and Practices of Transformational Development (Maryknoll, N.Y.: Orbis Books)

Nandy, A. 1990.
Indian Express, February

Neill, S., 1974.
Bhakti: Hindu and Christian (Madras: Christian Literature Society)

Neill, S., 1986.
A History of Christian Missions (London: Penguin)

Netland, H. 1991.
Dissonant Voices – Religious Pluralism and the Question of Truth (Grand Rapids, Mich.: Wm. B. Eerdmans)

Newbigin, L., 1982.
The Light Has Come: An Exposition of the Fourth Gospel (Edinburgh: Handsel Press)

Newbigin, L. 1986.
Foolishness to the Greeks: The Gospel and Western Culture (London: SPCK)

Newbigin, L., 1989.
The Gospel in a Pluralistic Society (Grand Rapids, Mich.; Geneva: Wm. B. Eerdmans; WCC)

Newbigin, L., 1995.
The Open Secret: An Introduction to the Theology of Mission rev. ed. (Grand Rapids, Mich.: Wm B. Eerdmans)

Ngada, N.H. 1986.
Speaking for Ourselves (Braamfontein: Skotaville)

Niebuhr, H.R. 1949.
The Nature and Destiny of Man: A Christian Interpretation 2v. (New York: Charles Scribner's Sons)

Niebuhr, H.R. 1951.
Christ and Culture (New York: Harper & Row)

Niebuhr, H.R. 1963.
The Responsible Self (New York: Harper & Row)

Nora, P. 1998.

Realms of Memory : Rethinking the French Past 3v. (*Les Lieux de mémoire).* (New York: Columbus University Press)

North-South, 1980.
North-South: A Programme for Survival (London: Pan Books)

Oddie, G.A. 1979.
Social Protest in India: British Protestant Missionaries and Social Reform, 1850-1900 (New Delhi: Manohar)

O'Donovan, J., 2003.
'Rights, Law and Political Community: A theological and historical perspective,' *Transformation* 20.1 (January) 30-38

Oommen, G.
The Struggle of the Anglican Pulaya Christians, Ph.D. Thesis, University of Sydney

Ouko, R. 1987.
Kenya Times, June 30

Padilla, R. 1989. 'The Politics of the Kingdom of God and the Political Mission of the Church in V. Samuel and A. Hauser (eds.) *Proclaiming Christ in Christ's Way: Studies in Integral Evangelism* (Oxford: Regnum)

Padilla, R., 1992.
'Latin American Evangelicals Enter the Public Square,' *Transformation* 9.3 (July) 2-7

Padilla, R., 1993.
'A Message for the Whole person,' *Transformation* 10.3 (July) 1-4

Painadath, S., 1993.
'Towards an Indian Christian Spirituality in the Context of Religious Pluralism,' in D. Veliath (ed.) *Towards an Indian Christian Spirituality in a Pluralistic Context: Papers and Statement of the Fourteenth Annual Meeting of the Indian Theological Association* (Bangalore: Dharmaram) 3-14

Paradkar, B.A.M. (ed.) 1969.
The Theology of Nehemiah Goreh (Madras: Christian Literature Society)

Parshall, P. 1980.
New Paths in Muslim Evangelism (Grand Rapids, Mich.: Baker Book House)

Petersen, D. 1991
'The Kingdom of God and the Hermeneutical Circle: Pentecostal Praxis in the Third World' in Dempster, M.W., Klaus, B.D. & Petersen, D. (eds.) *Called and Empowered: Global Mission in Pentecostal Perspective* (Peabody, Mass.: Hendrickson) 225-241

Petersen, D. 1996.
Not By Might Nor By Power: A Pentecostal Theology of Social Concern in Latin America (Oxford: Regnum)

Petersen, D. 1997.
'Towards a Latin American Pentecostal Political Praxis,' *Transformation* 14.1 (January) 30-33

Pieris, A. 1988.
An Asian Theology of Liberation (Maryknoll, N.Y.: Orbis Books)

Pinnock, C.H., 1992.
A Wideness in God's Mercy – The Finality of Jesus Christ in a World of Religions (Grand Rapids, Mich.: Zondervan)

Pomerville, P.A. 1985.
The Third Force in Missions (Peabody, Mass.: Hendrickson)

Pobee, J., 1982.
'Political Theology in the African Context', *Africa Theological Journal* 11, 168–172

Preston, R.H. 1983.
Church and Society in the late Twentieth Century: The Economic and Political Task (London: SCM Press)

Radhakrishnan, S. 1960.
The Hindu View of Life (London: Mandala Books)

Raiser, K. 1993.
'Promise and Power of Faith', in *Current Dialogue*, June

Ramachandra, V., 1996.
The Recovery of Mission (Carlisle: Paternoster)

Ramanujan, A.K. 1970.
The Interior Landscape (Bloomington, Ind.: Indiana University Press)

Ranger, T. 1965a
'The "Ethiopian" Episode in Barotseland, 1900-1905', *Rhodes-Livingstone Journal*, XXXVII (June)

Ranger, T. 1965b.
'African Attempts to Control Education in East and Central Africa, 1900-1939', *Past and Present*, 32 (December)

Ranger, T. 1969.
The African Churches of Tanzania (Nairobi: East African Publishing House)

Ranger, T. 1971.
'Christian Independency in Tanzania' in D.B. Barrett (ed.). *African Initiatives in Religion* (Nairobi: East African Publishing House)

Ranger, T. 1987.
'Religion, Development and African Christian Identity', in K.H. Petersen (ed.) *Religion, Development and African Identity* (Uppsala: Scandinavian Institute of African Studies)

Ranger, T. 1995.
Are We Not Also Men? (London, James Currey Publishers)

Ranger, T. 2002.
'Taking on the Missionary's Task: African Spirituality and the Mission Churches of Manicaland in the 1930s', in D. Maxwell (ed.) *Christianity and the African Imagination* (Leiden: Brill)

Ranger, T. 2007.
'African Initiated Churches' *Transformation* 24.2 (April) 66-72

Rasmussen, L.L. 1987.
'Creation, church and Christian responsibility' in Wesley Granberg-Michaelson (ed.) *Tending the Garden: Essays in the Gospel and the Earth* (Grand Rapids, Mich.: Wm. B. Eerdmans)

Rauschenbusch, W. 1916.
The Social Principles of Jesus (New York; London: Association Press)

Rayan, S., 1979a. *Breath of Fire - The Holy Spirit: Heart of the Christian Gospel* (London: Geoffrey Chapman)

Rayan, S., 1979b.

'Theology as Art', *Religion and Society* 26.2, 77-90

Rayan, S., 1994.
'The Earth is the Lord's' in D.C. Hallman (ed.) *Ecotheology: Voices from South and North* (Geneva; Maryknoll, N.Y.: WCC; Orbis Books)

Reed, R. 1996.
Active Faith (New York: Free Press)

Reglamento Local, 1992.
Reglamento Local: Manual de Doctrinas v Practicas de las Asambleas de Dios (San Jose, Costa Rica: Asociacion Cristiana de la Asambleas de Dios)

Richardson, A. 1953.
Genesis 1-2 (London: SCM)

Ro, B. R. (ed.) 1985.
Christian Alternatives to Ancestor Practices (Taichung: ATA)

Robin H.S.B., 1975.
An Introduction to Indian Christian Theology rev. ed. (Delhi: ISPCK)

Rocha, A.M. 1991.
'Comportamientos Sociales en el Protestantismo y en el Pentecostalism Popular Nicaraguense,' in Luis Samandu (ed.) *Protestantismos y Procesos Sociales en Centroamerica* (San Jose, Costa Rica: Editorial Universitaria Centroamericana) 202-203

Rolland, H. and Sider, R.J. 1996.
'Correcting the Welfare Tragedy', in Stanley W. Carlson-Thies and J. Skillen (eds.) *Welfare in America* (Grand Rapids, Mich.: Wm. B. Eerdmans) 454-79

Ross, A.C. 1994.
A Vision Betrayed: the Jesuits in Japan and China (Edinburgh: Edinburgh University Press)

Rowland, C. and Corner, M. 1990.
Liberating Exegesis: The Challenge of Liberation Theology to Biblical Studies (London: SPCK)

Rowland, C. 1993.
Revelation (London: Epworth Press)

Sahi, J., 1986.
Stepping Stones: Reflections on the Theology of Indian Christian Culture (Bangalore: ATC)

Samartha, S.J., 1991.
One Christ - Many Religions: Towards a Revised Christology (Maryknoll, N.Y.: Orbis Books)

Samartha, S.J. 1981.
Courage for Dialogue: Ecumenical Issues in Inter-Religious Relationships (Geneva: WCC)

Samartha, S.J. 1994.
The Pilgrim Christ – Sermons, Poems and Bible Studies (Bangalore: ATC)

Samuel, V.K. and Sugden, C., 1984.
'Dialogue with Other Religions – An Evangelical View', in B. R. Ro and R. Eshenaur (eds.) *The Bible and Theology in Asian Contexts – An Evangelical Perspective on Asian Theology* (Taichung: ATA) 265–289

Samuel, V.K, 1991.

'Mission in the Context of World Religions', in V. Samuel and C. Sugden (eds.) *A.D. 2000 and Beyond – A Mission Agenda* (Oxford: Regnum) 148–166

Samuel, V.K. and Sugden, C.N.M. (eds.) 1999.
Mission as Transformation: A Theology of the Whole Gospel (Oxford: Regnum)

Samuel, V.K., 2002.
'Mission as Transformation', *Transformation* 19.4 (October) 243-247

Samuel, V.K. and Sugden, C.N.M. 2003.
The Church in Response to Human Need (Wipf and Stock)

Sanneh, L., 1989 (& 1997).
Translating the Message: The Missionary Impact on Culture (Maryknoll, N.Y.: Orbis Books)

Schreiter, R..J. 1985.
Constructing Local Theologies (Maryknoll, N.Y.: Orbis Books)

Schmidt, B.E. 1995.
Von Geistern, Orichas und den Puertoricanern: zur Verbindung von Religion und Ethnizität.(Marburg: Curupira)

Schmidt, B.E. 1998.
'Der Wandel der Festkultur – der Tag des Señor de los Milagros in San Juan, in der südlichen Sierra Ecuadors," in B.E. Schmidt and M. Münzel (eds.) *Ethnologie und Inszenierung: Ansätze zur Theaterethnologie* (Marburg: Curupira) 295-314

Schmidt, B.E. and Bonilla, S.M., 2000.
Teufel und Heilige auf der Bühne: Religiosität und Freude bei Inszenierungen mestizischer Feste in Südamerika (Marburg: Curupira)

Schmidt, B.E. 2002.
Karibische Diaspora in New York: Vom Wilden Denken zur Polyphonen Kultur (Berlin: Dietrich Reimer Verlag)

Schmidt, B.E., 2006.
'*Fiestas Patronales* in the Ecuadorian Andes The Meaning for the Villagers and the Attitude of the Churches', *Transformation* 23.1 (January) 54-60

Schrage, W. 1988.
The Ethics of the New Testament D. E. Green tr. (Philadelphia, Pa.: Fortress Press)

Schubeck, T.L. 1993.
Liberation Ethics: Sources, Models, and Norms (Minneapolis, Minn.: Fortress Press)

Selvanayagam, I., 1998.
'Components of a Tamil Śaiva Bhakti Experience as Evident in Māņkkavācakar's Tiruvācakam' in David Emmanuel Singh (ed.) *Spiritual Traditions: Essential Visions for Living* (Bangalore: ISPCK,) 418-38

Semeador, 1994.
(August) 3

Shepperson G. and Price, T. 1958.
Independent African (Edinburgh: University of Edinburgh Press)

Shepperson, G. 1963.
'Church and Sect in Central Africa,' *Rhodes-Livingstone Journal* (33)

Sider, R.J. 1977.

Rich Christians in an Age of Hunger (New York; Downers Grove, Ill.: Paulist Press; InterVarsity Press)

Sider, R. J. (ed.) 1982.
'An Evangeelical Commitment to Simple Lifestyle,' in *Lifestyle in the Eighties*, (Exeter: Paternoster Press)

Sider, R.J. 1987.
'A Plea for MOI Radical Conservatives and More conserving Radical! *Transfonnation* (January-March) 11-16

Sider, R.J. 1989a.
'Christian Ethics and the Good News of the Kingdom' in V. Samuel and C. Sugden (eds.) *Proclaiming Christ in Christ's Way* (Oxford: Regnum) 127-128

Sider, R.J. 1989b.
'Toward a Biblical Perspective of Equality', Interpretation (April-June) 156ff.

Sider, R.J. 1997.
'Towards an Evangelical Political Philosophy and Agenda for Christians in the United States, ' *Transformation* 14.3 (July) 1-10

Sikand, Y. 1992.
'Religion and Religious Nationalism', *The Frontier*, 9 May

Simons, M. 1956.
The Complete Writings of Menno Simons (Scottdale, Pa.: Herald Press)

Simons, M. 2006.
'The Reason Menno Simon Does Not Cease Teaching and Writing,' written by, can be found at http://e-menno.org/menno/menno093.htm (accessed 30 November)

Singer, M. 1972.
When a Great Tradition Modernizes: An Anthropological Approach to Indian Civilisation (Chicago: University of Chicago Press)

Smedes, L. B. 1983.
Mere Morality: What God Expects from Ordinary People (Grand Rapids, Mich.: Wm. B. Eerdmans)

Smith, L. 1989.
'Recent Historical Perspective of the Evangelical Tradition,' in E.J. Elliston (ed.) *Christian Relief and Development: Developing Workers for Effective Ministry*, (Dallas, Tex.: Word Books)

Smith, W.C. 1981.
Toward a World Theology: Faith and the Comparative History of Religion (Philadelphia, Pa.: Westminster)

Sng, B.E.K. and Pang, C.C. (eds.) 1991.
Church and Culture – Singapore Context (Singapore: Graduates Christian Fellowship)

Snyder, H.A. 1985.
A Kingdom Manifesto (Downers Grove, Ill.: InterVarsity Press)

So, D.W.K. 2006.
Jesus' Revelation of His Father: A Narrative-Conceptual Study of the Trinity with Special Reference to Karl Barth (Waynesboro, Ga.: Paternoster)

So, D.W.K. 2006b.
'A paradigm of the holistic gospel developed from the theology of Karl Barth,' *Transformation* 23.3 (July) 130-141

Song, C.S. 1980.
Confessing Our faith Around the World (Geneva: WCC)
Song, C.S. 1982.
The Compassionate God (Maryknoll, N.Y.: Orbis Books)
Song, C.S., 1986.
Theology from the Womb of Asia (Maryknoll, N.Y.: Orbis Books)
Song, C.S. 1993.
Jesus and the Reign of God (Minneapolis, Minn.: Fortress Press)
Song, C.S. 1994.
Jesus in the Power of the Spirit (Minneapolis, Minn.: Fortress Press)
Stanley, B., 2007.
'Inculturation: Historical Background, Theological Foundations and Contemporary Questions,' *Transformation* 24.1 (January) 21-27
Stassen, G.H., Yeager, D.M. and Yoder, J.H. 1996.
Authentic Transformation: A New Vision of Christ and Culture (Nashville, Tenn.: Abingdon Press)
Stauffer, E. 1955.
Christ and the Caesars (London: SCM Press)
Steinberg, N. 1993.
Kinship and Marriage in Genesis (Minneapolis, Minn.: Fortress Press)
Stoll, D. 1991.
An unpublished paper presented to the Fundamentalism Project
Stott, J. 1964.
The Epistles of John (Tyndale Press, London)
Stott, J. and Coote, R. (eds.) 1980.
Down to Earth: Studies in Christianity and Culture. The Papers of the Lausanne Consultation on Gospel and Culture (Grand Rapids, Mich.: Wm. B. Eerdmans)
Stott, J. 1990.
Issues Facing Christians Today: New Perspectives on Social and Moral Dilemmas new ed. (London: Marshall Pickering)
Stott, J. (ed.), 1996.
Making Christ Known: Historic Mission Documents from the Lausanne Movement 1974-1989 (Carlisle: Paternoster Press)
Stronstad, R. 1984.
The Charismatic Theology of St. Luke (Peabody, Mass.: Hendrickson)
Sugden, C.N.M., 2003.
'Transformational Development: Current state of understanding and practice,' *Transformation* 20.2 (April) 71-79
Summers, C. 1994.
From Civilization to Segregation. Social Ideals and Social Control in Southern Rhodesia, 1890-1934 (Athens)
Summers, C. 2002.
Colonial Lessons. Africans' Education in Southern Rhodesia, 1918-1940 (Oxford: James Currey)
Sundkler 1976.
Zulu Zion and Some Swazi Zionists (Oxford: Oxford University Press)
Taylor, J.V. and Lehmann, D. 1961.

Christians of the Copper Belt (London: SCM Press)

Thangaraj, T., 1992.
'Towards a Singable Theology' in T.D. Francis and F.J. Balasundaram (eds.) *Asian Expressions of Christian Commitment* (Madras: Christian Literature Society) 163-72

Thangasamy, D.A., 1966.
The Theology of Chenchiah with Selections from His Writings (Bangalore: CISRS)

Thapar, R. 1990.
'Communalism and the Historical Legacy,' in *Social Scientist,* June/July

Thomas, M.M., 1990.
'The Holy Spirit and the Spirituality for Political Struggles,' *Ecumenical Review* 42.3-4, 216-224

Thomas, M.M., 1997.
'Christian Reflections on Indian Political Developments, ' *Transformation* 14.1 (January) 17-22

Thomas, P.T. (ed.) 1981.
Vengal Chakkarai v. 1 (Madras: Christian Literature Society)

Tomasino, A.J. 1992.
'History Repeats Itself: the "Fall" and Noah's Drunkenness', *Vetus Testamentum* 42, 128- 130

Torrance, T. (ed.) 1962.
'The Principles of Dogmatics According to Herrmann', in [Karl Barth] *Theology and Church: Shorter Writings 1920-28* (London: SCM Press)

Tracy, D. 1981.
The Analogical Imagination: Christian Theology and the Culture of Pluralism (New York: Crossroad)

Tracy, D. and Cobb, J. 1983.
Talking About God: Doing Theology in the Context of Modern Pluralism (New York: Seabury)

Upadhyaya, B. 1901.
'Varna Ashram,' *The Twentieth Century* (January-December) 1.1, 8–11

Vandana, 1989.
Waters of Fire 3rd. ed. (Bangalore: ATC)

Vandana (ed.) 1993.
Christian Ashrams - a Movement with a Future? (Delhi: ISPCK)

Vandana, 1993.
'Response II [to J.B. Chethimattam] from the Perspective of an Ashramic Spirituality' in Dominic Veliath (ed.), *Towards an Indian Christian Spirituality in a Pluralistic Context: Papers and Statement of the Fourteenth Annual Meeting of the Indian Theological Association* (Bangalore: Dharmaram) 99-117

Various Authors 1994.
Transformation 11.4 (October) 2–11, 33

Verhey, A. 1984.
The Great Reversal: Ethics and the New Testament (Grand Rapids, Mich.: Wm. B. Eerdmans)

Villafane, E. 1992.

The Liberating Spirit: Towardan HispanicAmerican Pentecostal Social Ethic (New York: University Press of America)

Wallis, J. 1981.
The Call to Conversion (Tring, Herts.: Lion); revised version: Wallis, J. 2005 *The Call to Conversion: Why Faith is always Personal but never Private* (London: HarperCollins)

Walls, A. 1996.
The Missionary Movement in Christian History (Maryknoll, N.Y.; Edinburgh: Orbis Books; T. &. T. Clark)

Walls, A. 2002.
The Cross-Cultural Process in Christian History (Maryknoll, N.Y.; Edinburgh: Orbis Books; T. &. T. Clark)

Walter, J.A. 1979.
A Long Way from Home: A Sociological Exploration of Contemporary Idolatry (Exeter: Paternoster)

Warrier, N.V.K. 1991.
'Proselylisation: A Causal Factor for Communalism' in *Minorities and Secularisn,* 223-9

Webster, J. 2000.
Barth (London: Continuum)

Webster, J.C.B. 1992.
Towards Dalit Liberation: From Indian Church to Indian Theology (Madras: Dalit Liberation Education Trust)

Webster, J.C.B. 1996.
The Dalit Christians: A History (Delhi: ISPCK)

Wei-Ming, Tu., 1984.
Confucian Ethics Today – The Singapore Challenge (Singapore: Federal Publications)

Wei-Ming, Tu., 1991.
'The Search for Roots in Industrial Asia: The Case of the Confucian Revival', in M.E. Marty and R.S. Appleby (eds.) *Fundamentalisms Observed* (Chicago and London: University of Chicago Press) pp. 740–781

Wenham, G.J. 2000.
Story as Torah: Reading the Old Testament Ethically (Edinburgh: T&T Clark)

Wilfred, F., 1998.
'Towards a Better Understanding of Asian Theology: Some Basic Issues,' *Vidyajyoti Journal of Theological Reflection* 62.12, 890-915

Willmer, H. 2001.
Review of *Mission as Transformation,* in *Transformation* 18.3 (July) 194-196

Wilson, E. A. 1983.
'Sanguine Saints: Pentecostalism in El Salvador,' *Church History* 52 (June) 186-98

Wilson, E.A. 1987.
'Latin American Pentecostals: Their Potential for Ecumenical Dialogue,' *PNEUMA*: *The Journal of the Society for Pentecostal Studies* 9.1, 85-90

Wilson, M. 1959.
Communal Rituals of the Nyakyusa (New York: Oxford University Press)

Wing-Hung, L., 1983.

Chinese Theology in Construction (Pasadena, Calif.: William Carey Library)

Wink, W. 1999.
Homosexuality and the Christian Faith: Questions of Conscience for the Churches (Minneapolis, Minn.: Fortress Press)

Wink, W. 1984.
Naming the Powers: The Language of Power in the New Testament (Philadelphia, Pa.: Fortress Press)

Wink, W. 1984.
Unmasking the Powers: The Invisible Forces That Determine Human Existence (Philadelphia, Pa.: Fortress Press)

Wink, W. 1992.
Engaging the Powers: Discernment and Resistance in a World of Domination (Minneapolis, Minn.: Fortress Press)

Wogaman, J.P. and Strong, D.M. (eds.) 1996.
Readings in Christian Ethics: A Historical Sourcebook (Louisville, Ky.: Westminster John Knox Press)

Wright, C.J.H. 1983.
Living as the People of God (Leicester: Inter-Varsity Press)

Wright, C.J.H. 1990.
God's People in God's Land (Grand Rapids, Mich.; Carlisle: Wm. B. Eerdmans; Paternoster)

Wright, C.J.H. 1992b.
'Family', in D.N. Freedman (ed.) *The Anchor Bible Dictionary* 2v. (New York: Doubleday) 761-769

Wright, C.J.H., 2002a.
'Family, Covenant and Kingdom of God,' *Transformation* 19.1 (January) 11-19

Wright, C.J.H. 2006.
The Mission of God: Unlocking the Bible's Grand Narrative (Downers Grove, Ill.: InterVarsity Press)

Wright, N.T. 1996.
Jesus and the Victory of God (London: SPCK)

Yoder, J.H. 1972.
The Politics of Jesus (Grand Rapids, Mich.: Wm. B. Eerdmans)

Yoder, J.H. 1984.
The Priestly Kingdom: Social Ethics as Gospel (Notre Dame, Indiana: University of Notre Dame Press)

Yoder, J.H. 1992.
Body Politics: Five Practices of the Christian Community before the Watching World (Nashville, Tenn.: Discipleship Resources)

Yoder, J.H.
The Royal Priesthood:Essays Ecclesiological and Ecumenical, M.G. Cartwright (ed.) (Grand Rapids, Mich.: Wm. B. Eerdmans)

Your Kingdom Come, 1980.
Report of the Melbourne Conference on World Mission and Evangelism 1980 (Geneva: WCC)

Yu, C.T. 1998.

'The Bible and culture in the shaping of Asian Theology,' *Transformation* 15.3 (July) 16-20
Ziegenbalg, B. 1718.
Propagation of the Gospel in the East (London: Joseph Downing)

Concept Index

Place Index

Name Index

Religion Index

GLOBAL THEOLOGICAL VOICES

Series Listing

David Emmanuuel Singh (Ed.)

Jesus and the Cross

Reflections of Christians from Islamic Contexts

The Cross reminds us that the sins of the world are not borne through the exercise of power but through Jesus Christ's submission to the will of the Father. The papers in this volume are organised in three parts: scriptural, contextual and theological. The central question being addressed is: how do Christians living in contexts, where Islam is a majority or minority religion, experience, express or think of the Cross? This is, therefore, an exercise in listening. As the contexts from where these engagements arise are varied, the papers in drawing scriptural, contextual and theological reflections offer a cross-section of Christian thinking about Jesus and the Cross.

2008 / 978-1-870345-65-1 / x + 226pp

Sung-wook Hong

Naming God in Korea

The Case of Protestant Christianity

Since Christianity was introduced to Korea more than a century ago, one of the most controversial issue has been the Korean term for the Christian 'God'. This issue is not merely about naming the Christian God in Korean language, but it relates to the question of theological contextualization—the relationship between the gospel and culture—and the question of Korean Christian identity. This book examines the theological contextualization of the concept of 'God' in the contemporary Korean context and applies the translatability of Christianity to that context. It also demonstrates the nature of the gospel in relation to cultures, i.e., the universality of the gospel expressed in all human cultures.

2008 / 978-1-870345-66-8

Young-hoon Lee

The Holy Spirit Movement in Korea

Its Historical and Doctrinal Development

This book traces the historical and doctrinal development of the Holy Spirit Movement in Korea through five successive periods (from 1900 to the present time). The first period (1900-20) was characterised by repentance and revival, the second period (1920-40) by persecution and suffering under Japanese occupation. The third period (1940-60) was a time of confusion and division while the fourth period (1960-80) was a time of explosive revival in which the Pentecostal movement played a major role in the rapid growth of Korean churches. In the fifth period (1980 to the present time), the Holy Spirit movement reaches out to all denominations. The book also discusses the relationship between this movement and other religions such as shamanism, and looks forward to further engagement with issues of concern in the larger society.

2008 / 978-1-870345-67-5

For the up-to-date listing of the Global Theological Voices Series, see http://www.ocms.ac.uk/docs/Global_Theological_Voices_Listing.pdf.

June 2008

Regnum Studies in Mission

Academic Monographs on Missiological Themes

(All titles paperback, 229 x 152mm)

Allan Anderson and Edmond Tang (eds.)
Asian and Pentecostal
The Charismatic Face of Christianity in Asia
(Published jointly with Asia Pacific Theological Seminary)

This book provides a thematic discussion and pioneering case studies on the history and development of Pentecostal and Charismatic churches in the countries of South Asia, South East Asia and East Asia.

2005 / 1-870345-43-6 / approx. 600pp

I. Mark Beaumont
Christology in Dialogue with Muslims
A Critical Analysis of Christian Presentations of Christ for Muslims from the Ninth and Twentieth Centuries

This book analyses Christian presentations of Christ for Muslims in the most creative periods of Christian-Muslim dialogue, the first half of the ninth century and the second half of the twentieth century. In these two periods, Christians made serious attempts to present their faith in Christ in terms that take into account Muslim perceptions of him, with a view to bridging the gap between Muslim and Christian convictions.

2005 / 1-870345-46-0 / xxvi + 228pp

Kwame Bediako
Theology and Identity
The Impact of Culture upon Christian Thought in the Second Century and in Modern Africa

The author examines the question of Christian identity in the context of the Graeco–Roman culture of the early Roman Empire. He then addresses the modern African predicament of quests for identity and integration.

1992 / 1-870345-10-X / xviii + 508pp

Richard Burgess

Nigeria's Christian Revolution

The Civil War Revival and Its Pentecostal Progeny (1967-2006)

Nigeria has become the arena of one of the most remarkable religious movements of recent times, reflecting the shift in the global centre of Christianity from the North to the South. This book tells the story of one sector of this movement from its roots in the Nigerian civil war to the turn of the new millennium. It describes a revival that occurred among the Igbo people of Eastern Nigeria, and the new Pentecostal churches it generated, and documents the changes that have occurred as the movement has responded to global flows and local demands. As such, it explores the nature of revivalist and Pentecostal experience, but does so against the backdrop of local socio-political and economic developments, such as decolonisation and civil war, as well as broader processes, such as modernisation and globalisation.

2008 / 978-1-870345-63-7 / xxii + 347pp

Gene Early

Leadership Expectations

How Executive Expectations are Created and Used in a Non-Profit Setting

The author creates an Expectation Enactment Analysis to study the role of the Chancellor of the University of the Nations-Kona, Hawaii, and is grounded in the field of managerial work, jobs, and behaviour, drawing on symbolic interactionism, role theory, role identity theory, and enactment theory. The result is a conceptual framework for further developing an understanding of managerial roles.

2005 / 1-870345-30-4 / xxiv + 276pp

Keith E. Eitel

Paradigm Wars

The Southern Baptist International Mission Board Faces the Third Millennium

The International Mission Board of the Southern Baptist Convention is the largest denominational mission agency in North America. This volume chronicles the historic and contemporary forces that led to the IMB's recent extensive reorganization, providing the most comprehensive case study to date of a historic mission agency restructuring to continue its mission purpose into the twenty-first century more effectively.

1999 / 1-870345-12-6 / x + 140pp

Tormod Engelsviken, Ernst Harbakk, Rolv Olsen, Thor Strandenæs (eds.)

Communicating the Gospel in the 21st Century

Essays in Honour of Knud Jørgensen

Knud Jørgensen is Director of Areopagos and Associate Professor of Missiology at MF Norwegian School of Theology. This book reflects the various main areas of Jørgensen's commitment to mission. At the same time it focuses on the main frontier of mission, the world, the content of mission, the Gospel, the fact that the Gospel has to be communicated, and the context of contemporary mission - the 21st century.

2008 / 978-1-870345-64-4 / 472pp

Tharcisse Gatwa

The Churches and Ethnic Ideology in the Rwandan Crises 1900-1994

Since the early years of the twentieth century Christianity has become a new factor in Rwandan society. This book investigates the role Christian churches played in the formulation and development of the racial ideology that culminated in the 1994 genocide.

2005 / 1-870345-24-X / approx 300pp

Gideon Githiga

The Church as the Bulwark against Authoritarianism

Development of Church and State Relations in Kenya, with Particular Reference to the Years after Political Independence 1963-1992

'All who care for love, peace and unity in Kenyan society will want to read this careful history by Bishop Githiga of how Kenyan Christians, drawing on the Bible, have sought to share the love of God, bring his peace and build up the unity of the nation, often in the face of great difficulties and opposition.' Canon Dr Chris Sugden, Oxford Centre for Mission Studies.

2002 / 1-870345-38-X / xviii + 218pp

Samuel Jayakumar

Dalit Consciousness and Christian Conversion

Historical Resources for a Contemporary Debate

(Published jointly with ISPCK)

The main focus of this historical study is social change and transformation among the Dalit Christian communities in India. Historiography tests the evidence in the light of the conclusions of the modern Dalit liberation theologians.

1999 / 81-7214-497-0 / xxiv + 434pp

Samuel Jayakumar

Mission Reader

Historical Models for Wholistic Mission in the Indian Context

(Published jointly with ISPCK)

This book is written from an evangelical point of view revalidating and reaffirming the Christian commitment to wholistic mission. According to Jayakumar, the roots of the 'wholistic mission' combining 'evangelism and social concerns' are to be located in the history and tradition of Christian evangelism in the past; and the civilizing purpose of evangelism is compatible with modernity as an instrument in nation building.

2003 / 1-870345-42-8 / x + 250pp

Julie Ma

Mission Possible

Biblical Strategies for Reaching the Lost

Written as Julie Ma hiked the mountains to share God's news, this is a missiology book for the church which liberates missiology from the specialists for every believer. Nevertheless, it serves as a textbook that is simple and friendly, and yet solid in biblical interpretation. This book links the biblical teaching to the actual and contemporary missiological setting, thus serving two important purposes. Examples are clearly given which aid understanding, and the biblical development is brought in to our contemporary setting, thus making the Bible come alive.

2005 / 1-870345-37-1 / xvi + 142pp

Myung Sung-Hoon and Hong Young-Gi (eds.)

Charis and Charisma

David Yonggi Cho and the Growth of Yoido Full Gospel Church

This book discusses the factors responsible for the growth of the world's largest church. It expounds the role of the Holy Spirit, the leadership, prayer, preaching, cell groups and creativity in promoting church growth. It focuses on God's grace (charis) and inspiring leadership (charisma) as the two essential factors and the book's purpose is to present a model for church growth worldwide.

2003 / 1-870345-45-2 / xxii + 218pp

Jemima Atieno Oluoch

The Christian Political Theology of Dr. John Henry Okullu

This book reconstructs the Christian political theology of Bishop John Henry Okullu, DD, through establishing what motivated him and the biblical basis for his socio-political activities. It also attempts to reconstruct the socio-political environment that nurtured Dr Okullu's prophetic ministry.

2006 / 1-870345-51-7 / xx + 137pp

Bernhard Ott

Beyond Fragmentation: Integrating Mission and Theological Education

A Critical Assessment of some Recent Developments in Evangelical Theological Education

Beyond Fragmentation is an enquiry into the development of Mission Studies in evangelical theological education in Germany and German-speaking Switzerland between 1960 and 1995. This is carried out by a detailed examination of the paradigm shifts which have taken place in recent years in both the theology of mission and the understanding of theological education.

2001 / 1-870345-14-2 / xxviii + 382pp

Bob Robinson

Christians Meeting Hindus

Analysis and Theological Critique of the Hindu-Christian Encounter in India

This book focuses on the Hindu-Christian encounter, especially the intentional meeting called dialogue, mainly during the last four decades of the twentieth century, and mainly in India itself.

2004 / 1-870345-39-8 / xviii + 392pp

David Emmanuel Singh, Bernard C Farr (Eds.)

Christianity and Cultures

Shaping Christian Thinking in Context

This volume is a way of marking an important milestone in the relatively short story of the Oxford Centre for Mission Studies (OCMS). The papers here have been exclusively sourced from Transformation, a quarterly journal of OCMS and seek to provide a tripartite view of Christianity's engagement with cultures by focusing on the question: how is Christian thinking forming or reforming through its interaction with the varied contexts it encounters? As Christianity has taken and still takes shape in multiple contexts, it naturally results in a variety of expressions and emphases. One can gain an appreciation of these by studying different strands of theological-missiological thinking, socio-political engagements and forms of family relationships in interaction with the host cultures.

2008 / 978-1-870345-69-9 / x + 260pp

Christopher Sugden

Seeking the Asian Face of Jesus

The Practice and Theology of Christian Social Witness in Indonesia and India 1974–1996

This study focuses on contemporary wholistic mission with the poor in India and Indonesia combined with the call to transformation of all life in Christ with micro-credit enterprise schemes. 'The literature on contextual theology now has a new standard to rise to' – Lamin Sanneh (Yale University, USA).

1997 / 1-870345-26-6 / xx + 496pp

Christopher Sugden

Gospel, Culture and Transformation

A Reprint, with a New Introduction, of Part Two of Seeking the Asian Face of Jesus

Gospel, Culture and Transformation explores the practice of mission especially in relation to transforming cultures and communities. Vinay Samuel has played a leading role in developing the understanding of mission as transformation, which he defines as follows: 'Transformation is to enable God's vision of society to be actualised in all relationships: social, economic and spiritual, so that God's will may be reflected in human society and his love experienced by all communities, especially the poor.'

2000 / 1-870345-32-0 / viii + 152pp

Al Tizon

Transformation after Lausanne

Radical Evangelical Mission in Global-Local Perspective

Lausanne '74 inspired evangelicals around the world to take seriously the full implications of the Gospel for mission. This was especially true of a worldwide network of radical evangelical mission theologians and practitioners, whose post-Lausanne reflections found harbour in the notion of "Mission as Transformation". This missiology integrated evangelism and social concern like no other, and it lifted up theological voices coming from the Two Thirds World to places of prominence. This book documents the definitive gatherings, theological tensions, and social forces within and without evangelicalism that led up to Mission as Transformation. And it does so through a global-local grid that points the way toward greater holistic mission in the 21st century.

2008 / 978-1-870345-68-2 / xx + 281pp

Hwa Yung

Mangoes or Bananas?

The Quest for an Authentic Asian Christian Theology

Asian Christian thought remains largely captive to Greek dualism and Enlightenment rationalism because of the overwhelming dominance of Western culture. Authentic contextual Christian theologies will emerge within Asian Christianity with a dual recovery of confidence in culture and the gospel.

1997 / 1-870345-25-8 / xii + 274pp

For the up-to-date listing of the Regnum Studies in Mission, see http://www.ocms.ac.uk/docs/Regnum_Studies_In_Mission_Listing.pdf.

regnum

Regnum Books International

Regnum is an Imprint of The Oxford Centre for Mission Studies
P.O. Box 70, Oxford, OX2 6HB
Web: www.ocms.ac.uk/regnum

In partnership with
Paternoster
Web: www.authenticmedia.co.uk/paternoster

June 2008